THE HISTORY OF SPAIN

THE HISTORY OF SPAIN

Peter Pierson

The Greenwood Histories of the Modern Nations
Frank W. Thackeray and John E. Findling, Series Editors

Greenwood Press
Westport, Connecticut • London

Library of Congress Cataloging-in-Publication Data

Pierson, Peter.
    The history of Spain / Peter Pierson.
        p.   cm.—(The Greenwood histories of the modern nations,
    ISSN 1096–2905)
    Includes bibliographical references and index.
    ISBN 0–313–30272–3 (alk. paper)
    1. Spain—History.   I. Title.   II. Series.
DP66.P53   1999
    946—dc21   98–22901

British Library Cataloguing in Publication Data is available.

Library of Congress Catalog Card Number: 98–22901
ISBN: 0–313–30272–3
ISSN: 1096–2905

First published in 1999

Greenwood Press, 88 Post Road West, Westport, CT 06881
An imprint of Greenwood Publishing Group, Inc.

Printed in the United States of America

The paper used in this book complies with the
Permanent Paper Standard issued by the National
Information Standards Organization (Z39.48–1984).

10 9 8 7 6 5 4 3 2

Contents

Series Foreword

The Greenwood Histories of the Modern Nations series is intended to provide students and interested laypeople with up-to-date, concise, and analytical histories of many of the nations of the contemporary world. Not since the 1960s has there been a systematic attempt to publish a series of national histories, and, as series editors, we believe that this series will prove to be a valuable contribution to our understanding of other countries in our increasingly interdependent world.

Over thirty years ago, at the end of the 1960s, the Cold War was an accepted reality of global politics, the process of decolonization was still in progress, the idea of a unified Europe with a single currency was unheard of, the United States was mired in a war in Vietnam, and the economic boom of Asia was still years in the future. Richard Nixon was president of the United States, Mao Tse-tung (not yet Mao Zedong) ruled China, Leonid Brezhnev guided the Soviet Union, and Harold Wilson was prime minister of the United Kingdom. Authoritarian dictators still ruled most of Latin America, the Middle East was reeling in the wake of the Six-Day War, and Shah Reza Pahlavi was at the height of his power in Iran. Clearly, the past thirty years have been witness to a great deal of historical change, and it is to this change that this series is primarily addressed.

With the help of a distinguished advisory board, we have selected nations whose political, economic, and social affairs mark them as among the most important in the waning years of the twentieth century, and for each nation we have found an author who is recognized as specialist in the history of that nation. These authors have worked most cooperatively with us and with Greenwood Press to produce volumes that reflect current research on their nation and that are interesting and informative to their prospective readers.

The importance of a series such as this cannot be underestimated. As a superpower whose influence is felt all over the world, the United States can claim a "special" relationship with almost every other nation. Yet many Americans know very little about the histories of the nations with which the United States relates. How did they get to be the way they are? What kind of political systems have evolved there? What kind of influence do they have in their own region? What are the dominant political, religious, and cultural forces that move their leaders? These and many other questions are answered in the volumes of this series.

The authors who have contributed to this series have written comprehensive histories of their nations, dating back to prehistoric time in some cases. Each of them, however, has devoted a significant portion of the book to events of the past thirty years, because the modern era has contributed the most to contemporary issues that have an impact on U.S. policy. Authors have made an effort to be as up-to-date as possible so that readers can benefit from the most recent scholarship and a narrative that includes very recent events.

In addition to the historical narrative, each volume in this series contains an introductory overview of the country's geography, political institutions, economic structure, and cultural attributes. This is designed to give readers a picture of the nation as it exists in the contemporary world. Each volume also contains additional chapters that add interesting and useful detail to the historical narrative. One chapter is a thorough chronology of important historical events, making it easy for readers to follow the flow of a particular nation's history. Another chapter features biographical sketches of the nation's most important figures in order to humanize some of the individuals who have contributed to the historical development of their nation. Each volume also contains a comprehensive bibliography, so that those readers whose interest has been sparked may find out more about the nation and its history. Finally, there is a carefully prepared topic and person index.

Readers of these volumes will find them fascinating to read and useful in understanding the contemporary world and the nations that comprise it. As series editors, it is our hope that this series will contribute to a heightened sense of global understanding as we enter a new century.

Frank W. Thackeray and John E. Findling
Indiana University Southeast

Preface

This narrative history of Spain for students and nonstudents alike reflects what educated Spaniards tend to know of their history. I hope the bibliography will prove useful to those who want to learn more. Although politics receives the chief emphasis, I have tried to weave into the text the concurrent history of society, religion, culture, and economics because people experience their history as a whole.

Spain is a country with powerful appeal and an exceptional history. Travel posters proclaim: *España es diferente* ("Spain is different"). I first visited Spain in 1956–1958, while serving in the U.S. Navy. I returned as a student in the summer of 1963 and spent 1964–1966 there as a Fulbright scholar. Since then I return to Spain every two or three years, and in my research and travel I have visited every part of the country.

I want to express my gratitude to Harry de Wildt, who knows Spain better than I do and who introduced me to much of its varied life; to my colleagues in the Society for Spanish and Portuguese Historical Studies, who have done much to further Americans' understanding of Spain and whose work I admire; to my friends and colleagues in Spain; and to my students at Santa Clara University over the years, who took my course on Spain and asked the kinds of questions and sought the sort of understanding I try to address here.

A NOTE ON USAGE

Geographical names used are those most familiar to English speakers. Seville has a long history of English usage. The Castilian Spanish form, the one we know best, appears on modern maps, although the latest may give the Basque, Catalan, and Galician versions used where those languages are spoken. These are included in the index. In the case of Aragón, I keep the traditional English form "Aragon," without accent, for the historic crown, dynasty, and kingdom that included Aragón itself, Catalonia, Valencia, and the Balearic Islands. In English we have also long used "pronunciamento," without the second, "i," for the Spanish word *pronunciamiento*, the pronouncement that begins a military uprising. Also familiar in English are "barrio," "burro," "guerrilla," "junta," and "macho."

The Castilian form is used for rulers' names, except when the English form has a long tradition, such as Ferdinand and Isabella, and appears in most histories of their reigns in English. Spain's Habsburg kings also ruled European lands where Dutch, Flemish, French, German, and Italian were spoken. For them Charles and Philip are used, except for the last, Carlos II, who was a contemporary of Charles II of England. For the rulers of the House of Bourbon, after French-born Philip V, the Spanish form is used. Medieval Aragonese rulers often used the Catalan form of their name, given in parentheses below. For Spanish Muslims, the form used is the one most often encountered.

Spanish and English Names
Carlos = Charles
Enrique = Henry
Felipe = Philip
Fernando (Ferran) = Ferdinand
Isabel = Isabella (or Elizabeth)
Jaime (Jaume) = James
José = Joseph
Juan (Joan) = John
Juana = Joanna
María = Mary
Pedro (Pere) = Peter
Rodrigo = Roderick
Santiago = St. James (the Greater)
Vifredo (Giufré) = Wilfred

Timeline of Historical Events

c. 40,000 B.C.	Modern humans appear in Iberian Peninsula
20,000–9000 B.C.	Evidence of prehistoric cave art
c. 1600 B.C.	Iberian immigration into Spain
c. 1100 B.C.	Phoenicians trade and begin colonies
c. 750 B.C.	Celts appear
c. 750–500 B.C.	Tartassian culture
c. 500–206 B.C.	Carthaginian dominion in south
217–19 B.C.	Roman conquest
19 B.C.– c. A.D. 450	Roman Spain; Judaism and Christianity appear
A.D. 409	Germanic invasions begin
c. 480–711	Visigothic kingdom
711–718	Moorish conquest; Muslim al-Andalus develops

718	Pelayo stops Moors at Covadonga; becomes king of Asturias
751–763	Galicia joins Asturias
755–1031	Umayyad dynasty
801	Charlemagne's Franks establish county of Barcelona
c. 809	County of Aragón appears
c. 813	Shrine of Santiago de Compostela
c. 840	Independent Navarre
c. 850	Christian reoccupation of region of Castile
879	Vifredo the Hairy establishes independent Catalonia
910	León becomes kingdom
929–1031	Caliphate of Córdoba, apogee of al-Andalus
930	Fernán González becomes count of Castile
970–1035	Sancho III the Great unifies most of Christian Spain
1008–1086	Muslim al-Andalus splinters into *taifa* kingdoms
1035	Castile and Aragón become kingdoms
c. 1043–1099	El Cid
1085	Castile occupies Toledo
1086–1143	Almoravids from Morocco rescue al-Andalus
1097–1128	Portugal becomes independent
1137	Catalonia and Aragón joined by their rulers' marriage
1143	Almoravid empire breaks up; *taifa* kingdoms reemerge
1156	Almohads from Morocco subjugate *taifa* kingdoms
1188	First assembly of a Cortes in León
1212	Kings of Castile, Aragón, and Portugal defeat Almohads at Las Navas de Tolosa
1229–1276	Jaime I of Aragon conquers Valencia and the Balearic Islands

1230	Castile and León united under Fernando III
1236–1252	Fernando III conquers Córdoba, Murcia, Jaén and Seville for Castile
1252–1492	Last Spanish Muslim kingdom of Granada
1282	Sicilian Vespers; Sicily comes under house of Aragon
1323	Aragon conquers Sardinia
1369	Enrique of Trastámara murders King Pedro; becomes king of Castile
1412	Compromise of Caspe gives crown of Aragon to Trastámara Fernando of Antequera
c. 1450–1556	Spanish cultural Renaissance
1469	Prince Ferdinand of Aragon and Isabella of Castile marry
1474–1504	Isabella reigns in Castile
1478–1480	Spanish Inquisition established
1479–1516	Ferdinand reigns in Aragon
1480–1492	Conquest of Granada
1492	Ferdinand and Isabella expel Jews from Spain; Isabella authorizes Columbus's voyage
1492–c. 1823	Spanish empire in Americas
1516–1556	Carlos I, first Habsburg ruler; becomes Holy Roman Emperor Charles V in 1519
1529–1578	Spaniards in wars with Ottoman Turks
1556–1598	Philip II
1556–1681	Spanish cultural Golden Century (*Siglo de Oro*)
1565	Spaniards begin conquest of Philippines
1568–1648	"Eighty Years War" of Dutch independence from Spanish Habsburgs
1571	Battle of Lepanto; Spain, Venice, and the papacy defeat Turkish navy

1580–1581	Philip II joins Portugal's empire to Spain's
1585–1604	War with England
1588	"Invincible" armada fails against England
1598–1621	Philip III
1609	Expulsion of Moriscos
1618–1648	Thirty Years War
1621–1665	Philip IV
1621–1643	Count-Duke of Olivares as chief minister
1635–1659	War with France
1640	Portugal becomes independent of Spain
1640–1655	Revolt of the Catalans
1659	Peace of the Pyrenees, victory for France
1665–1700	Carlos II, last Habsburg; low point in Spain's "decline"
1700–1746	Philip V, first Bourbon ruler
1702–1713/ 1714	War of the Spanish Succession; Aragón, Valencia, and Catalonia lose autonomy
1746–1759	Fernando VI
1759–1788	Carlos III and Enlightened government
1778–1783	Spain joins France against Great Britain during War of American Independence
1788–1808	Carlos IV
1792–1808	Manuel Godoy, chief minister
1793–1795	War against revolutionary France
1796–1802	War in alliance with France against England; ruin of Spain's American trade
1805–1808	Alliance with Napoleon
1808	Napoleon forces abdication of Carlos IV and his son Fernando VII; puts his own brother, Joseph Bonaparte, on Spanish throne

1808–1813	Risings against Napoleon in Madrid on May 2 opens Spain's War of Independence
1812	Liberal Constitution drafted by Cortes of Cádiz
1813	English duke of Wellington drives Joseph Bonaparte and French from Spain
1814	Fernando VII returns; rejects Constitution of 1812
1820	First military pronunciamento against government
1820–1823	Liberal government; Spain admits the loss of its overseas possessions except Cuba, Puerto Rico, Philippine, and outposts in North Africa
1823	French intervention topples liberal government; Fernando imposes a reactionary regime
1833	Isabel II (1833–1868); Regent María Cristina governs with liberal support; Liberals soon divide into Moderates and Progressives
1833–1839	First Carlist War and emergence of political generals
1837	Royalist Constitution includes a Cortes with limited representation
1841	General Espartero replaces María Cristina as regent
1843	General Narváez leads pronunciamento against Espartero
1848–1852	Carlist unrest in northern provinces; Second Carlist War
1854	Espartero and General O'Donnell overthrow Narváez regime
1855	New Constitution promulgated; Narváez back to power
1858–1863	O'Donnell in power; Spain active in Morocco, Mexico, and the Pacific
1863–1868	Rivalry of O'Donnell and Narváez
1868	Queen Isabel II deposed; First Cuban War of Independence (to 1878); clandestine Anarchist Party begins
1870	Amadeo of Savoy accepts Spanish crown; Third Carlist War ignites

1873	Amadeo abdicates
1873–1874	First Spanish Republic
1874	Restoration of Alfonso XII; government of Conservative Cánovas del Castillo
1876	New Constitution accepted; end of Third Carlist War; Basque privileges (*fueros*) abolished
1878	Clandestine Socialist Party formed; peace restored in Cuba
1881	Cánovas yields to Sagasta's Liberal Party to rotate parties in power
1885	Alfonso XII dies; Cánovas and Sagasta agree to rotate power for the sake of stability
1886	Alfonso XIII born
1888	Socialists led by Iglesias form the General Union of Workers (Unión General de Trabajadores [UGT])
1890	Universal manhood suffrage
1895	Beginning of Second Cuban War of Independence
1898	Spanish American War; Cuba independent; Spain yields Puerto Rico, Philippines, and Guam to the United States
1909, July	"Tragic Week" in Barcelona; mounting industrial and rural violence
1910	Anarchists form Anarcho-Syndicalist movement with workers syndicates (Confederación Nacional de Trabajadores [CNT]—National Confederation of Workers)
1914	Grant of partial autonomy, *Mancomunitat*, to Catalonia
1914–1918	World War I; Spain remains neutral and prospers
1917	General strike leads to crackdown by army
1918–1923	Postwar economic depression, unrest, and political confusion
1921	Military disaster at Annoual in Morocco
1923–1930	Dictatorship of General Primo de Rivera

1929–1936	World Depression
1931, April	Abdication of Alfonso XIII and proclamation of Second Republic; December, Constitution of 1931; women receive the vote; left and liberal parties dominate the government; Alcalá Zamora becomes president
1931–1934	Widespread rural unrest over land reform
1932	Catalonia receives wide autonomy in revived *Mancomunitat*
1933, November	Conservative parties gain majority in Cortes
1934, October	Asturian miners seize Oviedo; are crushed by army
1936, February	Popular Front of leftist parties wins elections to Cortes; July 18, generals rebel
1936–1939	Civil War
1936, October	Republic grants autonomy to Basque Country
1939, April 1	Nationalist rebels triumph
1939–1975	Dictatorship of Generalísimo Franco
1939–1945	World War II; pro-Axis Spain neutral
1946	Spain isolated by United Nations
1947	Franco declares Spain a constitutional monarchy
1948	Franco and Alfonso XIII's heir, Don Juan, provide that Don Juan's son Juan Carlos be educated in Spain
1948–1953	Cold War makes Spain an ally of the United States and North Atlantic Treaty Organization (NATO)
1953	U.S. agreement with Franco for U.S. air and naval bases in Spain
1954–1973	Spanish economy grows dramatically
1955	Spain joins United Nations

1973, December	Assassination of Admiral Carrero Blanco by radical Basque separatists
1975, November	Franco dies; Juan Carlos I becomes king
1976–1981	Centrist Suárez and the transition to democracy
1978	Democratic Constitution ratified; autonomy conceded to Catalonia and the Basque Country, with autonomy to Galicia and other regions to follow
1981, February 23	Right-wing coup attempt fails
1982	Spain joins NATO; Socialists (PSOE [Partido Socialista de Obrero Español]) win elections; Felipe González prime minister
1986	Spain joins European Community (EC); membership in NATO ratified by referendum
1991	First Ibero-American summit held in Guadalajara, Mexico
1992	Olympic Games in Barcelona; World Expo-92 in Seville
1993	Elections cost PSOE its majority, but Felipe González continues as prime minister
1996	In March elections, center-right Popular Party wins a plurality of seats in Cortes; its leader, José María Aznar, becomes prime minister

1

Spain Today

Spain at the end of the twentieth century is a nation of almost 40 million people. Its government is a constitutional monarchy with a democratically elected parliament called the Cortes that sits in Spain's capital, Madrid. Spain is a member nation of the European Community (EC). Today's democratic Spain is the product of a long and often troubled history. For much of the twentieth century Spain was governed by dictatorship, most recently during the years 1939 to 1975 under Generalísimo Francisco Franco. Franco died in 1975, and in 1978 Spain adopted its current democratic constitution.

Although Spanish is the language associated with Spain, what the world calls Spanish is more correctly called Castilian. Castilian or its regional dialects are spoken by almost three-fourths of Spain's people. But along much of Spain's east coast and in the Balearic Islands, Catalan, or variations of it, is spoken. In the northwest corner of Spain, Galician (*Galego*), akin to Portuguese, is the dominant language. These three languages are of the Romance language family, derived from Latin. In the Basque Country, people use the ancient Basque language, related to no other language on earth.

Spain's linguistic and historic regions form seventeen autonomous communities or regions, which are in ways similar to the states of the United States. From these regions Spain was forged, and even today some areas re-

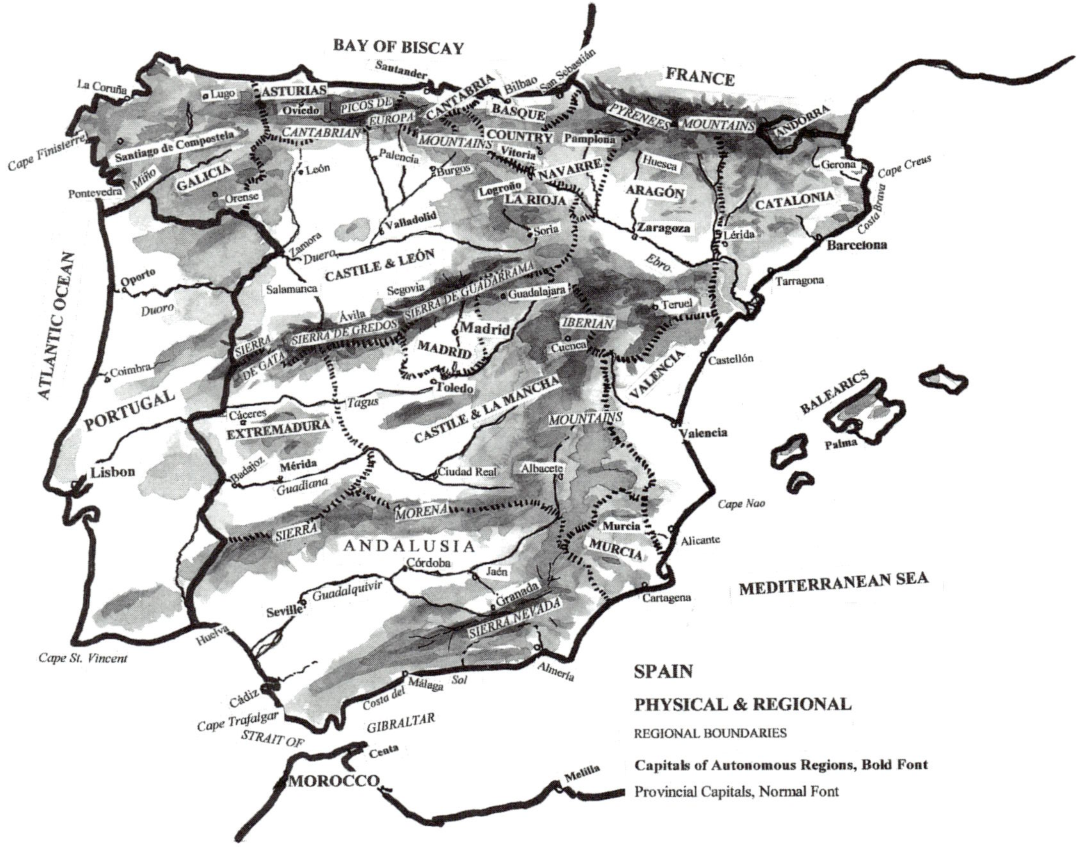

BAY OF BISCAY

ATLANTIC OCEAN

FRANCE

ANDORRA

PYRENEES MOUNTAINS

CATALONIA

Gerona
Cape Creus
Costa Brava
Barcelona
Tarragona
Lérida
Castellón

BALEARICS

Palma

Cape Nao

MEDITERRANEAN SEA

La Coruña
Cape Finisterre
Santiago de Compostela
Pontevedra
Vigo
GALICIA
Orense
Lugo

ASTURIAS
Oviedo
Gijón
CANTABRIA
Santander
PICOS DE EUROPA
CANTABRIAN MOUNTAINS
León
Palencia
Burgos
BASQUE COUNTRY
Bilbao
San Sebastián
Vitoria
NAVARRE
Pamplona
LA RIOJA
Logroño
Soria
ARAGÓN
Huesca
Zaragoza
Ebro

Valladolid
CASTILE & LEÓN
Duero
Salamanca
Segovia
SIERRA DE GUADARRAMA
Ávila
SIERRA DE GREDOS
IBERIAN
Teruel
Cuenca
Guadalajara
Madrid
MADRID
Toledo
Tagus
CASTILE & LA MANCHA
Ciudad Real
Albacete
VALENCIA
Valencia
Alicante
MURCIA
Murcia
Cartagena
Almería

PORTUGAL
Duero
Coimbra
SIERRA DE GATA
Cáceres
EXTREMADURA
Mérida
Guadiana
SIERRA MORENA
Córdoba
Guadalquivir
Jaén
Granada
SIERRA NEVADA
Sol

Lisbon
Huelva
Seville
ANDALUSIA
Cádiz
Cape Trafalgar
STRAIT OF GIBRALTAR
Costa del Sol
Málaga
GIBRALTAR
Ceuta
MOROCCO
Melilla

Cape St. Vincent

SPAIN

PHYSICAL & REGIONAL

REGIONAL BOUNDARIES

Capitals of Autonomous Regions, Bold Font

Provincial Capitals, Normal Font

Map 1

main in a state of tension with greater Spain. Most other European nations were stitched together in similar ways from historic regions, and in most, regionalism has also rekindled in strength. Most of Spain's autonomous regions contain several provinces, long the administrative subdivision of the country; the remainder consist of one province only.

GEOGRAPHY AND REGIONS

The kingdom of Spain measures 194,898 square miles (504,782 squre kilometers), which includes the Balearic Islands in the Mediterranean, the Canary Islands in the Atlantic, and the enclaves of Ceuta and Melilla on the North African coast. More than 190,000 square miles are on the Iberian Peninsula, of which Spain occupies 85 percent. Peninsular Spain is almost 20 percent larger than California, but in many ways it is comparable in climate and landscape. Except for the north coast and mountain regions, most of Spain is semiarid and receives less than twenty inches of rainfall a year, mainly between October and the end of April. Except along the northern coast, Spanish summers range from hot to very hot. Autumn and spring are pleasant. Winters on the mainland are cold, but only the mountains and highlands receive much snow. The southern coast and the Balearic and Canary Islands have agreeable year-round climates and are popular with tourists and retirees.

The Pyrenees Mountains, which crest at more than 11,000 feet, define Spain's northern land border and separate the Iberian Peninsula from the rest of Europe. Water bounds the remaining seven-eighths of the peninsula: the Atlantic Ocean on the north and west, the Strait of Gibraltar on the south, and the Mediterranean on the southeast and east. Most of the Iberian west coast is occupied by Portugal. Much of Spain is mountainous, and its vast center is a high tableland called the Meseta. Almost 70 percent of Spain stands above 1,640 feet (500 meters). In Europe, only Switzerland has a higher average elevation. Using a map (Map 1) as a guide, a survey of Spain's autonomous regions can serve to introduce Spain's geography.

The far northwest corner of Spain comprises the autonomous region of Galicia, which consists of the maritime provinces of La Coruña and Pontevedra, the province of Lugo, and the landlocked province of Orense. Galicia is hilly, green, and very wet and possesses significant forest lands. Its people speak Galician. Its landholdings tend to be small, and it is one of Spain's poorer regions. Though Galicia's harbors, such as Vigo, La Coruña, and the naval base at El Ferrol, are splendid and its fisheries excellent, they were long remote and difficult to access from the rest of Spain. Santiago de Compostela, site of a renowned shrine, is Galicia's regional capital and a university town.

Proceeding from Galicia eastward, the Cantabrian Mountains rise toward the jagged 8,000-foot summits of the Picos de Europa and divide the coastal region known as the Principality of Asturias, from the autonomous region of Castile and León to the south. Asturias, like Galicia, is wet, rugged, and green. Asturias was once rich in coal from which its capital, Oviedo, prospered, but the mines today are depleted, a serious problem for the region. Its slender coastal plain is better given to grazing than to crops, and the dairy industry dominates its agriculture. Its chief ports, Gijón and Avilés, fish, build vessels, and ship coal.

From the Picos de Europa the Cantabrian Mountains ramble east through the autonomous region that bears the name Cantabria. Its capital is the seaport Santander. With a more extensive coastal plain and easier access to the Spanish hinterland, Cantabria is more prosperous than Asturias or Galicia. The mountains continue into the autonomous region called the Basque Country (Euskadi, in its own unique language). Two Basque provinces, Vizcaya and Guipúzcoa, face the Bay of Biscay, and the third, Alava, straddles the mountains. By tradition Basques live from the sea, farm, or are mountain herdsmen. In modern times, the Basque Country has led the way in Spanish heavy industry. Its largest city, Vizcaya's capital Bilbao, bristles with smokestacks and factories. From the surrounding mountains come the iron ores, while the coal to fire the furnaces comes from Asturias. Guipúzcoa's capital, San Sebastián, is both an elegant summer resort and a busy shipping and fishing center. The regional capital of the Basque Country, Vitoria, long an agricultural backwater, is today a thriving industrial center. Basque agriculture rests on numerous small-holders with a tradition of mutual cooperation. Because the countryside is mostly hill and valley, dairying nowadays is most profitable. Autonomy and regional rights (*fueros*) within Spain are part of Basque history. These rights and autonomy were suppressed during the greater part of the period 1876–1975 but have been recovered since 1978 and include control over taxation and revenues. Most autonomous regions have only limited powers of taxation.

The Basque homeland laps into the mountainous region of Navarre, which straddles the western Pyrenees. Like the Basque Country, Navarre has a long history of autonomy and *fueros*, becoming part of Spain in 1513 through conquest. Like the Basque Country, Navarre controls its taxes and revenues. Its capital, Pamplona, is the scene of the fiesta of San Fermín, famous for the running of the bulls through its streets. Today it is also a major manufacturing center. In the rugged countryside, herding and grazing are a traditional way of life. Tucked along the southern border of Navarre and the

Basque Country is a tiny autonomous region called La Rioja, with its capital at Logroño, in the upper valley of the River Ebro. The Ebro's source lies high in the Cantabrian Mountains, and it is the only major Spanish river that flows to the Mediterranean. Spain's best-known red wines come from La Rioja.

East of Navarre, the autonomous region of Aragón rolls south from the Pyrenees. It begins in steep mountain valleys, then becomes a parched table-land, sliced through its center by the green swath of fertile soil watered by the Ebro. The valleys of the province of Huesca are sources of hydroelectric energy and grains. Aragón's capital, Zaragoza, is also capital of a province. Standing on the Ebro, it is a commercial and industrial center. South of the Ebro valley, Aragón rises again into rugged mountains, part of the Iberian system that runs north and south, and separates Mediterranean Spain from the interior. In the province of Teruel, mining is active. Aragonese speak Castilian Spanish, which in Aragón's rural dialect adds humor to Spanish comic movies.

As the Pyrenees roll eastward, its ridges descend to meet the Mediterranean and define the border between France and the autonomous region of Catalonia, where people speak Catalan and valleys become lush as they near the sea. On the Mediterranean shore in the province of Gerona, the Pyrenees and its southward extensions form a picturesque and wild stretch of coastline, some seventy miles long, called the Costa Brava, now dotted with tourist resorts. South of the Costa Brava, on the plain formed by the river Llobregat, stands the region's vigorous capital, Barcelona, the second largest city in Spain and capital of Catalonia and a province. Further south lies the province of Tarragona, while the province of Lérida forms Catalonia's rugged hinterland and abuts Aragón. With a history and language of their own, Catalans maintain a fierce sense of independence.

South of the delta formed by the Ebro where it reaches the sea, variations of Catalan continue to be spoken in the Valencian autonomous region, historically called the Levant. Its capital is Valencia, capital also of a province that encompasses a fertile plain abounding in citrus fruits and rice. To Valencia's north lies the province of Castellón, and to its south, round Cape Nao, the province of Alicante, famous for its beaches.

The Castilian language reemerges further south, in the autonomous region of Murcia, where history rather than any physical barrier defined the boundaries. Against a stark and arid landscape, irrigation and industry strive to lift Murcia from among Spain's poorest regions to a level of relative prosperity. Its seaport Cartagena has long been Spain's chief Mediterranean naval base.

Westward from Catalonia and Valencia, the land rises through the hills and mountains of the Iberian system, where Castilian reappears in the large autonomous regions of Castile and León and Castile–La Mancha. Near the highland city of Soria, the river Duero begins its course westward to the sea. Other rivers that rise in the Cantabrian Mountains or in the central cordillera that divides the Meseta join the Duero to form a broad valley, the heartland of historic Old Castile and León. The regional capital is Valladolid, also capital of a province, but the names of the region's other provincial capitals evoke equal or greater historic memories: Avila, Burgos, León, Palencia, Salamanca, Segovia, Soria, Zamora. Below Zamora, the Duero hits rough country, and for a brief span, its rapids separate Spain from Portugal until it turns and, now called the Duoro, courses through Portugal to the sea. Its pattern of descending from mountains, cutting across the Meseta, then tumbling via rapids into Portugal is repeated by the river Tagus further south and limits their usefulness for transport. Where they cut across the Castilian Meseta, steep banks hinder their use for irrigation.

South of the Duero the boundary that separates Spain and Portugal is determined mainly by rugged country with few inhabitants. The Spanish side gently rises toward the central cordillera that consists of the Sierra de Gata, the Sierra de Gredos, and the Sierra de Guadarrama. The westernmost, the Sierra de Gata, separates Castile and León from the rolling boulder-strewn autonomous region of Extremadura. The poorest region of Spain, Extremadura has its capital at Mérida, once a great Roman center, and includes the provinces of Badajoz and Cáceres. Livestock, cork, olives, tobacco, and some mining are its chief sources of income.

The Sierra de Gredos begins in Extremadura and connects with the Sierra de Guadarrama to separate historic Old Castile, now part of Castile and León, from historic New Castile, now the autonomous regions of Castile–La Mancha and Madrid. Madrid, Spain's capital and largest city, has a population of some 3 million and enjoys striking views of the Guadarrama. Its region is bordered by the provinces of Toledo and Guadalajara of Castile–La Mancha. From the sierras, scrub-covered tablelands roll southward toward the river Tagus, which rises in the Iberian Mountain system, in the province of Cuenca, and carves a valley across the tablelands to continue into Extremadura. Entering Portugal through a gorge, it meets the Atlantic at Lisbon. South of the Tagus low mountains punctuate the endless plains of La Mancha itself, the arid region made immortal by Don Quixote. In the sierras east of La Mancha rises the river Guadiana, to wend west through the provinces of Albacete and Ciudad Real, and turn south past Badajoz to mark the border between Spain and Portugal.

On the Spanish side of the lower Guadiana, the undulating Sierra Morena climbs to form the southern boundary of the Meseta and rolls eastward to separate the autonomous region of Andalusia from the rest of Spain. The

Sierra Morena's eastern reaches join other mountains that separate Castile–La Mancha from the Levant and give birth to the river Guadalquivir, which seventeenth-century poet Luis de Góngora called "the great king of Andalusia." The Guadalquivir flows west through a rich broad valley of red earth and grasses that turn golden in summer. The valley begins in the province of Jaén and extends through the provinces of Córdoba and Seville, with their fabled capitals rising from its banks. Below Seville, Andalusia's regional capital, the river meanders through marshlands till it reaches the Atlantic in the province of Cádiz. The city of Cádiz is Spain's chief Atlantic seaport. North of Cádiz, between the Guadalquivir and Guadiana, stretches the province of Huelva, watered by the Rio Tinto from which Columbus sailed in 1492. Huelva is the site of important copper mines.

South of the valley of the Guadalquivir more sierras rise. Beginning in low hills above Cape Trafalgar on the Atlantic, they gain altitude as they stretch eastward to the Sierra Nevada, in the province of Granada, which boasts mainland Spain's tallest peak, Mulhacén (11,420 feet; 3,478 meters). From the Sierra Nevada more sierras spread toward the Mediterranean like craggy fingers to define the arid valleys of the Andalusian province of Almería and link with the mountains of Murcia and the Iberian system. Along the coast of the provinces of Málaga and Granada, sierras plunging to the sea allow little more than slender plains. Spain's southern tip is anchored by the British-held Rock of Gibraltar. From Spain's southernmost town, Tarifa, Africa is less than ten miles away.

Andalusia, the most populous of Spain's autonomous regions and second largest in extent, is second only to Extremadura in poverty. Its economy is mainly agricultural, though it also has mines, fisheries, and light industry. While climate, mountains, and heath put natural limits on Andalusian agriculture, Andalusia possesses fertile irrigated valleys and has made holders of vast estates very rich. Labor was long provided by a multitude of poor field hands, who under a warm sun lived in whitewashed barrios that looked charming from a distance but were without plumbing or most other ordinary amenities. Although emigration to industrial centers has lately alleviated the problem, and forced landowners to modernize, pockets of real poverty persist.

Across the Strait of Gibraltar from Andalusia, the whitewashed Spanish cities of Ceuta and Melilla cling to the Moroccan shore and enjoy a status similar to that of an autonomous region. They survive, with the forbearance of Morocco, as the last of the fortresses Spaniards and Portuguese planted over 500 years ago on the North African coast to combat Barbary pirates. In those same years, Spaniards sailed into the Atlantic and conquered the Canary Islands, which now form an autonomous region. Known to the ancients as the Fortunate Isles, they were inhabited by native people called Guanches. Their lifestyle was Stone Age, but their resistance proved tenacious. They have disappeared, either destroyed or assimilated. The seven large and six small islands are divided into two provinces, Las Palmas and Santa Cruz de Tenerife. While the islands have important fisheries and raise subtropical crops, tourism forms their chief industry. On Tenerife stands Spain's tallest peak, Teide, a dormant volcano. Long a free-trade area, the Canaries remain, unlike the rest of Spain, outside the European Community.

In the Mediterranean Sea, the Balearic Islands of Majorca, Minorca, Ibiza, and Formentera form another island autonomous region and a single province. They were joined to Spain in the thirteenth century, when the kings of Aragon conquered them from the Moors. Their inhabitants speak dialects of Catalan and enjoy Spain's highest per capita income. Tourism is the principal industry, and the islands are a favored place for Europeans from colder climes to retire.

GOVERNMENT AND POLITICS

Spain's autonomous regions and fifty provinces exist within the framework of a unitary and indivisible Spanish state. Chief of state is King Juan Carlos I, who presides over Spain's constitutional government. The Constitution of 1978 places sovereignty with the Spanish people, who entrust it to the king. His powers are limited, and the actual conduct of government is the business of the prime minister, officially known as the president of the government. In Spain's peaceful transition from dictatorship to democracy, the role of King Juan Carlos has been crucial and at times heroic, which has given him significant moral authority both in Spain and in the wider world. Unlike some other European royal houses, Spain's royal family is not fabulously wealthy. The heir to the throne, Felipe, prince of Asturias, has become popular in his own right as an active military officer, aviator, and yachtsman who takes the ceremonial functions of his office seriously. His mother, Queen Sofía, and sisters have likewise become personally popular with most Spaniards.

The prime minister heads the executive branch of government and is elected by a majority of votes in the Congress of Deputies, the more important of the two chambers of Cortes. If none can muster a majority of votes in two month's time, the king dissolves the Cortes and calls for new elections. Ordinarily elections are held every four years. A prime minister can be removed only by a vote of censure. But as is often the case in parliamentary systems, a prime minister might resign when he or she cannot keep a majority of votes in Congress or sees a chance to increase that majority, which would mean new elections before the normal four-year term is up.

In the years since the restoration of democracy, Socialist Felipe González has held the post of prime minister longest (1982–1996) and has proved to be one of Europe's more remarkable political leaders of recent times. In 1996, José María Aznar, head of the center-right Popular Party, became prime minister. He is the protégé of Manuel Fraga Iribarne, whose long political career extends back to Franco's era, when he was among the regime's bright young men. In the 1980s, Fraga rallied the forces of the center and moderate right to form the Popular Alliance (AP [Alianza Popular]), now the Popular Party. The original democratic center-right coalition had come apart in 1981, following the resignation of Adolfo Suárez as prime minister. It was Suárez, another who had served Franco, who astutely managed the early transition of Spain to democracy after Franco's death. Suárez is now semiretired; the king has made him a duke. Fraga remains an important figure in his position as president of Galicia.

It is the task of the prime minister to select a deputy prime minister (vice president of the government) and form a cabinet. The cabinet includes ministers for foreign affairs, justice, defense, economy and finance, education and science, interior, public administration, autonomous regions, agriculture and fisheries, industry and energy, labor and welfare, transportation, tourism and communications, and culture. Most ministers are also members of the Cortes. While the cabinet meets periodically as a whole, most business is determined by five cabinet committees that consist of ministers and secretaries of state. The five committees are Autonomous Regions; Economic Affairs; Education, Culture, and Science; Foreign Affairs; and State Security.

Spain's Cortes, the chief legislative body, consists of two chambers: the more important Congress of Deputies and the Senate. The Congress, like the U.S. House of Representatives, reflects population. Senate membership is geographically based, although more populous regions receive additional senators. The Congress must pass all legislation and money bills and can override the Senate. The Constitution fixes the number of deputies at no less than 300 and no more than 400. In recent practice the number has been 350, or 1 deputy for each 114,000 Spaniards. Some 20 percent of the current deputies are women. Each of Spain's fifty provinces, established for administrative purposes in the last century, elects at least 1 deputy. The population of each province determines how many more it gets. In the election of deputies, party politics plays the decisive role, as citizens vote by straight-party tickets. Seats in the Cortes are distributed in proportion to the vote each party receives, in the order of priority set by the party. To assure themselves representation, in particular for their leaders, smaller parties often form coalitions with larger parties that share similar ideals. Although once elected, deputies are free to vote independently they tend to vote with the leaders of their party or coalition. In organization, both Congress and the Senate elect a president and a panel of vice presidents to direct debate and conduct business. Debate on the floor is tightly regulated. Both chambers use committees.

To the Senate each Spanish province elects four senators, except for the single-province Balearic Islands, which elect eight to match the number enjoyed by the two provinces of the Canary Islands; and tiny Ceuta and Melilla, which elect two. Each autonomous region also elects at least one senator, with an additional senator for each million inhabitants. Recently, membership has numbered around 250.

Like most continental European countries, Spain has a multiparty system, although two national parties have become dominant. Spaniards have long referred to parties by their initials, to the despair of non-Spanish students of Spain. The parties that dominate the Congress of Deputies in the 1990s are the Spanish Socialist Worker's Party (PSOE, [Partido Socialista de Obrero Español]) and the center-right Popular Party (PP [Partido Popular]), each with considerably over 100 seats. Another dozen national or regional parties hold seats, ranging in number from 1 to around 20. Among national parties, the largest has become the United Left (IU [Izquierda Unida]), a coalition of fragmented Communist parties and disaffected Socialists. The centrist Christian Democrats and traditional Liberals have lately joined forces with the Popular Party. The largest regional party is the Catalan Convergence and Union (CiU [Convergència i Unió]), a centrist party that averages close to 20 seats. An equally influential regional party, although it holds only 5 to 8 seats in the Congress, is the Basque Nationalist Party (PNV [Partido Nacionalista Vasco]). The middle-of-the-road PNV is the most important party in the troubled Basque Country and its local governments. For an effective voice and receipt of financial and administrative support in Congress, a party must hold at least 5 seats, which requires that members of parties with fewer than 5 seats must join with larger parties that hold similar views or form coalitions with others to reach at least 5. For those members who do not, a nondescript "mixed group" exists.

Historically the bureaucracy that carried out the aims of the government was bloated. Spanish governments bought support with government jobs in an economy that until recently did not create enough attractive jobs for the educated and energetic. Civil servants with a college diploma pushed papers; illiterates with the right connections became porters, opened doors, and carried papers back and forth. Government inefficiency became a national joke. The improved economy of the late twentieth century has at last provided adequate employment in the private sector, and the bureaucracy has been trimmed and become relatively efficient. At the top of the bureaucracy stands an elite corps of university-trained professionals. Many performed their jobs under Franco and, despite some complaints from the political left, continue to do their jobs under Spain's revived democracy. As this group retires, professionals who have entered civil service since 1975 and are more instinctively inclined toward democracy will replace them.

Spain's armed forces, like its bureaucracy, gradually became top-heavy. In the last century army officers became a crucial element in Spanish politics, and the army constituted the largest expenditure in the national budget. Since 1975, the officer corps has become more professional and amenable to democracy. Spain's army, navy, and air force currently number about 200,000, and Spain is a member of the North Atlantic Treaty Organization (NATO).

The Spanish judiciary, which is constitutionally independent, has taken shape over centuries and has a life of its own. Men—and since 1977, women—appointed to the bench have been characterized by probity and knowledge of the law and legal procedures. Instinctively conservative and adhering to the strict norms of legality, the judiciary has been little affected by changes in the form of government during the twentieth century. In the rhetoric of the left, the judicial system was long portrayed as a tool of the ruling classes. In 1988 the PSOE government extended civil rights in judicial proceedings, and in the 1994–1996 period it undertook major reforms of the court system, which included a provision for jury trials. In 1995 Spain's penal code, inherited from Franco's time, was thoroughly revised.

ECONOMY

Many attribute the success of Spain's democratic government, after several historical failures, to the modernization of its economy. Spain is no longer a land of extreme wealth and poverty, with little in between. A prosperous middle class is evident everywhere. In the mid-1990s, the average annual income for a Spanish household, about $26,000, reached 75 percent of the average for French and Italian households and 70 percent of North American household income. The ratio of motor vehicles to persons, a popular measure of prosperity, is 1:2.5 in Spain, 1:1.9 in Italy, and 1:1.3 in the United States.

In Spain's modernization, improvements in transport and communication have been particularly important. Lacking navigable rivers, Spain had to wait on railroads to build a modern national economy. Historically the mountains that crisscross the country limited wheeled transport and de-fined a hodgepodge of local and regional economies. Apart from coastal ar-eas that could be reached by ship, pack animals provided the chief means of getting goods from one place to another. The improvement of roads that be-gan in the eighteenth century added lumbering carts and wagons drawn by bullocks and mules to the traffic. The Basque Country and Catalonia, both accessible to the sea, were the first areas of Spain to industrialize. Today, with modern rail and highway transportation, manufacturing industries have sprung up almost everywhere, taking advantage of a hardworking la-bor force. That labor force is also literate, thanks to the unsung work of gen-erations of Spanish educators. At the beginning of the twentieth century, less than 50 percent of Spaniards were literate; now more than 90 percent are.

Well into the twentieth century, agriculture constituted the largest sector of Spain's economy. Today agriculture's share of the gross domestic product (GDP) hovers under 4 percent, and it employs at most 15 percent of the labor force. A historic problem for Spain is that scarcely half its land surface is ar-able, much of the soil is marginal, and only about 40 percent of the land is under permanent cultivation. Another 20 percent provides meadow and pasture. Of forest land, perhaps 15 percent is productive, the rest scrub. Some 10 percent of Spain is bare rock. Grains are the chief crop, although fruit production is important, with a large export market. Sheep and pigs ac-count for some 80 percent of Spain's livestock.

Manufacture, construction, transport, utilities, and mining, in descend-ing order, account for over 30 percent of GDP and 35 percent of employ-ment. International competition has forced retrenchment in Spanish heavy industry. The service sector, including retail trade, hospitality, finance, in-formation, education, and government, accounts for 60 percent of GDP and for almost half of employment. Tourism is particularly important to Spain's southern coast and islands, owing to the benign climate and the abundance of historic and artistic sites.

SOCIETY

Tourism also played a role in opening Spain's society to modernity, bringing together Spaniards with people from the rest of Europe, the Ameri-cas, and the world. Historically, Spanish society was ingrown, based firmly on family, urban barrio or rural village, and region. Great variety existed among the regions both in relative wealth and poverty and in personal de-meanor. Today travelers describe the pride of Spaniards from every region, a pride better described as an innate sense of personal dignity and worth, rather than the tetchy *pundonor* (point of honor) of romantic drama. Most Spaniards display a certain reserve, what the Castilians call *sosiego* (composure), although they tend to be generous and warm in dealing with strangers and hearty with their friends. The volatility some attribute to Spaniards applies mainly to Andalusians, although Spaniards, when compared to most other Europeans, seem capable of extraordinary passion in love and war, which Spanish literature and history both tend to bear out.

As Spain lies between the rest of Europe and North Africa, in their physical appearance Spaniards tend to reflect both European and North African characteristics. Most have brown or black hair, and complexions range from fair to swarthy. Some 17 percent of Spaniards are under fifteen years of age; 20 percent are over sixty. Life expectancy at birth is seventy-two years for men and eighty for women, about the same as in France or Italy.

Spaniards follow the Mediterranean pattern of living in urban centers, towns, or substantial villages. Three-fourths of the population live in communities of 10,000 or more people. Except in the extreme north and northwest, the isolated farmhouse or even hamlet is rare. At the core of a typical Spanish town is the main plaza (*plaza mayor*), flanked by a church and public buildings. Large cities have many plazas: one for the cathedral and others for major public buildings. The largest have multiple barrios, each with its own civic center, parishes, businesses, and character. The populations of Spanish cities tend to be concentrated, with most families living in owned or rented flats in apartment blocks. A few old noble families live in urban palaces surrounded by gardens. Suburban sprawl, with freestanding homes called *chaletes*, remains limited. Most who might afford a suburban chalet prefer to own a spacious condominium in an upscale apartment block and have a weekend house in the country or by the sea.

It is early to gauge the effect of contemporary culture on Spaniards, for whom it is still novel, and on that elusive mix of behavioral qualities known as the "Spanish character." Franco's dictatorship tried to keep much of modern culture at bay. Contemporary life in developed countries tends to homogenize personal behavior, while against it runs a small but noisy counterpoint of rebelliousness. Sensitivity to others is encouraged; egoism and idiosyncrasy are discouraged. Most Spaniards appear to retain their heartiness, dignity, and sense of propriety.

Modernity has touched and limited many of the traditional patterns of life, such as the large and late midday meal and the siesta. But come evening, men and women, old and young, still swarm to the streets to promenade in the daily *paseo,* to meet friends, to take a drink, and to savor tapas (appetizers and snack foods) in cafes and cafeterias before heading home. The *cafetería* holds a special place in Spanish life. A popular hangout for friends, neighbors, and associates, it serves espresso coffee, wine, beer, liquor, tapas, and light meals.

Spanish life carries a sense of vitality, and despite increased crime, most Spaniards feel relatively secure. Children roam the streets freely and feel attuned to the life of their elders. Young Spaniards, better educated than ever, do look somewhat longingly toward the United States, northern Europe, and Italy and seem eager to "be with it," but they seem to appreciate what they and their parents have. Old and young may differ on the relative openness of "sexual freedom." Discretion rather than puritanism has characterized the Spanish attitude toward sex. A "double standard" is the traditional norm for men and women, and attitudes toward prostitution remain ambivalent. The notion of "machismo" exists but seldom with the same intensity it does in Spanish America. As everywhere, "gay" life has only lately become open, although only rarely has there been compulsive hostility against gays among Spaniards.

The crime rate has increased significantly in Spain since the end of the repressive dictatorship. Although the crime rate remains among the lowest in the European Community, and much lower than that of the United States, some wax nostalgic about the virtual lack of serious crime under Franco. Most regard the illegal drug problem as particularly ominous and blame the drug traffic on Spanish Americans and North Africans. In some neighborhoods, vigilante groups have formed to combat drug dealers and users.

A group apart in Spain are the gypsies, or Romani, who number perhaps 3 percent of the population. Although some have assimilated with the larger Spanish society, many have not. Gypsies first appeared in Spain in the sixteenth century, and most settled in Andalusia, replacing expelled Muslims. They did not provide agricultural labor, as was hoped, but engaged in ironwork, entertainment, and barter with what many believed were stolen goods. They remained a small but distinct population with their own folkways and mutual support system. In recent times they have been most conspicuous as flamenco dancers and musicians, which has made some rich. Gypsy women and children still appear to live by begging, to the despair of other Spaniards and the confusion of tourists. The Madrid government has tried to find housing, which the advocacy group Gypsy Presence likens to prisons, for families of gypsy "squatters."

RELIGION AND CULTURE

Close to 95 percent of Spaniards are baptized Roman Catholics, but fewer than half are regular churchgoers. While the number of clergy pales compared to the number in the midnineteenth century, the presence of the Catholic Church still permeates Spanish life. Major rites of passage take place in church and with a priest—from baptism, first communion, confirmation, and marriage to last sacraments, funeral, and burial. So much of historic Spanish culture developed in the service of religion that in every city and town one sees splendid churches; Spanish museums are full of religious paintings and sculpture.

Cultural life in contemporary Spain, as elsewhere, is in flux. People watch television and wonder what became of the poets, novelists, and dramatists of yore. The years of Franco were not kind, and Spanish-American authors—not Spaniards—have recently won more world fame. However, two of the five Nobel Prizes in literature won by Spaniards have been awarded since Franco's death in 1975—in 1977, to poet Vicente Aleixandre; and in 1989, to novelist Camilo José Cela, who published mainly under Franco but bravely kept his critical independence. Spanish film has a large world market and has produced memorable works under directors such as Pedro Almodóvar.

While Spanish painting has of late produced no one to rival Pablo Picasso or Salvador Dalí, nowhere else are there artists of equal reputation. In the display of the heritage of art, Spain has added to its great museums like Madrid's Prado. New to Madrid are the Reina Sofía Art Center, which displays achievements of the twentieth century (including Picasso's famous *Guernica*), and the rich Thyssen-Bornemisza collection. Barcelona has a superb new Picasso museum, and in 1997 a spectacular Guggenheim Museum of Modern Art opened in Bilbao.

In music, Spanish symphony orchestras have come into their own and Barcelona and Madrid have world-class opera houses. The list of famous Spaniards on the opera stage is long and today includes Placido Domingo and Montserrat Caballé. In the popular music field Julio Iglesias is a superstar. Although young Spaniards have taken to rock music, Spain's own rock groups are little known outside the country. Flamenco, which had become mainly a tourist attraction outside Andalusia, is undergoing an international revival as an art form.

Sports occupy a big place in Spanish life. More a spectacle than a sport, the bull fight still has its aficionados, and most cities have an impressive *plaza de toros* (bull ring) despite opposition from animal rights activists and complaints from purists that things are not what they were. Among Basques, jai alai (also called pelota), a hard-ball indoor court sport, is popular. *Fútbol* (soccer in the United States), the great national attraction, packs huge stadiums and excites the wildest enthusiasm. When Madrid plays Barcelona or the Spanish national team vies for the World Cup, all of Spain is galvanized. Tennis, too, has become popular, as middle-class Spaniards flock to the courts, and Spanish tennis stars compete in international tournaments. Spaniards have also taken to golf. Bicycle clubs have sprung up all over, and on Sundays the back roads of Spain glow with cyclists clad in brilliant tights. Jogging, too, has gripped health-conscious Spanish yuppies.

Spain has come to resemble other modern Western and democratic nations. In spite of its transformation, its people have retained the warmth for which they have long been known, and the country's exotic differences make it special.

2

The Historic Foundations
of Spain

Before beginning with Spain's history the reader should recall that historically we are dealing with people biologically like ourselves but often different in the ways they thought and understood things. An imaginative effort should be made to understand their world as they perceived it. Over the last 200 years, our relation to the natural world has been radically transformed by science and technology. Life expectancy now extends to over seventy. Historically, infant mortality took the life of one child in four. Maybe half survived childhood diseases to reach age twenty, and one person in ten made it to age sixty. The conditions of life were hard: Most people walked wherever they went and scratched a living from the soil, anxious about weather and the threat of famine. People lived close to their domestic animals and feared predatory beasts. They had sexual urges; they raised families. They lacked pain-killing drugs. And they had no doubt that the workings of nature were governed by supernatural forces that could be capricious and had to be placated. Religion and its rituals were a part of the fabric of their daily lives. The luxury that the few at the top of society enjoyed depended on the labor of others, often slaves. The laws that governed behavior and provided continuity and some security were harsh, and the punishments were brutal. At all levels of organization—families, tribes, civilized communities, vast political aggregations called kingdoms and empires—conflict and war were endemic. As to why such strife exists within a species that can also be peaceable behavioral scientists disagree. From a historical viewpoint, plunder, territory, and later, ideology appear most often among the chief reasons for war.

Archaeologists believe that modern humans (*Homo sapiens*) first appeared in the Iberian Peninsula over 40,000 years ago. Related species such as Neanderthals preceded them. What further work will reveal cannot be known. Prehistoric cave paintings survive in several parts of Spain. Those found at Altamira in northern Spain from the Magdalenian Period (c. 15,000–9000 B.C.) are among the finest anywhere. The end of the Ice Age, around 10,000 B.C., led to new patterns in hunting and gathering, depicted by thousands of lively figure drawings on rocks in eastern and southern Spain.

Migrations of peoples into Spain continued from Europe beyond the Pyrenees, the Mediterranean, and North Africa. Evidence of the "Neolithic Revolution," the development of rudimentary farming and animal husbandry, appears after 6000 B.C., several thousand years later than it did in the Middle East. Spanish-made pottery also appeared, as did megalithic tombs, around 3500 B.C. After 3200 B.C. people began to work copper and also to fortify their villages, testimony to increased crowding and violence. With the coming of the Bronze Age around 2000 B.C., many villages were reestablished on heights for better defense. Rich in minerals, Spain had copper mines in the south and tin, necessary to make bronze, in Galicia.

Around 1600 B.C. the Iberians, who gave the peninsula their name, arrived in Spain. It is traditionally thought that they came from North Africa, but some believe that they followed Europe's Mediterranean coast to Spain. They clustered in fortified centers along the east coast and in southern valleys and dominated much of the region under a host of local kinglets. They mined silver in the Rio Tinto region and gold in the upper valley of the Guadalquivir, and their leaders wore elaborate jewelry. Their monuments included fine sculptures; the lovely bust of the *Lady of Elche* and the enthroned *Lady of Baza* are among the prized treasures of Madrid's National Archaeological Museum. The Iberians adapted the Phoenician alphabet to their language, which unfortunately has been lost. We can read little of it but place names.

Soon after 600 B.C. Celtic peoples crossed the Pyrenees into northwestern and central Spain. On the central Meseta they blended with the Iberians and established a distinctive Celtiberian culture. By the time the Celts arrived in Spain, we have the beginnings of history as we understand it, supported by written records. Phoenician seafarers and traders from the region of modern Lebanon, attracted by Spain's mines of copper, tin, gold, and silver, arrived on the coast of Spain before 1000 B.C.; legend claims they founded Cádiz, which they called Gadir, in 1100 B.C. After 800 B.C. Phoenician influence gave rise in the south to an Iberian culture the Greeks called Tartassian, which blended Middle Eastern and local elements. Some speculate that Spain was the Tarshish mentioned in the Bible. When Phoenicia fell to the Babylonians in 573 B.C., Phoenician colonies survived in southern Spain and included Cádiz and Malaca, today's Málaga. In the same years, on the Mediterranean coast of northeastern Spain, Greeks, who had colonized Massila (Marseilles, France), planted two small colonies at Emporion (Ampurias) and Rhoda (Rosas) on a flat stretch of the Costa Brava.

The south of Spain soon came under the hegemony of Phoenicia's most successful colony, Carthage, near today's Tunis. After the defeat of Carthage by Rome in a war over Sicily (First Punic War, 264–241 B.C.), Carthaginian general Hamilcar Barca extended Carthage's power in Spain. He landed at Cádiz and subjugated the remaining independent communities of the south. Before he died, he established on Spain's east coast in 228 B.C. a stronghold called Cartago Nova, today's Cartagena. Threatened cities to the north sought Roman aid, which in 218 B.C. led to the Second Punic War. From Spain, Hamilcar's son Hannibal led an army that included Iberian troops and war elephants overland to invade Italy. In response the Romans sent an army to Spain by sea, and under Scipio, the future Africanus, conquered Carthaginian Spain. Scipio next crossed to Carthage, forcing Hannibal to abandon Italy. At the Battle of Zama in 202 B.C. he defeated Hannibal and earned the name Scipio Africanus.

Scipio settled some of his veterans at Italica, near Hispalis (Seville), to begin the romanization of Spain. Rome divided Spain into two provinces, Hispania Citerior (Nearer Spain) and Hispania Ulterior (Further Spain). Over the next 200 years, ambitious Roman officials brought more and more of the peninsula under direct Roman control. The Celtiberian stronghold of Numantia, near modern Soria, required 20 years (153–133 B.C.) to subdue.

The conflict of rich and poor Romans over land possession in Italy led more and more poor Roman veterans to settle in Spain. They petitioned successfully for the extension of Roman civil rights and laws to Spanish towns. Spain was in the thick of the Civil War of 49–45 B.C., between Julius Caesar and Pompey the Great. Caesar defeated Pompey's supporters in Spain, and after Pompey's murder in Egypt, Caesar governed the Roman world. He rewarded many of his veterans with more land in Spain.

Following Caesar's assassination in 44 B.C., his nephew Octavius Caesar gained control of Rome and as Caesar Augustus ruled the Roman Empire. He completed the task of bringing the Iberian Peninsula under Roman rule and reorganized the provinces. The south became Baetica, its capital at Corduba (Córdoba); the east and north became Tarraconensi, its capital at Tarraco (Tarragona); and the west became Lusitania, its capital at Augusta Emerita (Mérida). Most of the chief cities of Spain not yet mentioned also existed: Barcino (Barcelona), Valentia (Valencia), Ilerda (Lleida or Lérida), Dertosa (Tortosa), Caesaraugusta (Zaragoza), Osca (Huesca), Legio (León), Toletum (Toledo), Segovia, Segontia (Sigüenza), Salamantica (Salamanca), Ocelum Duri (Zamora), Pallantia (Palencia), Lucus Augusti (Lugo), Aurium (Orense), and Pompaelo (Pamplona). These urban municipalities presided over administrative districts that were further divided into townships, whose boundaries many believe have undergone little change into modern times. An infrastructure of roads and public works supported commerce in a society that was largely agricultural but had important manufactures, mines, and forests. Large stretches of magnificent Roman road can still be seen wending upward from Arenas de San Pedro west of Madrid to cross the Sierra de Gredos. At Segovia a soaring aqueduct that rests on towering arches and brought mountain water to the inhabitants still stands. At Italica the remains of an impressive Roman amphitheater loom over other excavated ruins, while Mérida boasts a splendid theater. Across Spanish rivers Roman bridges survive at Córdoba, Mérida, and Alcántara.

The inhabitants of Roman Spain might best be called Hispani. For 200 years they knew peace and prospered. In A.D. 69 Emperor Vespasian conceded citizenship to the inhabitants of Hispanic towns, and in A.D. 212 almost all but slaves became Roman citizens. Latin gradually supplanted the other languages of the peninsula, except for Basque. Spanish-born contributors to high Latin culture included the rhetorician Marcus Annaeus Seneca and his more famous son, Lucius Annaeus Seneca, Stoic philosopher and playwright; their kinsman, the poet Lucan; Martial, famous for his epigrams; and Quintilian, the grammarian. Two of Rome's greatest emperors, Trajan (A.D. 98–117) and Hadrian (A.D. 117–138), were also born Hispani.

In the religious life of Spain the Romans added their pantheon of gods and goddesses to the Middle Eastern traditions the Iberians had acquired from the Phoenicians and the Druidic rites of the Celts. Mystery cults sprang up in Hispanic cities. Jewish communities settled in the peninsula, and Christianity followed them. St. Paul mentioned taking the Gospel to Spain (Romans 15:28), and pious legend claimed that the Apostle James the Greater (Santiago) preached in Spain, where his disciples buried him after his martyrdom in Jerusalem.

Hispano-Roman society was dominated by great landowners, referred to as *seniores,* which gives us *señor,* the Spanish word for lord, sir, and mister. While they kept mansions in major cities, they also built luxurious rural villas from which they oversaw their vast estates. Called *latifundia,* such vast estates would endure in varying forms till modern times and spread to Spanish America. Latifundios would come to pose a fundamental issue in the politics of modernization in Spain. They were most prevalent in the south and long worked by slaves. Extensive irrigation was necessary and demanded constant labor. Elsewhere smallholdings prevailed in regions that permitted cultivation, although many were worked by sharecropping arrangements under great landholders. In the mountains herding sheep and goats was a way of life, as was fishing along the coasts. Much of the land, then as now, was barren and sparsely inhabited.

Between A.D. 235 and 285 large-scale civil wars involving Roman merce-nary armies racked the empire until they were ended by Emperor Diocletian (284–305). He reorganized the sprawling province of Tarraconensis into three, with the southeast becoming Carthaginensis, its capital at Cartagena, and the far northwest becoming Gallaecia (Galicia), with its capital at Bra-cara (Braga in Portugal). Now five, Spain's provinces with Mauretania Tin-gitana, northern Morocco with its capital at Tingit [Tangier], formed the grand imperial diocese of the Spains.

Diocletian also tried to rid the empire of what he believed to be an impi-ous and disruptive Christian minority. In 304 he began the Great Persecu-tion, which did not last long in Spain. Previous persecutions were mainly local and sporadic. By the time Spain's most famous martyrs—St. Vincent of Zaragoza at Valencia and Saint Eulalia at Mérida—perished in the Great Persecution, Christianity had become well established. Christian churches existed in many towns, and around 310, nineteen Hispanic bishops assem-bled in the council of Elvira to discuss church discipline and morals. In 313 Emperor Constantine (306–337) legalized and favored Christianity. His chief religious adviser was Hosius, bishop of Córdoba. During the next sev-eral generations most Hispani became Christian, and in 392, Hispanic-born Emperor Theodosius I (379–395) outlawed paganism.

Diocletian and his successors imposed the burden of the reorganized em-pire upon the rich and powerful and demanded that they return to their civic obligations. Instead, the rich withdrew from the cities to their rural es-tates. Even there the government made demands on them but in compensa-tion gave them extensive jurisdiction over neighboring smallholders, tenant farmers, and the free but poor laborers who had largely supplanted the slaves. The groundwork of the systems called later seigneurial or feudal was thus laid, while urban life and the infrastructure of grand public works deteriorated. The public works that continued mainly involved the con-struction of defensive walls around the shrinking towns. Theodosius I was the last to preside over an intact empire. When he died in 395, his incompetent sons divided it into eastern and western halves, and the west began its chaotic collapse.

In A.D. 409 vast bands of Germanic warriors, accompanied by their women, children, animals, and worldly goods, entered Spain. Its population, between 4 and 6 million, was left almost defenseless by the disintegration of the legions. Citizen training at arms had been discontinued long ago; the ruling nobility feared the oppressed peasantry, who had been demilitarized during centuries of peace. The Roman count of Spain had perhaps 11,000 men to defend the peninsula against some 200,000 barbarians, including at least 50,000 warriors. The Sueves invaded Galicia and occupied several towns, plundering the countryside. Their Vandal allies numbered 130,000. Also rampaging through Spain were 30,000 Alans. In the same years Roman authorities had to contend with rebellious peasants, who at times controlled whole provinces and joined with marauding bands of barbarians.

Beyond the Pyrenees the Visigoths appeared, perhaps 200,000 strong. They had entered the empire in 376 in the region of the lower Danube River, and in 378 they defeated the eastern Roman emperor in battle at Adrianople. Theodosius pacified them and made them Roman allies. In 409 they rebelled and in 410 sacked Rome. They moved west to establish a kingdom in southern Gaul (now France), based on Toulouse. They made a new treaty with the Romans and aided Roman authorities in Spain against the Sueves, Alans, and Vandals. The Visigoths routed one branch of the Vandals, but the other, 80,000 strong, turned south to Baetica and in 429 crossed to Africa. When the Visigoths aided the Romans in Gaul to defeat Attila's Huns, the Sueves extended their sway from Galicia to much of Lusitania. Visigothic warriors returned to Spain at Roman invitation to drive the Sueves from Lusitania back to Galicia and crush more peasant uprisings. In the 490s, whole families of Visigoths began to settle in Spain, which was becoming part of the Visigothic kingdom, acknowledged as such by the eastern Roman emperor at Constantinople. No longer was there a Roman emperor in the west.

In 507 the Franks shattered Visigothic power at Toulouse, but the kingdom survived with its new capital at Barcelona. Subsequent Visigothic kings, as they consolidated power, transferred their seat to Mérida and finally to Toledo. King Leovigild (569–586) completed the destruction of the Galician kingdom of the Sueves. The Hispano-Roman aristocracy had offered some resistance to the Visigoths, but in the end, those who survived assimilated with the conquerors. The Visigoths, a warrior minority, needed them to maintain Roman administration and law; although for themselves, they referred to Visigothic tribal law. Because the land was productive, the Visigothic leaders did not interfere with the economy and mainly left the

Hispani in place to keep working. Visigoths not active in warrior retinues settled to farm or herd in thinly populated areas, mainly on the Meseta around Toledo and north of the central sierra in the valley of the Duero.

A lingering problem was religion. The Visigoths had converted to Arian Christianity, which the orthodox Hispano-Roman majority regarded as heresy. Arianism stressed Christ's humanity over His divinity and did not regard Him as equal to God the Father. The orthodox position, as defined by the Council of Nicea of 325, held that Christ was simultaneously true God and true Man and one with the Father. Not until the Third Church Council of Toledo in 589, convoked by King Reccared, did most Visigoths convert to orthodox Christianity. Their conversion furthered their assimilation with the surviving Hispano-Roman elite and their acceptance by the larger Hispanic population.

Among the ruling elite of the Visigothic kingdom, election, murder, and civil war alternated in the choice of kings. Church leaders, who mediated between rulers and ruled, became compromised. At times the Visigoths persecuted the Jews, thus alienating a significant part of the urban community. The larger Hispanic population remained passive and indifferent, but in hard times they became unruly. Yet sufficient stability and acquiescence were achieved to allow a crude late antique culture to flourish. In regions newly settled by Visigoths, churches were built and decorated, while the Visigothic elite showed a penchant for elaborate jewelry that included votive offerings of gold and precious gems in their churches. The chief intellectual light was St. Isidore, bishop of Seville (600–635), whose *Etymologies,* a hodgepodge of fact and fable, became the standard encyclopedia for early Medieval Europe.

A contested election for a king in 710 led to outside intervention and the collapse of the Visigothic kingdom. Exactly what happened and how remain murky. What makes most sense is that the enemies of King Rodrigo (710–711) invited Tarik, a Muslim chieftain from North Africa, to aid them in Spain. Legend speaks of a vengeful Count Julian, whose daughter Rodrigo had violated. Tarik had Julian besieged at Ceuta on the Moroccan coast, and the two may have struck a deal. Tarik landed with his people at Algeciras Bay, whose eastern shore is dominated by the great rock that took his name, Jebel al Tarik (Arabic for Mountain of Tarik), which usage has slurred to Gibraltar. At a battle on the road to Cádiz, supposedly near the Rio Guadalete, Rodrigo fell and Tarik triumphed. Rather than withdraw to North Africa, Tarik called for reinforcements. His superior, Musa, crossed the Strait with more people. They made allies among Rodrigo's enemies and proceeded to overrun the peninsula, driving the hold-outs —a few counts and bishops with their retinues— to places of refuge in the northern mountains.

By 718 the Muslim conquerors had incorporated the greater part of Spain into the world of Islam. Because they had launched their invasion from Mauritania, as Morocco was called, they were called Moors. With them the word *Andalusia* appears as *al-Andalus*. Today it applies to the south of Spain, the region that remained longest under Muslim rule. The romantically inclined think the word is Moorish for "land of the west" or "land of the evening star," but most experts believe the name derives from the Vandals, whose survivors were the first Germanic people the Arabs encountered in North Africa.

While the greater part of Europe was sunk in barbarism, Spain had become a part of the most dynamic civilization in western Eurasia. Islam, preached by the Prophet Muhammad, erupted from the Arabian peninsula soon after his death in 632, as reckoned by the Christian calendar. Inspired by the concept of *jihad* (holy war), Arab warriors ripped Egypt, Palestine, and Syria from the Byzantine Empire, the Greek-speaking heir to Rome. Although high culture endured at the Byzantine capital, Constantinople, the empire became largely defensive, preserving its past and clinging to religion in search of God's protection. In contrast, Islamic culture, confident of God's favor and glowing with success, embraced and reinvigorated the great legacies of Hellenistic Egypt and Syria, where ancient science survived.

At the pinnacle of the Islamic world stood the caliph, Muhammad's successor as leader of the faithful on earth and both a religious and political leader. As Arab conquests gained territory and booty, descendants of Muhammad's daughters, relatives, and associates vied for the office in bloody family feuds. By 661 the Umayyad family had triumphed. They established their capital at Damascus and saw Muslim warriors sweep west to Spain and into France, and eastward to overrun Persia and Afghanistan, and continue into Central Asia and northern India. Then in 744 more bloody civil strife broke out in Syria, and in 750 the Umayyads were overthrown. The victorious Abbasid dynasty succeeded to the caliphate and moved its capital to Baghdad. An Umayyad survivor, Abd-al-Rahman, escaped to Spain. There he persuaded the quarreling Arab, Syrian, Egyptian, and Berber elites, who dominated Spain's municipalities and regions, to recognize him as emir (commander) in defiance of the Abbasid caliphs.

From the time of the conquest, caliphs had appointed emirs to Spain and then removed them when they seemed too independent. Tarik and his superior Musa had been quickly recalled to Damascus. Subsequent emirs rose and fell with equal rapidity—some sent from Damascus or North Africa; others acclaimed by their warriors on winning a civil war. Commanders and governors ordered to Spain brought kinsmen and troops from their own place of origin, whether Arabia, Syria, or Egypt. Because Spain was close, many Berbers immigrated from North Africa and connected the politics of the two regions.

Despite frequent tumult in Spain, emirs led their troops on raids across the Pyrenees into France. In 732 the Frankish military leader Charles Martel (723–741) defeated a major marauding expedition at Poitiers. New unrest among the Berbers of Spain and North Africa limited further expeditions across the Pyrenees, and in time the Frankish kingdom that Charles Martel revived would assume the initiative under his grandson Charlemagne (768–814).

In Spain the larger Hispanic population continued as before, under new governors as well as under some old leaders left from Visigothic times who had switched sides and converted to Islam. Islam tolerated Christians and Jews as "Peoples of the Book," with whom Islam shared the traditions of the Bible and the prophets. Muslims believed that Jesus Christ was a prophet and thought Christians mistaken to believe in a Trinity and the Divinity of Christ. The Jews, no longer subject to sporadic persecution and strictly monotheistic like the Muslims, found their situation improved. Christians and Jews paid a special tax through their communities in place of the military service expected of Muslims. Many Hispani converted to Islam, especially noblemen eager to preserve their wealth and influence and peasants whose lot under the former regime had been servile. Called *muwalladun* in Arabic and *muladíes* in Spanish, the noble coverts intermarried with the conquerors and participated in government, while the peasant converts became free men. Those Hispani who remained Christian under Muslim rule, mostly members of well-organized urban congregations, came to be known as Mozarabs (Mozarabes, from the Arabic *musta'ribun*, "arabized") and regarded those who converted to Islam as renegades. Although Arabic became the language of government and business, Mozarabs and many *muwalladun* at home spoke the Romance languages derived from late Latin that would become Castilian, Catalan, Galician, and Portuguese. The interaction of Muslims, Christians, and Jews formed a distinctive dimension of Spanish medieval culture.

Abd-al-Rahman established his capital at Córdoba and effectively ruled most of Spain until his death in 788. While Muslim governors and elites of the principal Spanish cities enjoyed extensive authority in their own regions, Abd-al-Rahman and his successors asserted preeminence over them and proved able to quash their frequent revolts. Although the emirs selected some of their chief advisers and captains because they were kinsmen, they chose most for their talents and preferred to employ new men, who were dependent on them. Even talented slaves, converted to Islam, might rise high

in the emir's service. The emir's own succession to office was more prob-
lematic. Because each ruler might have four wives, as Islamic law allowed,
and many concubines, he usually had several sons. Though he often favored his first, the father might choose another son who seemed better
suited to the task of government. In the harem and among the court councillors and military commanders the politics of identifying the heir was a constant and often nasty business.

To deal with restlessness, the emirs built a professional army that numbered 40,000 under Abd-al-Rahman. Most were Berbers, but the ranks included many Slavs who had been enslaved as pagans in eastern Europe by
the Franks and sold in Spain. These troops, both mercenaries and slaves,
might be augmented by men called to service from the Muslim population.

Persistent unrest did not seem to hinder economic progress. As part of
the Islamic world, Spain traded mainly with North Africa and the Middle
East. To agriculture the conquerors introduced Middle Eastern techniques,
including irrigation on a more intensive scale than before, which increased
productivity. Roman Spain already knew grains, the grape, and the olive, to
which the Muslims added oranges, lemons, figs, dates, almonds, rice, and a
vast variety of vegetables. To flax and cotton, the Muslims added hemp and
silk. Beekeeping assumed a special niche in the economy. In Spain livestock
had been abundant since time immemorial, with cattle, oxen, sheep, pigs,
and horses. Among Visigothic settlers, herding had been a favored way of
life. The Muslims bred their superb Arabian horses to the already famous
Spanish stock to produce the elegant Andalusian breed; on a more humble
level, and more important, they greatly increased the use of the burro. Even
though there were asses in Roman Spain, it was mainly the ox that pulled
wagons and plows. In a Spain where most roads had become little more
than trails, the burro proved the perfect beast of burden, as well as a useful
helper to hardworking peasants.

Although the northern borderlands of Muslim Spain were troubled by
resurgent Christian principalities and revolts by local Muslim strongmen,
al-Andalus prospered. Its heartland was sheltered by the imposing barrier
of the central cordillera and centered on Córdoba and the valley of the
Guadalquivir. Córdoba became an almost wholly Muslim city after much of
its Mozarab population sought martyrdom by insulting the Muslim faith,
for which some paid with their lives and more with exile. Emir
Abd-al-Rahman I had commenced in Córdoba the Great Mosque, still one of
the wonders of the world despite later ill-advised alterations made after it
became a Christian cathedral. Emir Abd-al-Rahman II (822–852) added to
Córdoba's renown. Travelers from Christian Europe and the Middle East
found Córdoba a marvel, full of luxurious palaces and gorgeous gardens

alive with lush plants and playing fountains. It became known for cordovan leather, just as Toledo became famous for its steel blades. Like other Andalusian cities, Córdoba had a proud Jewish quarter. Córdoba's heyday came in the tenth century, when Abd-al-Rahman III (912–961) proclaimed himself caliph. At the time it may have had a population of 250,000 people. Outside the teeming city, on a gentle hill, the caliph built his spectacular summer palace, Medina Azahara, with, so it was described, 4,300 columns of white marble from Italy and green and rose from Tunisia. Andalusia had reached its pinnacle of splendor in world history.

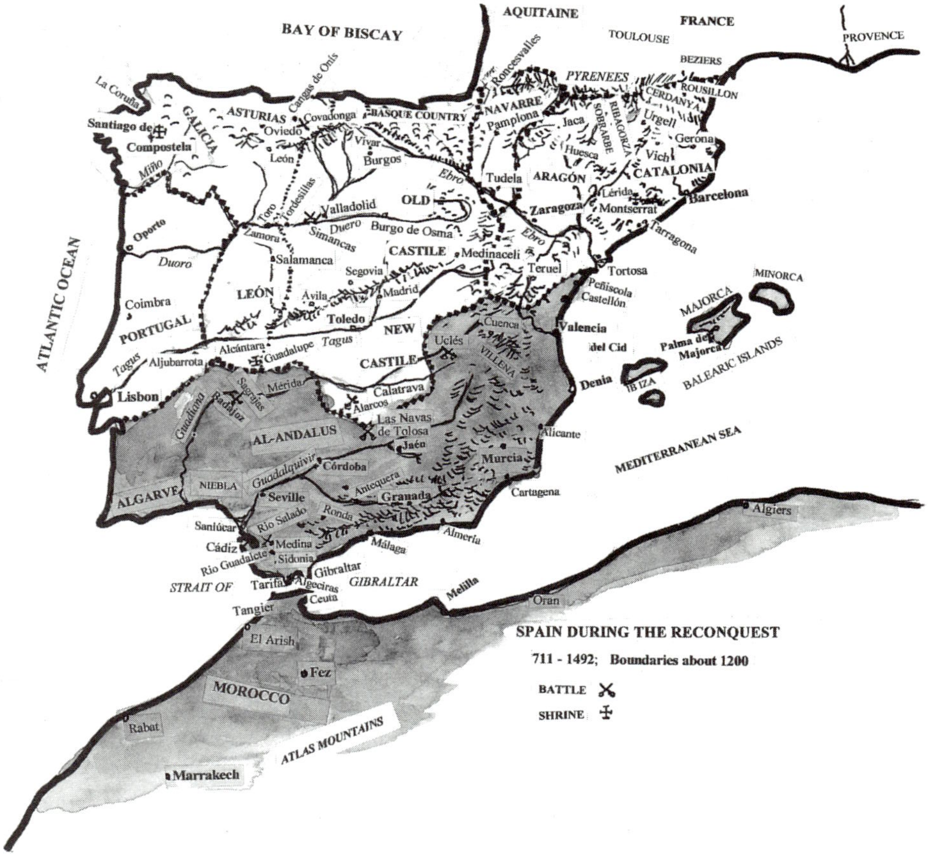
SPAIN DURING THE RECONQUEST
711 - 1492; Boundaries about 1200
BATTLE
SHRINE
BAY OF BISCAY
ATLANTIC OCEAN
MEDITERRANEAN SEA
AQUITAINE
FRANCE
TOULOUSE
BEZIERS
PROVENCE
ROUSILLON
CERDANYA
PYRENEES
Roncesvalles
NAVARRE
Pamplona
Jaca
SOBRARBE
RIBAGORZA
Urgell
Gerona
Vich
CATALONIA
Barcelona
Huesca
Tudela
ARAGÓN
Zaragoza
Lérida
Montserrat
Tarragona
Tortosa
Peñíscola
Castellón
Teruel
Valencia
del Cid
Denia
Alicante
Cartagena
MAJORCA
MINORCA
Palma de Majorca
IBIZA
BALEARIC ISLANDS
La Coruña
Santiago de Compostela
GALICIA
Miño
ASTURIAS
Cangas de Onís
Covadonga
Oviedo
León
BASQUE COUNTRY
Vivar
Burgos
Ebro
OLD
CASTILE
Valladolid
Tordesillas
Toro
Zamora
Duero
Simancas
Burgo de Osma
Medinaceli
Salamanca
Segovia
Madrid
Avila
LEÓN
Toledo
NEW
CASTILE
Oporto
Duoro
Coimbra
PORTUGAL
Tagus
Aljubarrota
Lisbon
Alcántara
Guadalupe
Uclés
Cuenca
VILLENA
Mérida
Sagrajas
Badajoz
Guadiana
Calatrava
Alarcos
Las Navas de Tolosa
Jaén
AL-ANDALUS
Córdoba
Guadalquivir
Murcia
NIEBLA
ALGARVE
Seville
Antequera
Granada
Ronda
Rio Salado
Sanlúcar
Cádiz
Medina
Sidonia
Rio Guadalete
Málaga
Almería
Gibraltar
Tarifa
Algeciras
STRAIT OF
GIBRALTAR
Tangier
Ceuta
Melilla
Oran
Algiers
El Arish
Fez
MOROCCO
Rabat
ATLAS MOUNTAINS
Marrakech

Map 2

3

Reconquest

The regions of Spain that successfully resisted the Muslim invaders were in the far north of the peninsula, mountainous, and poor (Map 2). The earliest success noted by chroniclers occurred in Asturias, where a refugee Visigothic nobleman, Pelayo, rallied local tribesmen. In 718, at the caves of Covadonga in the Picos de Europa, he defeated Moors sent to pursue him. The Asturians acclaimed him king. Before he died in 737, he made his capital at Cangas de Onís. His heirs consolidated their rule over Asturias, and Alfonso I (739–757) extended it into Galicia after its Berber garrison mutinied and withdrew. Alfonso led raids into the Duero Valley and turned its northern reaches into a no-man's land. In 810, King Alfonso II "the Chaste" moved his capital to Oviedo, a stronghold that covered the passes south. Outside Oviedo stands the tiny but remarkable Romanesque church of Santa María de Naranca, built around 840 as a royal hall and consecrated in 905 as a church.

For the Asturian kings, literate churchmen claimed legitimate rule over Christian Visigothic Hispania, however far-fetched that claim seemed in the ninth century. Around 813 a patron saint was found, with the location of the reputed tomb of Santiago (St. James the Greater), in Galicia. The shrine built over it, known as Santiago de Compostela, became the goal of a renowned medieval pilgrimage. Along the road to Santiago, which began in central

France, crossed the Pyrenees, and proceeded west through Burgos and León, sprang churches, monasteries, and cathedrals. The surviving shrine is one of Europe's finest twelfth-century Romanesque churches, with an eighteenth-century Baroque facade.

Christian principalities also emerged in the Pyrenees, while from the Frankish kingdom Charlemagne led several incursions into Spain and established a Spanish March based on Barcelona. His expedition of 778 is famous for the ambush in the Pass of Roncesvalles of his rearguard, commanded by Count Roland and immortalized in Old French by the epic *La Chanson de Roland*. Basques from Pamplona, rather than Muslim warriors, were the likely culprits. Although it was not mentioned in the epic, Charlemagne had destroyed the walls of Pamplona before he withdrew into France. The Pamplonans destroyed Roland and his rearguard in retaliation.

In the same years, Christianity revived among the region's population, which gave a new dimension to the border conflicts. Powerful Christian Basque families, supported by Frankish Aquitaine, wrested Navarre from local Muslim strongmen. In the Pyrenean valley of the river Aragón the town of Jaca many have been occupied by Christians as early as 760, but not until after 800 is the county of Aragón heard of. Other Pyrenean counties, some originally dependent on Frankish Toulouse and Aquitaine, included Ribagorza, Sobrarbe, Pallars, and Urgell.

Against these petty Christian principalities, Muslim Spain arrayed a chain of strongholds along the Duero and Ebro Rivers. Their governors did not always obey the emirs of Córdoba but often pursued their own interests in the vicissitudes of border warfare. Emir Abd-al-Rahman II led or sent forces north almost annually to harass the Christian north. When Vikings sacked Seville in 844, he defeated them and drove them from the country. He apparently fell victim to a harem intrigue, and his heir Muhammad I (852–886) was distracted by rebellions.

Christian rulers took advantage of the situation to gain territory through stubborn persistence. Asturian kings began to repopulate the area around León, not only with northerners but with Mozarabs from Andalusia, who drifted north to escape persecutions they sometimes courted. Alfonso III the Great (866–910) pushed Galicia's frontier into today's Portugal and tightened his grip over the northern half of the valley of the Duero. Around 882 he founded Burgos.

Aid from France fell off when Charlemagne's empire broke up. A band of Moorish raiders, supported by Córdoba, established a base on the French coast, not far from Marseilles. The counts of Barcelona, in theory vassals of France, were on their own. Vifredo the Hairy (d. 898), the semilegendary founder of independent Catalonia, combined his own inheritance of Urgell with the counties of Barcelona, Vich, Gerona, Ripoll, and Cerdanya. He pushed the frontier south to the sawtooth massif of Montserrat, where in the next century the historic Benedictine monastery of the Black Madonna appeared. Few areas in Europe are so rich in Romanesque monasteries and churches as the slopes of the Pyrenees in Catalonia.

In al-Andalus unrest persisted but mainly affected the elites, and Andalusia prospered in spite of them. When Abd-al-Rahman III became emir of Córdoba in 912, he spent his first twenty years quelling rebellions. He also battled the rulers of León and Navarre, who raided deep into Muslim Spain in search of plunder. In 920 he defeated the Leonese and in 924 sacked Pamplona. As he reasserted his authority in Spain, the unity of the world of Islam shredded. In 909 the Fatimid ruler of Tunis broke with the Abbasid caliph of Baghdad and claimed caliphal authority for himself. In 929, Abd-al-Rahman took the same step, invoking his Umayyad descent, and established the caliphate of Córdoba. Vested with the authority of caliph, he eliminated the last rebellions in al-Andalus.

In 932 King Ramiro II of León (931–951) crossed the Sierra de Guadarrama to sack Madrid, then a Muslim fortress. In 939, Abd-al-Rahman marched with a vast host to destroy León in what he called his "campaign of omnipotence." King Ramiro, Fernán González, count of Castile, and Toda, queen-mother of Navarre, rallied their people and on August 1, 939, at Simancas on the Duero defeated the caliph's "omnipotent" host.

Castile formed a new element in the struggle. As rulers of León extended their sway eastward along the north bank of the Duero and headwaters of the Ebro, they were checked by Moorish strongholds at Zaragoza and Medinaceli. Holding the land they had occupied and providing protection for the people who worked its soil required castles—and lots of them. Castles soon dotted the countryside and gave the region its name, Castile. Around 930 the king of León appointed Fernán González count of Castile. An ambitious border lord, Fernán González added to the region's population and took advantage of the fluid situation to make himself virtually independent.

Because of the dangers of frontier life, fighting men given lands by grateful princes had to offer generous terms to peasants who worked the soil and herded the animals. Castilian peasants remained free people; serfdom was not for them. When unhappy with their lord, peasants easily found another lord who would protect them. In some cases princes let the peasant settlers choose their lord. Landholding arrangements were many. A few owned land from time immemorial. Because much of the frontier had been a no-man's land, many acquired land by squatter's rights, secured by money payment to some higher authority. Lords usually ended up with a domain that included some land of their own, for which they usually made sharecropping arrangements with peasants, and lands owned by others, over which lords enjoyed seigneurial jurisdiction. They provided justice, collected fines, and charged dues for administration and defense. Payments were often in kind, and much business was done through barter, though money did circulate in Spain. Some of what lords collected they might have to pass on to the count or king, whose treasuries were still hoards. The moving frontier also affected lord and peasant relations in regions where serfdom had survived from Roman and Visigothic times, since lords often needed to offer their peasants freer conditions to prevent them from running off in search of something better.

Town life, which had been limited in Christian Spain, also quickened. Towns had been few and small in the north and west, although centers for commerce and markets did exist, and new towns appeared alongside those rebuilt on Roman foundations. Defense was the prime motive, since a concentration of people could build fortifications and provide centers of resistance to raids and shelter for peasants who worked the fields. *Burgos* basically means "fort." Valladolid seems to have begun as a Moorish stronghold. Rulers offered extensive privileges to the men and women who revived or established towns.

Both Burgos and Valladolid claim to speak the purest Castilian, which employs the *theta* sound for *c* before *e* and *i*, and the letter *z*; and often turns the Latin *f* into *h*, unique phenomena among Romance languages. Linguistic scholars believe it related to a local pre-Roman language, or perhaps Basque. Not until later did the Castilian dialect become the language of the court.

Abd-al-Rahman III maintained pressure on the Christian north, but his claim to be caliph embroiled him in North Africa, as it would his successor Hakam II (961–976). Against Christian rulers, Hakam alternated diplomacy and force. When he died, his heir, eleven-year-old Hisham II (976–1013), succeeded to the caliphate after his mother and his tutor conspired to strangle his uncle. By 981 the tutor, best known to history as al-Mansur ("the Victorious," 940–1002), eliminated all rivals and gained dictatorial power. He let Hisham reign as a figurehead and indulged him with pleasures. Once he had the upper hand in North Africa, al-Mansur turned on the Christian principalities of the north. Each summer he sent expeditions to keep them at bay, while exercising diplomacy to break up their leagues and force tribute from them. His most famous expedition sacked Santiago de Compostela in 997. Christians taken captive were paraded through Córdoba carrying the cathedral bells, to the delight of the Muslim mob.

When he died in 1002, the sheer power of the caliphate of Córdoba had reached its apogee, but its foundations were fragile. Al-Mansur controlled the bureaucracy through loyal slaves, and he used Slavic slaves and Berbers to man his large and costly armies. None of this was popular with the local elites or larger population. His eldest son held things together but died suddenly in 1008. His younger son, nicknamed Sanchuelo, lost the support of the army and was murdered. Hisham was dethroned and restored. Muslim dissidents, Catalan Christians, and mutinous Berbers sacked Córdoba and destroyed the caliph's summer palace. Over the next twenty years, more than a half-dozen Umayyad kinsmen claimed to be caliph, supported by this or that faction, till the last, Hisham III, was deposed in 1031 and hustled off to obscurity.

In the power vacuum created by the collapse of the caliphate, ambitious commanders and ever-restless local oligarchs took over the urban centers of al-Andalus. Muslim Spain splintered into some thirty *taifas* or faction-states, each with its own ruler. In Spanish history, they customarily appear as petty kings. Among the more important *taifa* kingdoms were Seville, Badajoz (which held much of Portugal), Córdoba, Granada, Málaga, Almería, Murcia, Denia (which included the Balearic Islands), Valencia, and Zaragoza. Despite the fragmentation of political authority, the economic prosperity of al-Andalus continued, and the cultural momentum acquired under the caliphs attained new heights in poetry, architecture, philosophy, and science. The initiative, however, was about to shift to the backward Christian north.

Most of the Christian principalities of the north had come, through inheritance or conquest, under the sway of Sancho III the Great, king of Navarre (1004–1035), save for Galicia and the county of Barcelona. Both Navarre and Barcelona benefited from developments north of the Pyrenees, which included the revival of the Church by the monks of Cluny in France and the use of mailed knights on big horses to overpower enemies on the battlefield. By means of shrewd diplomacy, Navarre suffered least from the annual campaigns of al-Mansur.

Sancho's eldest son, García, inherited Navarre. Another son, Fernando, count of Castile (1029–1065), married the heiress of León and in 1038 combined Castile with León. Another, Ramiro, was given Aragón with the title king, to which he added Ribagorza and Sobrarbe on the death of his brother Gonzalo. Medieval proprietary monarchy was taking form. A region and its people, with the obligations to provide government, justice, and defense, became a form of property to be passed from parents to children. It was not the republic—*res publica*, "public thing"—of the Romans, although the word was still used. Nor was the office of ruler elective, as it had been for the Visigoths, although powerful lords, with some legal support, reserved the right to make or unmake a ruler if a family line died out or a ruler failed to rule effectively. Most churchmen, given the circumstances of the times, agreed that hereditary monarchy provided more stability than elective monarchy, and they blessed rulers with the concept that he or she ruled "by the Grace of God."

By now, we have already seen enough names of kings and dates of reigns, and we shall see more. Do not despair. The destinies of their countless subjects were intertwined with theirs, with their successes and their failures. Their names and dates are convenient devices for historians to summarize in few words situations and developments that involved infinitely more than the printed page can sustain.

Alhough once more fragmented, the Christian north had become tougher through the new military techniques and religious revival and confronted an even more fragmented al-Andalus, weakened by faction and lulled by prolonged economic prosperity. We have reached that fluid moment in Spain's history when a personality like El Cid could flourish. Not long after his death in 1099, El Cid (*sidi*, "lord," from Arabic *sayyid*) became the subject of epic poetry and historical chronicle. The greatest, *The Poem of My Cid* (*El poema del mio Cid*), appeared in Castilian no later than 1207, although it lay till 1779 in a remote monastery near Burgos. The historic Cid was born Rodrigo Díaz in the town of Vivar, near Burgos, according to tradition, not long after 1040, with 1043 most likely. His father was connected to the court of Castile and placed Rodrigo in the household of Prince Sancho, where he learned letters as well as military skills. By 1063 he was in battle alongside Sancho, who aided the emir of Zaragoza against King Ramiro of Aragón. Ramiro, founder of the kingdom of Aragón, was fatally wounded. Sancho's father, King Fernando I, died in 1065 and once more divided his kingdoms. Sancho became king of Castile. The second son, Alfonso, became king of León, and the youngest, García, king of Galicia. An unedifying family saga follows. In 1071, Sancho and Alfonso despoiled García of Galicia. Sancho next forced Alfonso into exile at Toledo. Then partisans of Alfonso and their sister Urraca, who took Alfonso's side, murdered Sancho. Opinion blamed Urraca and Alfonso, who hurried from Toledo to claim both Castile and León. The legend grew that Rodrigo Díaz, before pledging fealty to Alfonso, made him swear that he had no part in Sancho's murder. Alfonso VI (1072–1109) would prove a successful king, but in tales of El Cid, he comes off as a scoundrel.

At first Rodrigo served Alfonso, but according to the poem, Rodrigo's enemies at court persuaded Alfonso to exile him. A case can be made that Rodrigo exceeded his authority. In the epic, he leaves his family behind and with his followers heads for the borderlands. The epic is rich in the names of places that still exist. In it, Rodrigo plundered Moorish strongholds and sent gifts to King Alfonso. Fact suggests that he served the emir of Zaragoza for pay against the count of Barcelona and the king of Aragón. His successes earned him acclaim as a war leader, "El Cid."

In 1085 King Alfonso VI occupied Toledo. The fall of a leading *taifa* capital alarmed other *taifa* rulers, who summoned help from the Almoravids of North Africa. Recent converts to Islam, the Almoravids formed a zealous and puritanical sect and had conquered the western Sahara and Morocco. Yusuf, Almoravid chief and founder of Marrakech, crossed to Spain in 1086 with a disciplined host of Senegalese, Berber, and desert warriors. At Sagrajas, near Badajoz, he defeated Alfonso, who escaped and clung to Toledo. Yusuf became distracted by developments in Morocco and did not return to Spain until 1090. Muslim zealots formed Almoravid parties in the *taifa* kingdoms, denounced the laxity of their rulers, and favored Yusuf's empire.

Alfonso reconciled with El Cid and sent him to assist the *taifa* kinglet of Valencia, a foe of Yusuf's. When Yusuf's partisans threatened to seize Valencia in 1094, El Cid took it for himself. His defense of Valencia features prominently in the poem. After his death in 1099, his wife Jimena had to abandon it. But El Cid did well: Jimena retired comfortably and his daughters married into the princely houses of Navarre and Barcelona. Tales of their marriages to the Infantes (princes) of Carrión, their humiliation, and El Cid's revenge are fiction.

Attitudes and religious feelings in the Spain of El Cid were changing rapidly. In the year of his death, crusaders stormed Jerusalem. In Spain, the Almoravids revived the *jihad*, holy war, and the Christians responded. In 1086 Alfonso went back on his generous terms to the Muslims of Toledo. He allowed the destruction of Toledo's Great Mosque and its replacement with a Christian cathedral. The Almoravids were tolerant of neither Mozarab Christians nor Jews. The days of ambitious border lords fighting on both sides were largely past. The southward advance of the Christian states became the *Reconquista*, the Reconquest, under the banner of the Cross. "¡Cierra, Santiago y España!"—"Close for Santiago and Spain!"—became their battle cry.

The disintegration of the Almoravid empire over the next generation, coupled with succession squabbles among the Christian kingdoms, allowed the *taifa* kingdoms to revive. Their legendary luxury continued, and the intellectual life of al-Andalus reached new peaks. The most influential thinker was Averroës, born in Córdoba in 1126. A distinguished physician, he served the Almohad rulers of al-Andalus and died in 1198 at their court in Marrakech. He is most famous for his commentaries on Aristotle, which had a profound impact on medieval Christian philosophy. Another renowned thinker and physician was Moses Maimonides (1135–1204), the best-known Jewish philosopher of the Middle Ages and author of *Guide for the Perplexed*. His family hailed from Córdoba, but Almoravid intolerance caused them to relocate, first in Spain and later to Morocco. He spent most of his career in Cairo. The twelfth would be the last century of cultural greatness for al-Andalus, to which Granada would provide but an afterglow. When the Almohads, who supplanted the Almoravids in Morocco, began to intervene in the defense of al-Andalus from the Christians, they drew their chief support from Muslim zealots who shared the intolerance of the Almoravids.

Alfonso VI outlived El Cid by ten years. Although he held on to Toledo, he suffered a series of defeats on the battlefield, and at the disaster at Uclés in 1109, he lost his only son. His daughter, Queen Urraca (1109–1126), succeeded him. Widow of a knight-adventurer, Raymond of Burgundy, Urraca was succeeded by her son Alfonso VII (1126–1157), aged twenty-one. Determined to restore the glory and preeminence of the kingdom of León, Alfonso had himself crowned emperor in 1135 at the cathedral of León. His imperial pretensions had little effect.

In 1139 his cousin Afonso Enriques, prince of Portugal (1128–1185), proclaimed himself king of Portugal and in time won papal confirmation. Their grandfather Alfonso VI had given the frontier region of Portugal to his illegitimate daughter Teresa and her husband Henry of Burgundy (Raymond's cousin). Teresa inspired their son's desire for an independent kingdom, which he achieved.

While Portugal became independent, Aragón became bigger. King Alfonso the Battler (1104–1134) conquered Zaragoza in 1118 and pushed his frontier ever southward. In a daring raid on Granada, he liberated a large number of Mozarabs, whom he resettled in his own kingdom. When he died, Navarre chose a French dynasty, while the Aragonese persuaded Alfonso's brother Ramiro, a monk, to leave the monastic life and become their king. Ramiro II the Monk (1135–1137) reigned long enough to marry and sire a daughter, Petronilla. She was betrothed to Ramón Berenguer IV, count of Barcelona (1131–1162), with Aragón as her dowry. Ramiro retired to his monastery, and Ramón Berenguer became the effective ruler of the potent federation of Aragón and Catalonia. Because Aragón was a kingdom, it gave the federation its name. Historians refer to the federation as the Crown of Aragon to keep the inland kingdom, with its Castilian dialect, apart from the Catalan-speaking county. The kingdom, its capital at Zaragoza, and the county, its capital at Barcelona, each kept its separate laws and institutions and were held together by their ruler only in personal union.

This established a precedent for Spain's future growth. The kings of greater Aragon usually reigned from Barcelona, the booming seaport that made Catalonia wealthy. By contrast, the economy of old Aragón was rural, based on the agriculture of the valleys of the Ebro and its tributaries and herding in the mountains. In the Ebro valley many Muslims, under Christian rule called *mudéjares* (Mudejars), remained to work the soil. Catalonia also had an agricultural base, which was marginally richer than old Aragón's. Both had an active warrior nobility whose feudal relationships among themselves, a pyramid of lords and vassals, approximated the feudal system of France and differed from the seigneurial system of Castile and León, with its direct tie between the king and every lord. The nobles of Aragón and Catalonia also enjoyed a firm legal grip over their peasants, whose status was closer to that of the serfs of France than to that of the relatively free villagers of Castile. The roots of Aragonese feudalism and serfdom are Frankish.

Ramón Berenguer added Lérida and Tortosa to his dominions but also became involved in the politics of Provence, where his nephew was count, and with Italy, through the maritime ambitions of Barcelona. His son, Alfonso II, continued to pursue dynastic interests in Provence which embroiled Aragon in the conflicts of southern France.

The would-be emperor, Alfonso VII of León, divided his own inheritance and bestowed Castile upon his eldest son, Sancho III (1157–1158), and León on his youngest, Fernando II (1157–1188). Sancho's early death and his succession by Alfonso VIII (1158–1214), aged three, left the field to Fernando. Fernando backed Alfonso in Castile but compensated himself with territory. He repopulated his kingdom south of the Duero and revived Salamanca. He pushed his frontiers southward beyond Badajoz, and he encouraged the establishment of Spanish crusading orders. Already Knights Templar and Knights of St. John served in Spain. The Spanish orders began with the Knights of Calatrava, followed by the Knights of Santiago. The Knights of Alcántara appeared soon after. The orders were given strongholds that still rise stark on the Spanish landscape and were endowed with lands and peasants, *encomiendas* (commanderies), to support their crusading activities. *Encomiendas* made the orders rich and careers in them desirable for younger sons of nobles, who did not fancy becoming monks and whose older brothers inherited the family estates. Knights took the monastic vows of poverty, chastity, and obedience but changed St. Benedict's injunction from "work and pray" to "fight and pray."

Fernando II had trouble with Portugal, which feared his pretensions, as well as with Castile and Aragon. In a series of meetings, he and the other rulers came to agreements regarding the conquest of Moorish Spain, temporarily shored up by the Almohads. Each Christian kingdom was basically allotted the territory south of its current border to conquer. When Alfonso

IX (1188–1230) succeeded Fernando to the Leonese throne, he was only eighteen. To win support against rival factions and foreign threats, he summoned to León an assembly that included clergy, nobles, and townsmen and was called the *Cortes*, the name still used for Spain's parliament. It was arguably the first parliament in Europe. The Cortes came to meet frequently in medieval Spain and gave urban interests a voice against the powerful landed nobility.

Alfonso IX had territorial differences with his cousin Alfonso VIII of Castile, but under papal pressure, the two cousins renewed the crusade against the Almohads. In 1195 the Castilians suffered a crushing defeat at Alarcos, when the Leonese failed to appear. Infuriated, Alfonso of Castile allied with Portugal against Alfonso of León, who in turn allied with the Almohads. When the pope intervened in 1197, Alfonso of León yielded. He married Alfonso of Castile's eldest daughter, Berenguela, and undertook a pilgrimage to Santiago as penance. But when the Church preached a crusade in 1212, León did not heed the call. Alfonso of Castile, joined by Pedro II of Aragon and Afonso II of Portugal, did and led Spain's crusaders to victory at Las Navas de Tolosa, shattering the power of the Almohads. The Christian allies had developed a devastating combination of heavy and light cavalry, backed by infantry, that routed the Almohad light horsemen and opened al-Andalus to conquest.

After Alfonso of Castile died, followed by his only son, Castile passed to Fernando III (1217–1252), son of Berenguela and Alfonso of León. In 1230, on Alfonso IX's death, Fernando permanently united the two kingdoms of Castile and León. Fernando III the Saint, after whom California's San Fernando mission and valley are named, conquered Córdoba (1236), Murcia (1243), Jaén (1246), and Seville (1248). When he captured Seville, he mocked his Muslim enemies by riding his horse up the massive Giralda tower, the minaret for Seville's Great Mosque.

The vanquished Moors retained only the mountainous kingdom of Granada, where most Andalusian Muslims eventually relocated. For Fernando, his triumphant warriors, and their successors, the big task was to repopulate and make the lands they had won productive. In the time it took, much of the long and arduous work of the Moors to irrigate the valley of the Guadalquivir and make it rich came undone. It was several centuries before western Andalusia again approached the population and prosperity of its Moorish days, and even then, its production focused on a few cash crops, such as olives, wine, and to a lesser extent, grains. The number of livestock using the land for grazing increased greatly.

From the opening of the Duero valley to the conquest of western Andalusia, the repopulation of Christian Spain had centered on cities, towns, and villages. This was both in the Mediterranean tradition and necessary for security on a shifting frontier. Isolated homesteads and hamlets were rare, save in the more secure far north. In the earlier years of the reconquest, people who migrated to newly conquered frontier regions insisted on their liberties and privileges (*fueros*). Towns and villages in Castile had became relatively self-governing under their councils, mostly elected by householders (*vecinos*), although the kings or *señores* retained ultimate jurisdiction over them. Spanish women, too, enjoyed specific rights in a land where female succession to the crown or lordships was possible in the absence of brothers. Women did, in a rough and tumble world, need strong husbands. Marriage was the norm, and the only other option was the religious life. Widows succeeded husbands as heads of households while their children were minors, and women's dowries gave them rights. Fathers, whether from love, family pride, or both, remained concerned for their daughters even after they had married. El Cid's legendary pursuit of the Infantes who abused his daughters, their wives, is a case in point.

In newly conquered Andalusia, however, privileged towns and villages were less numerous and the rights of their inhabitants less secure. The Castilian and Leonese nobles who participated in its conquest acquired vast estates, and *latifundios* prevailed. The Spanish peasants who replaced the Moors in the south became in general more dependent on their *señores*, for whom they usually labored by the day, rather than tend plots of their own.

After the spectacular surge of reconquest under Fernando III, his son Alfonso X (1252–1284), known as "the Learned," presided over the flowering of medieval Castilian culture from the lovely alcázar (citadel) of Seville. Alfonso wrote and collected poetry, although Galician rather than Castilian was the favored poetic language. He had histories written and, in his most significant achievement, had the laws of the kingdom codified in the *Siete Partidas* (Seven Sections). Although the Cortes did not ratify the *Siete Partidas* until later, they became the foundation for legal training and affected judicial decisions. In Toledo a school of translators flourished who transmitted Arab philosophy and science to Christian Europe, including Averroës's commentaries on Aristotle. Spain's first universities appeared at Salamanca and Valladolid.

Alfonso wasted his energies seeking election as Holy Roman Emperor by appeals to the pope and German princes. His sons began to jostle for power after his eldest died, leaving behind two boys, the Infantes de la Cerda. Alfonso's last years were troubled by conflict with his oldest surviving son, Sancho el Bravo, who was determined to displace his nephews. On Alfonso's death, Sancho IV donned the crown. Civil war with his nephews and other brothers, and their ambitious supporters, erupted at once. Aragon,

Portugal, and France became involved. Sancho held his own but died in 1295, leaving the crown to his son Fernando IV, aged ten. Fernando's mother, María de Molina, proved herself one of the more remarkable women in Spanish history, as she manipulated noble and urban factions in the Cortes and parried the ambitions of foreign princes till Fernando came of age. He did not last long. Marching to conquer Granada, he took sick and died. From retirement María de Molina emerged to defend the rights of her one-year-old grandson, Alfonso XI (1312–1350), against untrustworthy kinsmen, among them Infante Don Juan Manuel (1282–1348), political theorist, poet, and warrior. After she died in 1321, the kingdom nearly came apart. Alfonso came of age in 1325, and with the cooperation of the Cortes, he restored effective government. In 1340 at the Rio Salado, he smashed the last major Moorish invasion of Spain from North Africa. In 1350 he died of the Great Plague that swept Europe.

The Great Plague hit Barcelona, the heart of Aragonese power, hard and plunged it and Catalonia into a long depression. In the years after Las Navas de Tolosa Aragon had undertaken its own reconquest, lost most of its holdings in southern France, and gained dominions in Italy. King Pedro II of Aragon (1196–1213), after Las Navas de Tolosa, fell in France the next year at the Battle of Muret in another kind of crusade, called by Pope Innocent III to uproot the so-called Albigensian heresy. King Philip II Augustus of France used it to crush the powerful nobles of southern France, where Pedro held the counties of Beziers and Provence.

Pedro's son Jaime I (1213–1276), aged five when his father died, lost Beziers and Provence, but his uncle kept Aragon intact. When Jaime came of age he proved an energetic warrior and is known to history as "the Conqueror." In 1229, at age twenty-one, he used the maritime might of Barcelona to conquer Majorca in the Balearic Islands. Its Muslim population was expelled and replaced by poor Catalan peasants, lured to work domains distributed to the nobles and knights who participated in the conquest. The remaining Balearics were conquered from Majorca; and while more of the Muslim population was expelled, others were made serfs or even slaves by the conquerors.

Jaime next conquered the Moorish kingdom of Valencia. Here, unlike Majorca, most of the Muslim rural population was kept to work the irrigated plains under Aragonese and Catalan overlords. Urban Muslims were expelled, and in 1263 many Muslim peasants rebelled and suffered expulsion. Yet Valencia remained a sort of colony, in which Muslims outnumbered the Christian population of 30,000 by over 3:1. Not until the late 1400s did Christians equal the subject Muslims, in number.

Barcelona was the great commercial and maritime center of the Crown of Aragon, though both the city of Valencia and Palma de Majorca also enjoyed vigorous economies and prospered from shipping. When the opportunity arose for King Pedro III (1276–1285) to claim the Crown of Sicily, he could muster the naval might he needed. In 1282 the Sicilians rebelled against their French-born ruler, Charles of Anjou, in the uprising called the Sicilian Vespers, because it began at vespers time on Easter Monday. The rebels turned to Pedro because he was the husband of Constance of Sicily, daughter of popular King Manfred, from whom Charles had conquered both Naples and Sicily. Although Charles had the backing of the papacy and France, Pedro won Sicily, which he bestowed on his younger son, Jaime. Jaime hung on to it, with aid of the formidable Catalan admiral Roger de Lluria, who defeated all of Charles's fleets. In Catalonia, Catalans and Aragonese repelled an invasion from France. In return for their vote of money for the war, the Catalan and Aragonese nobles and urban rich exacted extensive privileges from Pedro's successor, Alfonso III. In time the Crown of Aragon settled its differences with France and the papacy and secured Sicily for the junior branch of the dynasty.

Aragon's expansion into the Mediterranean embroiled it with the rivalry of Genoa and Pisa and led to the arduous conquest of the island kingdom of Sardinia. Perhaps the most dazzling story of these years deals with a Grand Company of some 6,500 Catalan mercenaries, who hired themselves in 1303 to the Byzantine Empire in its struggle with the emerging Ottoman Turks. When the suspicious Byzantines murdered the company's leaders, the Catalans mutinied and marched into fragmented Greece. In 1311 they seized the duchy of Athens, presented it as a fief to the faraway Crown of Aragon, and held it for two generations before it fell in 1381 to the rulers of Corinth.

When the Great Plague stuck the Aragonese kingdoms, King Pedro IV (1336–1387), called "the Ceremonious" for a treatise he wrote on courtly life, survived. Medieval Catalan poetry flourished, Aragon had its university at Lérida, and the kingdom produced a philosopher of unique genius in Ramón Llull. King Pedro, as best he could, maintained Aragonese influence in the western Mediterranean. In the next generation, a Castilian dynasty would succeed to the Crown of Aragon.

4

Union and World Empire

Alfonso XI of Castile fathered a son, Pedro, by his queen, plus a brood of ille-gitimate children with his mistress Leonor de Guzmán. While a teenager, he had fallen in love with Leonor, a beautiful widow of Seville. Their eldest sons were the twins Enrique, count of Trastámara, and Fadrique. Echoing in literature the scandalous love of the king and his favorite, the archpriest of Hita authored his *Libro de Buen Amor* (Book of Honest Love). Its real subject was not honest love but crazy, illicit love, and it introduced one of Spanish literature's most memorable characters, the elderly procuress Trotaconven-tos ("convent hustler").

Alfonso XI fell victim to the Plague in 1350, and Pedro succeeded to the throne. Pedro had Leonor disgraced, and his mother had her executed. In 1355 Pedro had Leonor's restless son Fadrique assassinated. Enrique and his other brothers rebelled. Pedro received the support of Seville and other towns. Enrique gained the support of most nobles, whom Pedro's pro-urban policies alienated. Pedro made an alliance with England, caught up in the Hundred Years War with France, and Edward the Black Prince marched into Castile and defeated Enrique. After Edward returned to France, the conflict swung in Enrique's favor. In 1369, Enrique cornered Pedro at Mon-tiel in the Sierra Morena and, with his henchmen, stabbed him to death. En-rique of Trastámara was now King Enrique II of Castile (1369–1379). He and his heirs gave Pedro a bad name, and their chronicles denigrated him as Pedro the Cruel. Historians still have difficulty sorting through the positive and negative aspects of Pedro's reign.

Enrique's noble backers expected to be rewarded, and to them, he and his Trastámara successors conceded domains, offices, and titles. Called *ricos hombres* (powerful men) and later grandees, the great nobles had long vied for power with the towns of Castile and gained the upper hand in the years of civil war that began with Sancho IV. The Cortes met often in a quest for stability, and through the Cortes the towns tried to enlarge their jurisdictions and improve business conditions. The civil wars cost Castile's kings money, and the towns, with their concentrations of wealth, tried to buy the royal favor with subsidies. Alfonso XI chose to impose throughout the kingdom a tax on all sales and business transactions, the *alcabala*, a tax from Moorish times that might reach 10 percent. The towns could no longer buy royal favor so easily, and only the largest maintained a precarious freedom from the grandees. The number that sent delegates to the Cortes fell to seventeen. In the political, economic, and social life of Castile, the grandees, with their vast estates dominated.

The grandees were joined by a teeming and ambitious lesser nobility, called hidalgos and caballeros. Nobles tried to avoid taxes and instead offered the king their swords and armed retainers. Towns fought back with armed leagues, *hermandades*, but the kings, except for Pedro, favored one or another faction of the nobility. The nobles had no program of government, but, rather, each sought only the extension of his own power and wealth. They could be rallied for a crusade but little else. With the favor of the crown, they garnered under their seigneurial jurisdiction most of the villages of the kingdom and many a goodly town.

Not left behind in the accumulation of jurisdictions and estates were bishops, monasteries, and crusading military orders, often the beneficiaries of noble and royal wills. Endowing the Church was considered a pious work that helped one toward salvation. However badly noblemen and kings behaved on earth, they believed in heaven, purgatory, and hell. They likely expected purgatory for their misdeeds, but that was a way station on the road to heaven. Hell was eternal.

In the contest to control land, vast flocks of sheep infringed on arable soil as they crossed Extremadura, La Mancha, Castile, and León in their annual migrations from lowlands in winter to greener highlands in summer. The sheep owners formed a guild, the Mesta, to protect their interests against cultivators of the soil, who complained of damage caused to crops by the sheep. The sheep owners profited from the wool shorn each year and shipped to looms in Flanders and Italy. From that profit, fat payments were made to the crown, which put its authority on the side of the Mesta against complaining cultivators.

Enrique's son and successor, Juan I (1379–1390), attempted to conquer Portugal in 1385, when its original line of kings died out. Defeated at Aljubarrota by new Portuguese King João I, he was driven back to Castile. He faced another conflict with John of Gaunt, English duke of Lancaster, who married King Pedro's daughter and claimed Castile in her name. To settle it, Juan arranged that his nine-year-old son Enrique marry Lancaster's daughter Catherine. Enrique III (1390–1406) became king at eleven. He saw himself a crusader, and when of age, he used the ideal of the crusade against Granada to rally support. Castilian vessels raided the coast of Morocco and probed the Canary Islands.

The crusading fervor stirred by Enrique helped inflame the wholesale attacks on Jews that began in 1391. Although estimates of the size of Spain's Jewish population in 1391 vary widely, it most likely stood around 200,000, in a larger population of over 4 million. Spain's Jews had long suffered sporadic intolerance, though Muslim al-Andalus proved kinder to them than Christian Spain until the Almoravids arrived. Most Jews lived in towns and engaged in a wide variety of trades and crafts. Apart from their distinctive religion, what made them conspicuous was money lending. Christian, Jewish, and Islamic law forbade usury, charging interest on loans, between believers, but a Jew could charge interest on a loan to a Christian, and vice versa. As there were so many more Christians than Jews, some Jews found money lending gave them both profit and influence, since kings and noblemen were great borrowers and could favor or protect their Jewish creditors. Kings and nobles recognized the financial skills of Jewish money lenders and employed them to manage their treasuries and collect taxes, not the most endearing of occupations. Kings also sometimes turned on them. King Pedro of Castile, accused of coddling his Jewish creditors, had a distinguished Jew who served on his royal council, Samuel Halevi, cruelly executed, then confiscated the victim's goods, although he continued to do business with other Jews.

The Great Plague seems to have been a watershed in Christian-Jewish relations. Many Christians blamed the presence of Jews for what they believed to be punishment by God. Dominican and Franciscan friars intensified their intolerance of Jews. Determined to convert Jews to Christianity, they held public debates with rabbis and became ugly when they lost. Yet Jews remained in Spain, whereas England and France had expelled them. Matters came to a head in 1391 when the administrator of the archdiocese of Seville preached against the presence of Jews and incited mobs to riot. Authorities lost control, and countless Jews were murdered. Only by conversion to Christianity did many save their lives. From Seville the wave of intolerance, murder, and forced conversion engulfed most of the major cities and towns of Castile and Aragon. Though it has been argued that genuine conversions of Jews to Christianity in Spain exceeded forced conversions, most historians believe that considerably more conversions were forced. Occasionally a rabbi converted, and a great fuss was made over it. Many Jews who converted under pressure saw that their children were raised devout Christians for their own safety. But whether resentful or sincere, these converts, called *conversos*, remained suspect. They and those converted from Islam, whether by persuasion or pressure, were forever New Christians. Though the Old Christian majority was admonished to treat New Christians with charity, in practice they often did not.

Enrique III was not thirty when he died, but his one-year-old heir, King Juan II (1406–1454) and Castile enjoyed the good fortune of an effective regent in Don Fernando, Enrique's brother. Fernando governed the south, while Queen-Mother Catherine of Lancaster governed the north. In a successful campaign against Granada, Fernando captured the Moorish stronghold of Antequera and became known as Fernando of Antequera. In 1412 the Cortes of the Crown of Aragon elected him to succeed King Martín, who had died in 1410 without an heir.

When Fernando of Antequera departed for Aragon, Queen-Mother Catherine assumed the regency of all Castile. She died in 1418, and Juan II was declared of age the next year. Fernando's sons, the Infantes of Aragon, Juan, Enrique, and Pedro, intended to dominate him. He was betrothed to their sister María. When Juan, the oldest of the three, left to marry the heiress of Navarre, Enrique, headstrong, barely twenty, and grand master of Santiago, seized the boy-king. He rushed the king's marriage to María and demanded Juan's sister in marriage for himself. The boy king, with the aid of his favorite courtier, Don Alvaro de Luna, escaped. Enrique was foiled, and Alvaro de Luna became ruler of Castile in all but name. The illegitimate son of a powerful nobleman, nephew of the archbishop of Toledo, and grandnephew of Anti-Pope Benedict XIII, he was handsome, graceful, and fifteen years older than Juan. Juan made him constable of Castile, the highest military office in the land, and bestowed vast estates on him.

The Infantes of Aragon would not accept Luna's position and troubled Juan's long reign with endless intrigues and frequent civil wars. After each round of civil war, both winners and losers seemed to benefit at the crown's expense. The estates of the grandees grew ever larger, while the court of Castile blossomed under the influence of the Italian Renaissance and late chivalric culture. A leader of the noble opposition, the marquis of Santillana, Don Iñigo de Mendoza, proved the greatest chivalric poet of the age. He also emerged from the civil wars as the most powerful person in the kingdom. The noble opposition wore Luna down and forced Juan to have him beheaded in 1453. Juan died the next year.

Our medieval family dramas enter their last act. Juan had married twice. By his first queen, he had his initial heir, Enrique IV. By the second, he had Isabella and Alfonso. To Enrique, growing up in the hothouse atmosphere of a cultivated court, the poetry of chivalry meant more than the reality of the crusade. Luna paired him with a poet when he placed Juan Pacheco in his household as a page. Enrique bonded with Pacheco and made him marquis of Villena. He mainly failed with women, becoming known as "the Impotent." After his first marriage was annulled, he married Princess Juana of Portugal. She gave birth to a daughter, Juana, but most believed that Juana's father was Don Beltrán de la Cueva, captain of the guards. The unfortunate daughter came to be called Juana la Beltraneja.

The marquis of Villena, along with his uncle, Archbishop Carrillo of Toledo, and his brother, Don Pedro Girón, master of Calatrava, manipulated Enrique to dominate the government. Widespread opposition to their pretensions led to more civil wars. Castile slipped into anarchy, and none seemed safe. Fighting men who served this or that faction turned to plunder at the end of each civil war and oppressed peasants rose in revolt. Towns mustered their militias for the fray. Enrique enjoyed little respect, and his foes forced him to renounce Juana and accept his half-brother Alfonso as his heir. When Alfonso died—many suspected poison—he accepted Isabella. Enrique insisted that he should decide whom Isabella should marry and pledged her to his crony, the master of Calatrava. On his way to claim her, the master dropped dead, which Isabella took to be a sign from heaven. Independently she decided to marry Prince Ferdinand of Aragon. In October 1469, Ferdinand slipped into Castile disguised as a mule driver, because King Juan II of Aragon, his father, was caught up in a civil war and could spare no men for escort. Hastily the couple married in Valladolid.

In response, Enrique asserted that Juana was legitimate and his rightful heiress. He betrothed her to King Afonso V of Portugal to ensure that she would have a powerful champion. But when Enrique died in late 1474, Isabella was acclaimed in Segovia as queen-proprietress of Castile. Together with Ferdinand she rallied more than enough support to defeat Afonso of Portugal in 1476 at the Battle of Toro. Afonso never married la Beltraneja, who died in a Portuguese convent, outliving Isabella by twenty-six years.

Isabella and Ferdinand had started the business of bringing order to Castile when Ferdinand became king of Aragon and Sicily in 1479. Unruliness had also plagued Aragon during the reign of Ferdinand's father, King Juan II. Juan had been king of Navarre by marriage to its heiress Blanche and fathered Charles, prince of Viana. In 1458, Juan succeeded his brother Alfonso V (1416–1458) to the Crown of Aragon and the kingdom of Sicily. Alfonso, called the Magnanimous, had spent most of his reign in Italy, where he conquered the kingdom of Naples from the Angevin dynasty. A Renaissance prince, Alfonso patronized the arts at his court in Naples. He left the kingdom of Naples to his illegitimate son Ferrante.

King Juan faced old problems that in the 1460s led to new violence. Catalonia's economic decline following the Great Plague steadily deepened. The situation of Catalan peasants became worse than almost anywhere else in the peninsula, and the powers of the landlords were summed up as the "six bad customs." To meet rising costs and pay war taxes, landlords increased their exactions from the peasants. Bloody uprisings followed. Juan sided with the peasants, provoking violent opposition from the nobility and Barcelona's urban oligarchy, who had invested in land when commerce declined. Charles of Viana, already at odds with his father over Navarre, rallied the Catalan opposition. Civil war ensued. Charles's early death deprived Juan's enemies of leadership, but they refused to recognize Ferdinand, Juan's son by his second marriage to Castilian María Enríquez. Juan slowly gained the edge and by 1472 had beaten Barcelona into submission. A compromise settlement left most of the powers and privileges of the nobles and oligarchs intact, though in practice they reduced their exactions from the peasantry, who remained armed and ready to rebel again if sufficiently provoked.

In 1479, the Crown of Aragon and, above all, its once richest part, Catalonia, stood economically far behind Castile and still seethed with barely resolved tensions. In the union of the crowns, Aragon was the junior partner, but its king, Ferdinand, was a fit match in intelligence and political acumen for Isabella. Both shared those elusive qualities of leadership that allowed two human beings to take full advantage of the inherent authority of kingship and affect the destinies of millions.

After their victory at Toro, Ferdinand and Isabella took up the restoration of order. To look after royal interests in important towns, they appointed agents, *corregidores*, who became a fixture of government. To deal with brigands they encouraged the formation of a *Santa Hermandad*, a Sacred Brotherhood of the towns. The towns formed companies of archers to police the highways and byways and hunt down bandits. Judges often accompanied them so that culprits could be tried and punished on the spot.

Ferdinand and Isabella also needed money. Although the Cortes proved generous, previous Trastámara rulers had given away too many regular sources of royal income to their backers. These included not only lands but mineral, forest, and grazing rights, salt flats, and customs houses. While

Ferdinand and Isabella cajoled nobles into surrendering several important towns such as Cádiz, Gibraltar, and Plasencia, most of what had been alienated to the nobles was left in their hands. To try to take more back might turn them against the crown. But Ferdinand and Isabella did arrange for the pope to appoint Ferdinand grand master of each of the Spanish military orders when the current grand master died. Thus, the crown gained control of their vast estates, mostly in New Castile and Andalusia, which increased its revenues.

In this the nobles, after some grumbling, acquiesced. After all, they, along with the bishops and rich church foundations, still dominated most of Spain. The Velasco family lorded over the region from Burgos to Santander, and its chief became constable of Castile and duke of Frías. The head of the Enríquez family bore the titles admiral of Castile and duke of Rioseco and dominated the area around Valladolid. The Toledo family, headed by the duke of Alba, dominated León from Salamanca south. The area around Segovia came under the duke of Alburquerque; around Soria, under the duke of Medinaceli. The Rioja region was the territory of the Manrique de Lara duke of Nájera, whose power reached into Navarre. The province of Guadalajara came under the duke of Infantado, chief of the extensive Mendoza clan. The Girón family held estates in the Duero valley as counts of Ureña as well as territory in Andalusia around Osuna, which later gave them a ducal title. The duke of Béjar and count of Miranda, of the Zúñiga family, dominated northern and central Extremadura. Southern Extremadura was the province of the Figueroa family, in time dukes of Feria. Rivals in western Andalusia were the Guzmán dukes of Medina Sidonia and the Ponce de León dukes of Arcos. Around Córdoba the Fernández de Córdoba family dominated, as marquises of Priego and counts of Cabra. The big man in Murcia was the Fajardo marquis of los Vélez.

In Aragón illegitimate scions of the royal house held the titles of duke of Segorbe and duke of Villahermosa, with estates scattered from the Pyrenees to the plains of Valencia. More powerful were the Sandoval marquises of Denia and Borja dukes of Gandía, both from Valencia. The Borja family owed its fortune to forebears who entered the papal service. Two, Calixtus III and Alexander VI, became pope. Catalonia had no nobles who matched their fellows in Castile, Valencia, or even Aragón in wealth and power. Of them the most prominent was the duke of Cardona.

To rally and occupy this powerful nobility, in 1480 Ferdinand and Isabella launched a crusade to conquer the Muslim kingdom of Granada. Italian political theorist Niccolo Machiavelli thought it a brilliant move that left Ferdinand free to reform government. He believed that Ferdinand, more than any other contemporary ruler, best combined the desired qualities of the lion and the fox.

The war against Granada proved arduous. Ruled by the Nasrid dynasty, last of the *taifa* kings, Granada was divided by quarreling factions. Yet in their mountains the Moors resisted tenaciously. Through narrow gorges Ferdinand led his people, his cannon battering the walls of Moorish strongholds. Isabella rode round Castile, collecting recruits, horses, and supplies and, with her churchmen, whipping up zeal for the crusade.

Reform of the Church was much on her mind. Monasteries and convents of men and women had become lax; bishops were too often corrupt and venal. Cardinal Mendoza, archbishop of Toledo, though a fine statesman and sometimes called "the third king of Spain," sired several bastards. Bawdy tales about the indiscretions of the clergy abounded. In 1495 Isabella found the ideal person to oversee reform, a pious, learned, and yet formidable Franciscan named Francisco Ximénez de Cisneros. He succeed Mendoza as the archbishop of Toledo, and by the time he died in 1516, the Spanish Church had been purged of many of the abuses that provided fuel for the Protestant Reformation elsewhere. Isabella, who patronized the arts, and Cisneros believed education important for the faith and well-being of her subjects, and Cisneros founded a new university at Alcalá de Henares. Its curriculum emphasized the humanities, whereas Spain's older universities stressed theology and law. Cisneros supervised a pioneering compilation of scripture in Greek, Hebrew, and Latin that became known as the Complutensian Polyglot Bible. Isabella encouraged the establishment of printing presses in Spain, and in 1492 humanist scholar Antonio de Nebrija presented her with a grammar of Castilian, at a time when grammar meant Latin. In secular literature appeared the prose dialogue *La Celestina*, attributed to Fernando de Rojas. A romance about Calisto and Melibea, it takes its title from their bawdy go-between Celestina and had a profound influence on the development of the novel.

Isabella also regarded as a major concern the possibility that *conversos* would revert to Judaism or practice it in secret, pretending to be Christian. This was backsliding, a grievous sin, at a time sin was seen as a cancer that would destroy the soul and doom the sinner forever to hell. Suspicion of *conversos'* sincerity and popular hostility toward practicing Jews led to riots in which the property and lives of *conversos* and Jews were endangered. Isabella and her advisers decided to take charge by establishing a Spanish Inquisition and sought the necessary authority from the papacy. The original papal inquisition, rooted in the Middle Ages and nearly defunct, inquired into the beliefs of Christians to make sure that none was heretical. Those holding such beliefs were punished, and those who advocated them, along with those who would not repent, were "relaxed" to the secular authorities and put to death, usually by burning at the stake. Burning symbolically purged the community of promoters of error. The Spanish Inquisition came under a royal council, the only one with jurisdiction over both Castile and Aragon. The rulers nominated the Inquisitor General, or Grand Inquisitor, whom the pope confirmed, and he and his fellows councillors appointed the regional inquisitors, priests schooled in theology and canon law. Usually three inquisitors each were assigned to the most important provincial bishoprics. Assisting them were agents called familiars (*familiares*) and secret informers. Their jurisdiction extended only to baptized Christians, and *conversos* became their prime target. The Inquisition quickly channeled the sporadic mob violence directed at *conversos* into a juridical procedure that satisfied the mob and enjoyed the acceptance of ordinary Old Christians until its final suppression in the nineteenth century. For *conversos* and Muslim converts, called Moriscos, it remained a potential terror. While there were rules of evidence, the position of those accused, as in contemporary criminal courts, was guilty until proven innocent. During interrogation, torture might be employed, though according to the rules, not so much that false confessions might result. Not until the eighteenth century did European justice systems begin to drop judicial torture.

The punishment of those convicted by the Inquisition began in a grand ceremony called an *auto de fe* (act of faith). Inquisitors and civil authorities would preside, and large crowds gathered for the spectacle. After the preaching of sermons, the convicts would be paraded, wearing dunce caps and clad in yellow poncholike habits called sanbenitos on which lists of their errors and transgressions were written. Most common was blasphemy, for which those convicted paid fines. Witches the Inquisition more often regarded as dupes rather than willing agents of the devil, and witch crazes were few in Spain, save in remote mountain areas. Heretical beliefs or reversion to Judaism or Islam meant long imprisonment or even death. Most serious was the promotion of heresy, which meant death by burning. If any person convicted to death repented, he or she would be garroted—strangled—before the fire was lit. Otherwise they would burn alive. While there were public burnings, usually those convicted to burn would be led off to a fenced *quemadero* (place of burning) on the edge of town, accompanied by clergymen, police, and the executioners, and burned there. While the Spanish Inquisition deservedly has a bad reputation as a means of thought control, in its rules of evidence it was probably a notch above most contemporary courts, clerical or civil.

The war against Granada ended on January 2, 1492, with the surrender of Boabdil, the last Moorish king. He and most of his principals left for exile in

Morocco. The pass from which he last looked over the city of Granada and his Alhambra Palace is called the "Last Sigh of the Moor." His bitter mother purportedly chastised him: "Do not weep like a woman over what you could not defend like a man." The remaining Moorish population, abandoned by their leaders, were allowed by treaty to practice Islam. Assailed by zealous Christian missionaries, they rose in revolt in 1499 but were savagely crushed and given the choice of conversion to Christianity or expulsion from Granada. Mostly simple folk and unwilling to give up their ancestral livelihoods, the majority accepted Christianity and became Moriscos. Few conversions proved sincere. They continued to speak Arabic and dress in Moorish fashion, maintained their public baths, and avoided eating pork, while they surreptitiously practiced Islam. Hard workers, they enriched the nobles to whom Ferdinand and Isabella gave estates in Granada after its conquest, and for a time the nobles sheltered them from prying inquisitors and royal agents.

The fall of Granada also led to the expulsion of Jews from Spain. Isabella and her clerical advisers, such as Grand Inquisitor Tomás de Torquemada, himself of *converso* stock, feared that practicing Jews tempted *conversos* to backslide and decided to expel all Jews who would not accept Christianity. Ferdinand seems to have stalled her decision because he believed Jewish financial expertise was useful, until Granada fell. *Converso* money lenders may have favored expelling Jews to get rid of competition. Within weeks of Granada's fall, the edict of expulsion was promulgated and implemented in Castile and Aragon. As Jews who would not convert began to flee to Portugal, Ferdinand and Isabella put pressure on the Portuguese king to expel Portugal's Jews, which he did, though less wholeheartedly. Of the Sephardic tradition, Iberia's Jews began a new diaspora. A few migrated to the Low Countries or Italy but most left for North Africa or the Ottoman Turkish Empire. Most proved hostile to the Spanish crown, although some maintained commercial ties with *converso* relatives. Their Spanish dialect, called Ladino, would produce a rich body of literature, much of it nostalgic poetry for their lost homeland.

In the same weeks that Isabella ordered the Jews expelled, she signed a pact with the Genoese adventurer Christopher Columbus to undertake a voyage to reach Asia by sailing west. As history shows, he discovered a world unknown to Europeans. The consequences for Spanish and world civilization would prove immense. Two years later Ferdinand turned his interests to Italy, when King Charles VIII of France conquered Naples from Ferdinand's cousins. Ferdinand's diplomacy and the tactical brilliance of Gonzalo de Córdoba, the grand captain, won Naples for Ferdinand and gave Machiavelli more to write about. The Italian Wars (1494–1559) provided fields of glory for Spanish fighting men and later harnessed the energies of Italy and Spain to check the expansion of the Ottoman Turks in the Mediterranean. In the long run they led to Spain's involvement in all the power rivalries of western Europe. The Castilian thrust across the Strait of Gibraltar became a sideshow, though it brought the conquest of Melilla, Oran, and Tripoli and allowed Spaniards to plant a citadel in the harbor of Algiers, the chief Barbary corsair lair.

While Ferdinand focused on Italy, the American discoveries took on a life of their own and became the envy of Europe. Legally, Spain's overseas empire was Castile's. Subjects of the Crown of Aragon were excluded, along with all other Europeans. Castile had previously held only the Canary Islands, which provided Columbus with a safe stop for repairs and adjustments on his epochal voyage of 1492. Queen Isabella followed Columbus's efforts closely. Before she died in 1504, she saw to it that proper government, courts of law, and church institutions were established in Santo Domingo, the first capital of the Indies, and forbade the enslavement of American Indians. In 1503 she chartered a House of Trade (Casa de Contratación) in Seville which included royal officials, leading merchants, and shipowners, to regulate commerce with the Indies. Further expeditions sailed to map the New World, and in the reign of Isabella's grandson, the survivors of Magellan's crews became the first men ever to circumnavigate the globe.

To gain wealth and spread Christianity were the professed goals of Spaniards who embarked on the risky voyage to a barely known New World. The most spectacular conquests, Mexico by Hernán Cortés and Peru by Francisco Pizarro, came in the next reign. Imposing order on the unruly conquistadors, especially in Peru, proved a daunting task for viceroys sent from Spain. Administration of the growing empire was conducted from court, at first by the Council of Castile, then after 1522, by the Council of the Indies, which did what it could to supervise viceroys, captains-general, and law courts (*audiencias*) over 3,000 miles away. Laws promulgated by Isabella's successors were well intended and provided for humane treatment of the Indians. Early abuses were chronicled in savage detail by Fray Bartolomé de las Casas, who influenced Spanish legislation. But legislation was one thing, reality another, and in the rough and tumble of the New World the conquistadors and their descendants maintained a harsh ascendancy over the surviving native population. Disease was the big killer. Smallpox, fatal to 20 percent of Europeans, wiped out nearly all of the Caribbean Indian population, close to 90 percent of Mexico's Indians, and perhaps half the Indians of Peru. Its impact varied in the rest of the Americas, as Europeans came into contact with native peoples.

A handful of Indians, mainly of princely rank, married into the ranks of the conquistadors and their descent. Intermarriage with the conquered elite is a traditional tactic of domination. A son of a conquistador and an Inca princess, Garcilaso de la Vega el Inca, wrote a remarkable history of Peru that blended both Spanish and Inca accounts. The history of the Aztecs was written through the collaboration of a Spanish friar, Bernardino de Sahagún, and Aztecs and included marvelous illustrations of the conquest from an Aztec perspective. The good friar's purpose, however, was to learn Aztec history and ways to further their conversion to Christianity. In 1532, an Indian neophyte, Juan Diego, believed he saw an apparition of the Blessed Virgin as an Indian maiden, Mexico's Virgin of Guadalupe. (Spain's Guadalupe is closely associated with the late reconquest.) Mexico's Indians now had their own patron saint. With zeal and determination, the first friars fanned out through the Spanish conquests to convert and protect other Indians. By 1600 they had been largely replaced by comfortable parish priests of Spanish or mixed descent, who feared that the Indians' conversions had been superficial and used the confessional to test Indians' beliefs. Through a concordat with the papacy, the crown nominated bishops and usually provided good men, but their task was immense. The Inquisition also came to the New World. On the frontiers the old fervor survived, and missions spread to New Mexico, to Arizona, and in the eighteenth century, to Alta California. In Paraguay the Jesuits tried with some success to establish a Christian utopia, despite slave raids from Brazil. When the Jesuits were expelled in 1769, their utopia collapsed.

Those who crossed the Atlantic in search of fortune hoped to live like great lords. To provide labor, as the Indian population died from disease, demoralization, and abuse, they imported West Africans. The West African slave trade was already long established. The victims were acquired through raids, often by rival local tribes. The Arabs and Berbers of North Africa transported slaves by caravan across the Sahara. The Portuguese, as they worked down the African coast in search of a route to India, cut into the slave trade by sea. While the market for slaves in Europe was limited, as the free labor supply was large and cheap, the Portuguese found markets in Madeira and the Canary Islands, where colonizers founded sugar plantations. The New World proved yet another and vastly larger market for the traffic in Africans that the Portuguese conducted, and by 1520, it was well under way. In Spain people remained squeamish about the business, although they admitted that it seemed vital to the prosperity of their New World colonies, and it was provided for in law. The galley slavery they accepted in the Mediterranean seemed a different matter, a consequence of capture in the crusade and *jihad*, especially as manifested in piracy.

Spain's achievement in the New World is immense, as the history of the Spanish-speaking American republics attests. However, the legacy of the conquistadors, men of Spain's lower nobility eager to live like great lords, has posed persistent problems. Moreover, Spaniards who came later to defend and administer the empire added to the prestige of the armed forces or bureaucracy as fit careers for bright young men. Though Spaniards were always industrious and not lacking in business acumen, neither heavy industry nor large-scale business became characteristic of Spanish America, though matters are changing. While geography plays a significant role in every case, cultural attitudes rooted in late medieval Spain cannot be dismissed—although they remain elusive and make historians nervous in dealing with them.

Some of the same observations might be applied to the Philippines. Their conquest was undertaken from Mexico in 1565, long after Isabella's death, by an expedition of 350 men commanded by Miguel de Legazpi. Crossing the Pacific, Legazpi touched at Guam, which he claimed for Spain, before landing on Leyte to make Spain's empire the first in world history on which the sun never set. After establishing a stronghold on Cebu, Legazpi founded Manila in 1570. A brisk trade with China soon opened, and each year thereafter the Manila galleon would cross the Pacific, laden with porcelains, precious gems, and silks. Down the California coast it sailed until it reached Acapulco. Its rich cargo would then be transhipped to Spain. The Catholic religion and many Filipino names still reflect the legacy of Spain.

Isabella died in 1504, Ferdinand in 1516. Their emblem had been a yoke and five arrows. The arrows stood for the five kingdoms of Spain: Castile, León, Aragon, Navarre, and Granada; the yoke stood for the two of them who worked in tandem to advance the five kingdoms. For their achievements, the pope acknowledged them as *reyes católicos,* "Catholic kings." They are buried side by side in the royal chapel of Granada, where their grandson, King Carlos I, gazed at their tombs and exclaimed, "So small a space for so much glory!"

EUROPE IN THE AGE OF PHILIP II

SPANISH HABSBURGS

AUSTRIAN HABSBURGS

Map 3

5

Imperial Spain

Carlos I of Spain is better known as Holy Roman Emperor Charles V. Of the Habsburg dynasty, he was born in 1500 in Ghent, Flanders, of today's Belgium. His advent to the Spanish throne was the unforeseen result of Ferdinand's foreign policy. Ferdinand had disputes with France over Catalonia's borderlands and Navarre and conflicting claims in Italy. He sought allies among France's foes, and in the diplomacy of the times, he arranged for the marriages of their children to his. He and Isabella had five, a son and four daughters. Isabel, the eldest, married King Emmanuel the Fortunate of Portugal. In 1497, Prince Juan and the second daughter, Juana, married the daughter, Margaret, and son, Philip, of Holy Roman Emperor Maximilian I. An Austrian Habsburg, Maximilian had differences with France over the Low Countries, which Philip had inherited from his mother, Mary of Burgundy. Maximilian also differed with France over interests in Italy. Yet another ally of Ferdinand was Henry VII Tudor of England, whose son Henry VIII married the youngest of Ferdinand's daughters, Catherine of Aragon, in 1509. The next youngest, María, married Emmanuel of Portugal after her sister Isabel died.

Prince Juan died in 1498, only eighteen. His lovely tomb at Avila evokes thoughts of what might have been, had he lived. When his sister Isabel died in 1500, followed by her infant son, Juana became the heiress of her parents.

A high-strung princess, she desperately loved Philip, known as "the Hand-some." He philandered, and she came mentally unraveled. Dutifully she bore him six children. After Queen Isabella died, Juana and Philip claimed Castile and embarked from Flanders for Spain. They left their heir Charles in Brussels with his widowed aunt Margaret. Ferdinand reluctantly vacated Castile to Juana and Philip and withdrew to Aragon. All admitted that Queen Juana seemed too unstable to rule, but the Castilian Cortes hesitated to grant regency power and the title of king to Philip, a foreigner sur-rounded by foreign cronies. Philip suddenly took sick and died, shattering his pregnant wife's feeble composure. She had his coffin opened as the body was transported across Castile to be placed near Isabella's coffin in Gra-nada. Ferdinand hurried back to Castile, where the Cortes granted him re-gency power to act for his distraught daughter. He confined her to a rundown palace at Tordesillas, where she gradually lost touch with the world round her. History knows her as Juana *la loca* (Joan the Mad). Ferdi-nand, occupied by the affairs of Aragon and Italy, left Cardinal Cisneros to serve as lieutenant general of Castile.

Ferdinand did not fancy the idea that Charles, growing up in Brussels, would succeed to Aragon, Sicily, and Naples, as well as to Castile, and so he married Germaine de Foix. Despite the use of love potions, she did not pro-duce an heir. When Ferdinand died in 1516, Queen Juana and her son Char-les were accepted as heirs to Aragon.

From the Low Countries, Charles, aged sixteen, set sail for Spain with a tribe of greedy Flemish nobles, headed by the Sieur de Chièvres. Cardinal Cisneros awaited Charles to give him good advice but died before they met. The Castilian Cortes acknowledged Charles as king alongside his mother but insisted that both sign all decrees and laws to make them valid. When Charles rewarded his Flemish followers with choice Spanish plums, con-sternation ensued. Chièvres played chief minister and nominated his teen-aged nephew to be archbishop of Toledo. Charles's Dutch tutor, Adrian of Utrecht, became bishop of Tortosa, while Charles's popular brother Ferdi-nand was dispatched to Austria.

After receiving a grant of money from Castile, Charles traveled to Aragón and was acclaimed king in Zaragoza. Some confusion exists about the legendary coronation oath. It was claimed that Aragonese nobles ac-cepted their king by swearing "We, who are as good as you are, accept you, who are no better than we are, as our lawful sovereign so long as you uphold our laws, rights and privileges; and if not, not." It took eight months' hag-gling to get money. Charles headed for Barcelona to meet the Cortes (Corts) of Catalonia. Early in 1519, he learned that his grandfather Emperor Maxi-milian had died. Charles inherited the Habsburg Austrian lands, while

Maximilian's bribes to the seven German electors won him the imperial title. Now Holy Roman Emperor Charles V, he postponed visiting Valencia and at the beginning of 1520 hurried back to Castile to get more money. The Castilian Cortes proved reluctant so he dragged them with him to Santiago, near La Coruña, where his fleet waited. A sermon by Bishop de la Mota of Badajoz about the benefit of Charles's imperial destiny to Castile did not impress them. By a scant majority of eight to seven, with one abstention and neither Toledo nor Salamanca represented, they voted Charles the subsidy he requested. Despite news that Toledo had revolted, Charles sailed and left Adrian of Utrecht as his regent to keep order.

Charles was acknowledged emperor at Aachen, and in April 1521, at the Diet of Worms, he held his fateful confrontation with Martin Luther. Luther stood his ground, and Charles responded that he would support the Church of Rome, even if it cost him his life's blood. At that moment blood was spilling in Spain. The delegates to the Cortes of Santiago had returned to angry constituencies. Several were mobbed; one was lynched. Throughout Castile rebellion erupted. Instigated by urban communal governments, it is known as the Revolt of the Comuneros. The rebels formed a national junta, headed by Juan de Padilla of Toledo and Juan Bravo of Segovia. They denounced government by foreigners and a king who abandoned Spain for Germany. They urged Queen Juana to resume her throne. They only confused Juana and they alienated the nobility when their revolt spread to villages under noble jurisdiction. When Charles brought the constable and the admiral of Castile into the regency government, and decreed the twenty-five most powerful to be grandees of Spain, the nobles rallied to him. In April 1521, royalist cavalry routed the Comunero host at Villalar and had Bravo and Padilla executed. Inspired by Padilla's widow, María Pacheco, Toledo held out until early 1522. Another revolt had erupted in Valencia and was put down by nobles. Soon afterward Charles returned to Spain, mastered the Spanish language, and pardoned most of the rebels. He met with the Cortes, improved the administration of government which he staffed with Spaniards, and in 1526 married a redheaded Portuguese princess, Isabel. When she gave birth in 1527 to their son, Philip, in Valladolid, Spaniards believed they again had one of their own to inherit the throne. The couple had two other children who survived, María and Juana.

Charles matured through the decade of the 1520s, guided by the suave Italian hand of his chancellor, Mercurino Gattinara, and came to be admired in Spain in his own right. Queen Juana was almost forgotten in her rooms at Tordesillas. The years 1522 to 1529 were the most he spent in Spain, where his ministers refined its system of government by councils. To advise him on grand policy, he had his Council of State. For administration there were the councils of Castile, the Indies, and Aragon. A Council of War managed his armed forces, and a Council of the Hacienda (Treasury) oversaw his finances. Each council had its secretaries, who formed a budding bureaucracy.

Charles had a war with France, which his generals waged in the Low Countries and Italy, where they captured King Francis I at Pavia in 1525. Shipped to Madrid to make peace, Francis went back on the terms when he reached home. The pope joined him when he renewed the war, and in 1527, Charles's soldiers got out of hand and sacked Rome. Francis disputed Charles's inheritance at every turn, including Castile's claim to monopoly in the New World. "The sun shines on me as it does on your master," he told Charles's ambassador, "and I should like to see the clause in Adam's will that allots him ownership of the world." Two sensible women prevailed, Charles's aunt Margaret, and Francis's mother, Louise of Savoy. They hammered out "the Ladies' Peace" of 1529. By its terms Francis married Charles's sister Eleanor, widow of Emmanuel the Fortunate.

More ominous to Charles than war with France was the threat posed by the expansion of the Ottoman Empire under Sultan Suleiman the Magnificent. In 1520 Suleiman captured Belgrade and, in 1522, drove the Knights of St. John from the Island of Rhodes. In 1530 Charles gave the Knights the island of Malta as a new base. The great disaster came in 1526, when Charles, on his honeymoon at Granada, learned that his brother-in-law, King Louis of Hungary and Bohemia, had been killed and his army annihilated by the Turks on the distant Danube. The Holy Roman Empire lay open to attack, and in 1529, the Turks besieged Vienna. Vienna held out, but in 1530 Charles embarked for Austria, accompanied by many Spaniards. At Bologna in Italy the pope crowned him emperor. He would be the last Holy Roman Emperor to receive the crown from a pope's hands. In Germany he temporized with the Protestants so he could assemble an army in which Spaniards marched beside Germans. In 1532 he and his brother Ferdinand paraded along the Hungarian border. Charles had conceded Austria to Ferdinand, who also became king of Bohemia and unoccupied Hungary. When Charles returned to Spain, he organized a Spanish-Italian expedition against Tunis, in order to isolate Algiers, where Suleiman's admiral Khair-ed-Din Barbarossa had driven the Spaniards from its waterfront citadel. In 1535 Charles's vast armada, commanded by Genoa's Andrea Doria, landed an army that conquered Tunis. To govern Tunis, Charles selected a Muslim prince hostile to the Turks. To intimidate its Muslim population, he had his engineers build the fortress of La Goleta, which he garrisoned with Christian soldiers.

In triumph Charles returned via his kingdoms of Sicily and Naples, then proceeded to Rome. He lectured the pope and cardinals in Spanish about his services, the need for an ecumenical council to deal with Lutheranism, and the perfidy of Francis I, who allied with the Turks. A brief war erupted between Charles and Francis before Pope Paul III arranged a shaky truce and brought the two together for personal meetings.

In 1539, Charles lost his wife, Empress Isabel, but found little time for grief. In 1540 he traveled to the Low Countries to deal with troubles there. The next year he proceeded first to Germany, where again he failed to settle the Lutheran issue, then on to Genoa, to coordinate an expedition against Algiers. The army had scarcely landed in late 1541 before the weather turned foul and scattered the fleet. Over the objections of Hernán Cortés, conqueror of Mexico, the bedraggled army reembarked and a humbled Charles returned to Spain.

Francis I declared war on Charles in 1542. In 1543 Charles made his sixteen-year-old son Philip his regent in Spain, then headed for the Low Countries to coordinate the war against France. To guide Philip, Charles chose Fernando de Valdés, archbishop of Seville and Grand Inquisitor; the duke of Alba, his best general; and Francisco de los Cobos, his financial expert. Before sailing, he sent Philip a set of remarkable secret instructions about government and the people who served it. He warned Philip that nobles tended to seek gain at the crown's expense, while bureaucrats tried to line their own pockets, and he named names. He advised Philip to guard his thoughts and to flatter people as necessary but give nothing away. He warned Philip that women might be employed to win his favor. Worried that sex might tempt the teenaged prince, Charles arranged that he marry a Portuguese princess, María, who was his own age. Two years later she gave birth to a son, Don Carlos, then two weeks afterward, she died. In time Don Carlos would prove a problem.

In 1545 Charles obtained a truce with France while Pope Paul assembled an ecumenical council at Trent. The council clarified the religious issues for Charles, who marched against the German Lutherans. In April 1547, his army, which included a large Spanish contingent under Alba, smashed his enemies at the Battle of Mühlberg. A great equestrian portrait by the Venetian painter Titian, now in Madrid's Prado, commemorates the victory. Charles assembled the Germans at Augsburg in 1548 in hopes of putting the religious issue to rest and arranging the imperial succession to allow Philip to succeed his uncle Ferdinand. In neither quest did Charles succeed.

Early in 1552 a revived league of German Protestant princes struck a secret deal with Henri II, the new king of France, and chased Charles from Germany. While Ferdinand patched up a truce in Germany that led to the Religious Peace of Augsburg (1555), Charles failed against Henri II. Embittered, he withdrew to Brussels but saw a chance to get England back as an ally when his cousin, Catholic Mary Tudor, daughter of Henry VIII and Catherine of Aragon, succeeded Edward VI to the English throne. He arranged for her to marry Philip, though she was thirty-eight. Dutifully Philip embarked in 1554 for England and left his nineteen-year-old sister Juana as regent. Juana was the widow of Prince João of Portugal, whose posthumous son Dom Sebastian she had just borne.

As husband of Queen Mary, Philip became England's titular king. With England again an ally, Charles signed a truce with the French king and took the opportunity to abdicate his inheritance to Philip. Early in 1555 Queen Juana had died, leaving Philip's succession unimpeded. In January 1556 Philip became king of Castile and Aragon.

Leaving Philip to settle matters in the Low Countries, Charles sailed to Spain. For his retirement he selected the monastery of Yuste in the wild Sierra de Gredos. He had a small dwelling built against its chapel and could hear Mass through a special door from his bedroom. There he prayed and ruminated, though he still followed the affairs of the world and showered advice on Regent Juana and Philip. In September 1558 he died.

Philip had been successful in the north. With England as an ally, his armies defeated the French at the Battle of St. Quentin in 1557, and in 1559 he made peace with Henri II at Cateau Cambrésis. Queen Mary of England had died in 1558, without child, and England passed to her half sister, Elizabeth I. Although Philip feared that Elizabeth would return England to Henry VIII's Protestantism, he preferred her to her Catholic rival, Mary Queen of Scots, wife of the Dauphin of France. He did not trust France, but for the sake of peace, he married Henri's daughter, Elisabeth de Valois, aged thirteen. He was ready to return to Spain, above all to repair his finances. In 1557 he had been forced to declare bankruptcy and renegotiate the huge debts he had inherited from Charles, to which the last war added more. War required, Philip admitted, "money, money, and more money."

Philip faced not only money problems on his return to Spain. In Seville and Valladolid the Inquisition had discovered cells of people harboring Protestant ideas. When Charles learned about them from Regent Juana, he thundered back that Protestant heresies had to be uprooted at first sight, lest they disturb the community and lead to rebellion, civil war, and the loss of the kingdom. Juana and Philip agreed. She presided over a major *auto de fe* at Valladolid in the spring of 1559, and Philip presided over a second after his return in the autumn. Others were held in Seville. Some 60 people went to the stake, and perhaps 200 were given other punishments. Having nipped Spanish Protestantism in the bud, the Inquisition stepped up its assault on the writings of the great Dutch humanist scholar Erasmus, which seemed too critical of Church institutions and traditional theology. To protect Castilian collegians from dangerous ideas, Philip forbade them to study outside the peninsula, save for the universities of Rome and Bologna in the Papal States. It mattered little, since most Spanish students were career oriented, with law school, which led to government jobs, the favorite choice. Serious, if sporadic, efforts were made to limit access to universities, and church and government posts to those of "pure" Old Christian descent. While the Inquisition worried about religious controversies and backsliding among *conversos*, it paid little heed to science. The idea of Copernicus, that the earth went round the sun, did not bother the Spanish inquisitors. Spanish students showed little interest in abstract science, and those pursuing medical degrees took no more than they had to.

To find money Philip first tried to make tax collection more efficient and to recover revenues from mineral rights, salt flats, and customs houses conceded to grandees during the previous century. Yet during his reign he sold lands and other jurisdictions to them and to municipalities for hard cash. He received generous grants from the Cortes of Castile, pleased to see him in Spain again, and lesser sums from the Cortes of Aragón, Catalonia, and Valencia. Steadily increasing during his reign were revenues due him from the New World.

The mines of the New World had become a significant source of income and a major prop of Spain's power in Europe. Most lucrative were the mines of Potosí, a virtual mountain of silver discovered in 1545 in Upper Peru (today's Bolivia) and made immensely productive by the employment of mercury brought from Spain. In its peak years, 100,000 people, white, black, and Indian, free and slave, worked Potosí. Almost from the start, pirates, and in wartime privateers, threatened the transatlantic routes that brought American gold and silver to Spain's coffers. Spain made its merchant ships sail in convoy. In time two fleets a year sailed, one to New Spain, as Mexico was called, and the other to Tierra Firme, the Spanish Main (the coast of today's Venezuela and Colombia). To escort the fleets and chase pirates from the Caribbean, Philip established an armada of a dozen galleons, the principal warships of the age. The stiff tax imposed on merchant ships to pay for their escort would over time contribute to the decline of Spain's merchant marine.

Philip would have preferred to concentrate on providing good government for his subjects and took particular care in making judicial and episcopal appointments. He established separate councils for Italy and Flanders, as the Low Countries were called in Spain. However, larger problems involving the defense of his imperial interests occupied too much of his time (see Map 3). Though Philip preferred diplomacy, he became engulfed in costly wars. The religious wars against the Ottoman Turks in the Mediterranean and North Africa were popular with Spaniards, and the Cortes were willing to find money for them. Wars against Catholic France were less popular, though they had a long tradition. What posed the chief drain on Spain's resources, the Revolt of the Netherlands, was perceived as a dynastic rather than Spanish concern, and as the original determination to combat Protestants as heretics faded, finding money to suppress the revolt became thoroughly unpopular.

In 1555 the Turks seized two of Spain's North African strongholds, Tripoli and Bona. In 1559, Philip permitted his viceroy of Sicily and the Knights of Malta to attempt the recovery of Tripoli. They failed and suffered heavy losses in men and shipping. In 1562 storms cost Philip a squadron of galleys and forced him to dun the Cortes for money to build more. When the Turks besieged Malta in 1565, Philip organized a powerful relief armada in time to drive them away. The next year, Suleiman the Magnificent, Charles's implacable foe, died, and Philip had a brief respite. He needed it to deal with mounting troubles in the Netherlands and the rebellion of the Moriscos of Granada. To the Netherlands he dispatched an army under the duke of Alba to impose order. To subdue the Moriscos, who controlled a remote and rugged part of Granada known as the Alpujarras, he appointed his twenty-three-year-old half brother, Don John of Austria, an illegitimate son of Charles V, who overrode rival local authorities and pacified the Alpujarras by the end of 1570. In the aftermath, the Moriscos of Granada were dispersed throughout Old and New Castile in an effort to assimilate them into the Old Christian majority of Spaniards.

The Morisco rebellion was still aglow when in 1570 the new Ottoman sultan, Selim II, invaded the Venetian possession of Cyprus. Turks had already seized control of Tunis, although the fortress of La Goleta held out. Venice sought allies through Pope Pius V, who turned to Spain. After contentious negotiations, Pius, Spain, and Venice formed a Holy League. Philip agreed to foot half the costs and obtained the supreme command for Don John. Through him Philip meant to direct the League's strategy. For Cyprus it was too late, although at the Battle of Lepanto, on October 7, 1571, Don John and the League armada of over 200 galleys and six heavily gunned galleasses defeated the Turks' near 300 lighter and less well-gunned galleys. After achieving little in 1572, mainly because Philip was distracted by developments in France and the Low Countries, the League broke up in 1573, when Venice defected. Later that year, Don John recovered Tunis, but the Turks retook it in 1574 and kept it. Don John was preoccupied with Genoa, where he assisted the government of Philip's allies to maintain control. Genoa did Philip's banking and was troubled by his skyrocketing debts, incurred to maintain a big army in the Low Countries and a big armada in the Mediterranean. In 1575 Philip had to declare bankruptcy and renegotiate his debts with his Genoese creditors. He summoned the Cortes of Castile and cajoled them into tripling the basic tax rates. He was fortunate to see his revenues slightly more than double. None doubted that the burden on Castile's tax base had become dangerous, but the wars, which Philip believed justifiable in defense of religion and his patrimony, demanded it.

The revolt in the Low Countries would lead to the division of the region between the Spanish Netherlands (today's Belgium and Luxembourg) and the Dutch Republic. For five generations of Spanish soldiers it meant "trailing a pike in Flanders." The seeds of the revolt were many and included national differences and resistance to taxation over endless dynastic conflicts with France. However, the chief problem was religion. Before he returned to Spain, Philip learned of the spread of Calvinist Protestantism among the Low Countries' population. To check it, he had Rome establish fourteen new bishoprics, in addition to the four long there, and assign two inquisitors to each. Traditionally the Low Countries had been relatively tolerant and held small numbers of Lutherans and Anabaptists, as well as Jewish refugees from Spain and Portugal.

Most of the Low Countries' population opposed the new bishoprics, despite the efforts of Philip's governor-general and half sister Margaret, an illegitimate daughter of Charles V and duchess of Parma, to establish them. The principal nobles, led by William the Silent, prince of Orange, joined the opposition and demanded an end to the inquisition and a moderation of penalties for heretics. Although Philip temporized, he did not give in. In 1566 riots erupted in most of the chief towns. Calvinist mobs looted Catholic churches and preached from their pulpits. Local authorities were slow to react, and on receiving the news, Philip was stunned. He knew that he ought to visit the Low Countries and settle matters with the States General, but he agreed to the duke of Alba's plan that an army precede him to ensure order. He put Alba in charge of what history knows as the Army of Flanders and reluctantly prepared to follow.

His main worry was his son, Don Carlos. Now twenty-one, Don Carlos had proved to be unstable and erratic in his behavior. Most, save his indulgent father, thought him unfit for the business of kingship. In 1568, Philip learned that Don Carlos meant to flee court and confined him. He died of fevers six months later.

Alba found the situation in the seventeen provinces that comprised the Low Countries worse than he expected. Margaret resigned and left him with the government. He subdued the opposition, but it cost money; Philip told him to find the money locally. Alba browbeat the States General and tried to impose new taxes unilaterally. Rebellion revived on land and sea.

Protestant Queen Elizabeth I grew nervous about Alba's big army and
Catholic talk of invading England, and aided the rebels, who were mainly
Protestants. French Protestant Huguenots also aided them. Philip tried am-
nesty to win peace and replaced Alba, but he would not yield on the matter
of keeping the Low Countries Catholic. The revolt raged on, "a voracious
monster," according to one minister, "that devours the men and treasure of
Spain." With a simultaneous war against the Turks, Philip could not pay his
soldiers, who mutinied and ran amok and drove Catholics to join the rebels.
Don John, the hero of Lepanto, became governor and dismissed the army.
Failing to appease the rebels, he again resorted to arms. Distressed, Philip
became involved in scandal when he permitted his secretary Antonio Pérez
to have Don John's secretary murdered as a security risk.

But religious division also plagued the rebel ranks, and Don John's successor, Alexander Farnese, Margaret's son and, after 1586, duke of Parma,
won the Catholics back and established an obedient "Spanish" Netherlands
that consisted of the ten southern provinces. The seven northern provinces
formed the Dutch Republic (which we often call Holland, from its richest
province), under its States General and the House of Orange.

At first Philip had little money and few men for Parma, because the death
in 1578 of King Sebastian of Portugal, on a mad crusade against Morocco,
opened the succession to the Portuguese throne. Philip claimed Portugal by
right of inheritance through his mother and made his claim good with an
army led by the duke of Alba and an armada commanded by the marquis of
Santa Cruz. In early 1581 Philip entered Portugal and summoned its Cortes
to acclaim him king. Portugal retained its laws, institutions, and the administration of its empire in Asia and Brazil. When Philip left in 1583 for Madrid,
he made his nephew Archduke Albert his viceroy in Lisbon. In Madrid he
established a Council of Portugal to advise him on Portuguese affairs.

Once Portugal and its empire were added to his worldwide dominions,
Philip regularized the pay of Parma's Army of Flanders. While Parma re-
captured Antwerp, Queen Elizabeth signed a treaty of alliance with the
Dutch, which led to open war. Already some of her subjects, like Sir Francis
Drake, had raided Spanish commerce in the Caribbean and the Pacific. In
1586 Drake ravaged the Caribbean and in 1587 struck Cádiz as Santa Cruz
struggled to form an armada. Concerned about costs, Philip devised a complicated scheme whereby Santa Cruz would cover the passage to England
of Parma and the Army of Flanders. By February 1588 Santa Cruz had assembled a vast but motley armada of Spanish, Portuguese, and Mediterranean ships, but then he died. The duke of Medina Sidonia, a naval
administrator rather than a sailor, took command and with the assistance of
his admirals got the armada into the English Channel. The English fleet

proved more maneuverable and far better at gunnery and frustrated the armada's attempt to "join hands" with Parma. Forced into the North Sea, Medina Sidonia returned to Spain by sailing north of Scotland and around Ireland. Storms slammed the battered armada, and nearly half its ships and more of its men were lost, the men mostly to disease.

Philip ascribed the defeat to God's punishment of sin, then pressed on. A siege mentality grew in Madrid. The Dutch held on, Parma reconquered little more, and after his death in 1592, his successors lost a bit. France under its new king, Henri IV of the Bourbon dynasty and once a Huguenot but now a Catholic, declared war on Philip. With his people fighting in France, too, Philip rebuilt his armadas and renewed his attacks on England. His armed forces were stretched thin, his royal officials scrambled to maintain them, and to sustain Spain's war effort, he had to enlist the cooperation of local powers whose enthusiasm would not last. To foot the bills, he summoned the Cortes and appealed to their loyalty to him and to God. They voted him money on stiff terms that allowed urban governments to dump more of the tax burden onto ordinary folk. The amounts were reckoned in millions of ducats and known as the *millones*. Although treasure from the Indies managed to get through English blockades, rising taxes and war costs began to impair the economy of Castile. Major epidemics in the years round 1600 added to Spain's woes.

Yet during Philip's reign, Spanish Golden Age culture flourished. Lope de Vega commenced writing for the Madrid stage. El Greco, born on Crete and trained in Venice, painted his masterpieces in Toledo. St. Theresa of Avila inspired religious reform and revival, while St. John of the Cross wrote perhaps the finest mystical poetry in any language.

Before Philip died in September 1598, he obtained peace with France. He tried to solve the dilemma of the Low Countries by transferring them to his daughter Isabella, sometimes called the Great Infanta, and her husband Archduke Albert. But when Albert died in 1621 they had no heir, and the Low Countries reverted to the Spanish crown. Isabella continued to govern the ten obedient provinces until her death in 1633. The Dutch Republic persisted in its independence.

Philip III (1598–1621), an indolent youth of twenty when he became king, allowed his favorite minister (*valido*), the duke of Lerma, to run the government. Spain made peace with England in 1604 and a Twelve Years' Truce with the Dutch in 1609. The power of Spain still seemed awesome, and a few years of peace did the economy no harm. Yet many feared that things had gone seriously wrong, and men known as *arbitristas* bombarded the government with proposals of what might be done to improve matters. Little was done save to expel the Moriscos, who had not assimilated into Old Christian society. After 1609 over 200,000 Morisco men, women, and children were dumped on the beaches of North Africa.

Four years earlier in Seville a novel appeared, the first part of *Don Quixote de la Mancha*, by Miguel de Cervantes. The complete novel is one of those rare great books into which we can read almost anything. Cervantes fought at Lepanto, where his left hand was maimed. Later captured by Algerian corsairs, he spent five years as a slave. When ransomed and returned to Spain, he took up writing plays, with little success. He landed a government job collecting taxes for the armada. An audit of his accounts put him in jail, where he supposedly conceived *Don Quixote*. The gaunt old don, pursuing his chivalric dreams, seems a fit symbol for an exhausted Castile, persisting in wars it could not afford.

But Castile protested through its Cortes and, increasingly, through tax evasion and resistance to recruiting. It was the Habsburg dynasty, its dependent ministers, and a handful of loyal grandees who persisted in the struggle. The Count-Duke of Olivares, the *valido* of Philip IV (1621–1665) becomes the archvillain. An intelligent but overbearing man, determined that his sovereign should be the world's greatest, Olivares took up with energy the wars that began to sputter out in Philip III's last months. In the Holy Roman Empire, the Army of Flanders intervened in support of the Viennese Habsburgs in what would become the Thirty Years War. Then the Dutch War resumed. Olivares mobilized Spain's resources, and in 1625 the Spaniards won a spate of victories. But the French, guided by the brilliant Cardinal Richelieu and fearful of revived Spanish power, played the role of spoiler, aiding the Habsburgs' enemies and bringing the Swedes into the conflict. In 1628 near Havana, Cuba, the loss of a silver fleet to the Dutch proved a setback. With desperate effort Olivares gathered new forces, and in 1634, Philip IV's younger brother, the Cardinal-Infante Don Fernando, defeated the Swedes at Nordlingen in Germany. In 1635, France entered the war openly. The array of powers against Spain became overwhelming, while in Spain opposition to Olivares mounted. Spain's best admiral called him a fat, desk-bound bureaucrat without knowledge of war and got thrown into prison. In 1639, the Dutch virtually destroyed Spain's last major armada in the Battle of the Downs.

Olivares had long urged that Spain's kingdoms form a Union of Arms for common defense, but Aragón, Catalonia, and Portugal opposed him. When he lodged Castilian troops in winter quarters in Catalonia, close to southern France, the Catalans in 1640 rose in revolt. As more Castilian troops marched against Catalonia, Portugal took the opportunity to rebel and proclaim the duke of Braganza as King João IV. Soon after, Olivares nipped in the bud a conspiracy to make the ninth duke of Medina Sidonia king of Andalusia. The whole peninsula seethed with revolt and sedition.

In the Netherlands, in 1643 after the Cardinal-Infante died, the French at the Battle of Rocroi inflicted on the Army of Flanders its greatest defeat. When the gun smoke cleared, most of its Spaniards lay dead, still in their ranks. In Spain Philip IV dumped Olivares, who soon went mad and died in 1645. A new ministry sought peace, and to end the war with the Dutch, Philip IV acknowledged the republic's independence in 1648. Before he died in 1665, he also acknowledged the independence of Portugal. He did recover Catalonia. His last portraits, painted by Diego de Velázquez, reveal a broken but still proud man. Velázquez is arguably Olivares's greatest legacy to Spain. Olivares brought the promising young Sevillian painter to court in the 1620s. There Velázquez painted portraits of the king and royal family and the bombastic Olivares. He painted the remarkable *Surrender of Breda*, one of the Spanish triumphs of 1625. In it, the commander of the Army of Flanders, Ambrogio Spinola, a Genoese banker turned Spanish general, graciously receives the surrender of the Dutch. While the Dutch pikes droop, those of the Army of Flanders stand upright, causing Spaniards to call the painting *Las lanzas* (the Lances). The most charming of Velázquez's paintings is called *Las Meninas* (the ladies-in-waiting). While the artist stands at his easel, painting the king and queen—whose reflections can be seen in a mirror—their daughter Margarita and her ladies-in-waiting burst into his studio. A court dwarf, her son, and a pet dog also appear in the picture. When Margarita left for Vienna to marry Emperor Leopold I, Philip had the huge canvas hung in his small office as a memento of a happy moment.

At his death, Philip IV was hardly a happy man. He had yielded the northern Netherlands and Portugal and had seen Spain broken by war. He had given his eldest daughter, Maria Teresa, as bride to Louis XIV, king of France and arbiter of Europe. She had renounced all rights to Spain for herself and her heirs, though most legal experts thought she could not justly renounce the rights of her heirs. Philip's only other surviving child was Prince Carlos, who succeeded to the Spanish throne in 1665, not quite aged four.

The reign of Carlos II is often considered the low point of Spain's long history. With the death of playwright Calderón de la Barca in 1681, Spain's cultural Golden Age ended. Yet sometime in the later 1680s the economy and population began to show faint signs of recovery. Carlos II, a product of excessive inbreeding between the Habsburgs of Madrid and Vienna, never knew good health. He had an indifferent education, and people in the streets believed that his mother, Mariana of Austria, regent during his minority, cast him under a spell: He is thus known as Carlos *el hechizado* (the be-witched).

His uncle, Don Juan José de Austria, provided some energy to govern-ment and Spain's meager war efforts. Son of Philip IV and an actress, he was ever at odds with the queen-mother and her lowborn *valido*, Fernando de Valenzuela. Don Juan José led a faction of grandees, who again became ac-tive in government. When he finally got the upper hand in 1676, he had Va-lenzuela exiled and initiated a series of needed reforms. He died at age fifty in 1679 and was followed in office by a string of grandees who survived in office through intrigue and made use of government professionals. The best was the count of Oropesa, chief minister between 1685 and 1691, when he fell victim to infighting. The government's main achievement was reform of the currency, which had become so debased as to be nearly worthless.

As the sickly Carlos grew up and in 1679 married a niece of Louis XIV, ru-mor grew that he was impotent. The question of the Spanish succession be-came the overriding issue of European diplomacy. Spain's former enemies, England and the Dutch, did what they could to prop up sagging Spanish fortunes against the mounting power of Louis XIV. After the death of Don Juan José, Spain took little initiative abroad. Shipments of silver from the New World became intermittent as pirates and enemy fleets infested the Caribbean. In 1697, a French fleet in combination with a force of buccaneers sacked Cartagena de Indias, capital of the Spanish Main.

Making peace in 1697, Louis XIV and his chief foe, William III, king of England and leader of the Dutch Republic, developed a plan to partition Spain's empire between the Bourbon and Habsburg dynasties to avoid an-other ruinous war. The Italian share would go to Louis's second grandson, Philip, duke of Anjou. Spain, the Spanish Netherlands, and the overseas possessions would go to Emperor Leopold's younger son, Archduke Char-les. Leopold strenuously objected, claiming all belonged to the Habsburgs. In Madrid, Louis's and Leopold's ambassadors intrigued for influence with Spanish ministers of state and members of the royal household. The queen-mother died in 1696, but the pro-Habsburg faction at court continued under the direction of Carlos's second wife, Mariana of Neuberg, and her German entourage. To dominate the king, she implied that she was pregnant with the heir he so desperately wanted. But when Carlos died on November 1, 1700, and his will was read, France had won. The Spaniards around Carlos, led by Archbishop Portocarrero of Toledo, wanted their world empire to re-main intact. Though humiliated on the battlefield and the high seas by the French, they preferred the Bourbon candidate to the Habsburg candidate. Louis XIV not only had Europe's most powerful army; he also had a strong navy, which Emperor Leopold did not. The will stipulated that Philip of Anjou had to accept the entire inheritance, which meant that Louis would have to reject the partition agreements. If Philip did not, then Spain and its empire would pass to Archduke Charles. Charles hardly intended to reject the offer; if he did, the whole would pass to the duke of Savoy. A week after Carlos II died, the news of his will reached Louis XIV at Versailles. After weighing his options and giving Leopold a chance to agree to partition, Louis dispatched Philip to Spain. In February 1701, seventeen-year-old King Philip V arrived in Madrid. His House of Bourbon replaced the House of Habsburg on Spain's throne.

From the reign of Charles V into the reign of Philip IV, the Spanish Monarchy—as contemporaries called Spain, the king's other European dominions, and Castile's overseas empire—had seemed the greatest power in Europe. Philip II had been the first sovereign in world history on whose dominions the sun never set. However, when he died in 1598, the structural weaknesses of a world monarchy that depended overmuch on Castile and American treasure had become apparent to many. The treasure did not cover the gap between revenues and expenditures, and the other kingdoms of the monarchy did little more than pay their own ordinary expenses. In any emergency, Castile covered the difference, to the detriment of its own fragile economy.

Outside Madrid, the chief architectural monument of the Habsburg era, the Escorial, built by Philip II, rises on the slopes of the rugged Sierra. Geometric and austere, it looks over the stark Castilian countryside rolling southward. Part palace and part monastery, it is above all a mausoleum to Spain's kings since Charles V, and its vastness resounds with echoes of faded glories.

6

Tradition and Enlightenment

In February 1701, Madrid gave enthusiastic welcome to teenaged King Philip V. Philip employed mostly Spaniards on his Council of State, though he did include Frenchmen. Confused by the problems of government, he corresponded with his grandfather Louis XIV in search of advice. Cardinal Portocarrero presided over government, and the Cortes of Castile met in grand assembly and voted the king money. In late summer Philip journeyed to Catalonia to meet his bride, thirteen-year-old María Luisa of Savoy. The Catalan Corts voted him a rich subsidy, despite strong separatist sentiment. Philip married María Luisa at Figueras; the young couple were soon smitten with each other. Full of energy, she gave the sometimes melancholy Philip crucial support. Even more crucial was the chief lady of her household, the princess of Ursins, handpicked by Louis XIV. Already aged sixty, Ursins arguably saved the Spanish throne for the Bourbon dynasty through her astuteness.

The Habsburgs of Vienna had not given Spain up, and Austrian armies marched on Philip V's Italian possessions. Louis XIV provoked the English and Dutch into war when he sent French troops into the Spanish Netherlands to secure them for Philip. Thus erupted in 1702 the War of the Spanish Succession, which arrayed the Grand Alliance of Emperor Leopold, England, the Dutch, Savoy, and Portugal against Spain and France. Philip left his tender bride as regent in Spain and hurried with Spanish troops to defend his Italian possessions.

Philip's victories in Italy temporarily saved Naples and Sicily for his crown, but the English navy sank Spain's treasure fleet off Vigo. Emperor Leopold proclaimed his younger son, Archduke Charles, as King Charles III of Spain. Charles provided a rallying point for Spaniards who opposed the House of Bourbon and feared Philip would extend to Spain the centralization of government apparent in Louis XIV's France. Many grandees feared the loss of influence over their provinces, while dominions subject to the Crown of Aragon feared the loss of autonomy. Philip hurried back to Spain to shore up his government against growing unrest. Louis XIV sent him French troops, commanded by the duke of Berwick, illegitimate son of deposed King James II of England.

In 1704 an English fleet landed Charles III in Portugal, then surprised Gibraltar and accepted its surrender in Charles's name. In 1705 an army of Portuguese, English, and Dutchmen invaded Spain, while an English fleet bombarded Barcelona into submission. Austrian and English troops occupied it for Charles III, cheered by Catalan separatists. Charles reached Barcelona in November to find that Valencia and much of Aragón had also rallied to him. The allied armies next converged on Madrid and forced Philip and his queen to flee to Burgos. In June the allies paraded into Madrid and by late summer held Zaragoza. But the people of Castile proved hostile to them and made their situation tenuous, despite their victories in the field. Philip V acknowledged Castile's loyalty and clung doggedly to his throne. Allied troops, isolated by Berwick's reinforced army and popular hostility, abandoned Madrid late in 1706. Philip remained with Berwick; the queen returned to Madrid to cheers. In the spring of 1707, Berwick defeated the allies at Almansa and drove them from Aragón and Valencia. Philip deprived Aragón and Valencia of their traditional privileges and institutions as punishment for rebellion. In both kingdoms, the opposition had been undermined by conflicts between nobles and commoners. On both he imposed Castilian forms of government. That summer, the queen gave birth to an heir, Prince Luis. She bore a second son, Fernando, in 1713.

In 1708 Charles III married in Barcelona and proved as stubborn as Philip. Though most of Spain seemed secure in Philip's hands, the English took Minorca. In 1709 Louis XIV sought to end the war. He agreed to abandon Philip and even to subsidize the allies but denied their request for French troops to aid them against his grandson.

The princess of Ursins refused Louis's command to return to France and remained with Philip and María Luisa to bolster their morale and rally support. Alone, Philip's army of Spaniards and a few Irishmen could not withstand the allies. Philip again abandoned Madrid, and Charles III marched in, welcomed by none but a few disgruntled grandees. The general population, disgusted by so many Protestants in the allied army, remained loyal to Philip V.

In 1710 French soldiers again joined Philip's Spaniards after Louis XIV rejected the allies' terms. Together Spanish and French forces soon had the allies in retreat. In 1711, Charles III's older brother, Emperor Joseph, died, and Charles inherited Austria and was elected Emperor Charles VI. He returned to Vienna but did not yield his claim to Spain. He thus alarmed his allies with the specter of the European empire of Charles V all over again. Philip, in contrast, renounced all rights to France. Because the allies were as war weary as their enemies, they ignored Charles VI and opened peace negotiations at Utrecht, where in 1713 a treaty was signed by everybody but Charles, who settled a year later. By the Peace of Utrecht, Philip kept Spain and its overseas possessions. Charles VI received Naples, Milan, Sardinia, and the Spanish Netherlands, which became the Austrian Netherlands. The duke of Savoy got Sicily. England won trading concessions in the Spanish empire, including the lucrative African slave trade, and kept Gibraltar and Minorca.

In 1714 Philip reconquered Barcelona. To punish the Catalans, he stripped Catalonia of its ancient privileges, as he had stripped Aragón and Valencia of theirs, and went further, suppressing its universities.

Bourbon Spain was no longer a union of crowns but had become a unified kingdom. It had its capital in Madrid, centralized departments of government, and a single Cortes rendered largely ceremonial. The historic kingdoms became administrative regions and were each subdivided, giving Spain some thirty provinces. The old organization of government by councils, given to passing the buck among councillors, gave way to a government of ministries, each headed by a single responsible minister, on the French model. Although unpopular and associated with Finance Minister Jean Orry, a Frenchman, the reforms in government and finance were effective and doubled Philip's annual revenues. Not happy with centralized government, the old grandees largely withdrew from public service, though they maintained palaces in the capital for its social whirl. Philip and his Bourbon successors proved generous in bestowing new titles on their public servants and soon created a titled nobility beholden to them. From Madrid the ministries worked to revive the economy of Spain and rebuild its army and navy.

Tuberculosis took Philip's queen in February 1714, which left him depressed. Government routine carried no interest for him. His clinging to the aged princess of Ursins became ludicrous, and he was urged to marry again. An ambitious Italian cleric, Giulio Alberoni, agent in Madrid for the duke of

Parma, persuaded Ursins that Elizabeth Farnese, Parma's stepdaughter and heir, was the right match for Philip. When Elizabeth arrived in Spain, Alberoni met her at the frontier and gained her confidence. At her first interview with Ursins, she had the old princess packed out of the kingdom. She soon dominated Philip, and in 1716, she bore his son, Carlos, for whom she expected Parma, if not more.

Alberoni, backed by the queen, emerged from the Parmesan embassy to become in effect chief minister of Spain. The pope confirmed him as bishop of Málaga and in 1717 made him a cardinal. Aware that Austrian rule in Emperor Charles VI's Italian possessions made people yearn for the good old days of Spanish government, Elizabeth and Alberoni sent the rebuilt Spanish fleet with troops aboard to reconquer Sardinia and Sicily. The English, who feared the revival of Spanish naval power in the Mediterranean, overwhelmed the raw Spanish fleet off Cape Passaro. Alberoni threatened to send the Stuart pretender, James III, in a Spanish armada against England and its new Hanoverian king, George I. But the rest of Europe, France included, ganged up on Spain and forced it to withdraw from Sardinia and Sicily. Alberoni was sacked. In 1720, by the Peace of the Hague, Philip V and Emperor Charles gave up their claims to each other's territories, and all agreed that Elizabeth's son Carlos would inherit Parma. Charles VI joined Sicily to Naples, to reconstitute the kingdom of the Two Sicilies, and the duke of Savoy got Sardinia.

The energies Spain showed in rebuilding its army and navy were indicative of a return to prosperity. The population, measured at 7.5 million at the end of the War of the Spanish Succession, would pass the 9 million mark by midcentury. Emigration to the Americas averaged 15,000 hopeful folk a year, and Spain's shipping and American trade revived. In Madrid competent statesmen, such as José Patiño and the marquis of la Ensenada, gave firm direction to government. Queen Elizabeth Farnese continued to connive, now for her second son, Felipe. The king kept his dignity in public and alternated between bouts of hunting and fits of deep depression.

The royal couple built the extravagant summer palace of San Ildefonso de La Granja, with its soaring fountains, on a forested slope above Segovia. There Philip hankered to retire, and in January 1724, he abdicated in favor of sixteen-year-old Luis. Luis died that August, and Philip V dutifully resumed the throne, although his fits of depression continued. Elizabeth's moment came in 1733, when the War of the Polish Succession allowed her to further her ambitions for Carlos. With the first Bourbon family compact she got French support. Carlos marched from Parma, aided by Spanish troops and a fleet, and chased the Austrians from Naples. He obtained the Two Sicilies by the Peace of Vienna in 1738, at the price of Parma to Austria.

A fire in 1734 gutted the gloomy old Alcázar of Madrid, which Philip hated, and allowed him and his queen to begin construction of the current royal palace. Philip's energies were revived when the War of Jenkins' Ear with England erupted in 1739 over disputed commercial rights. It began after a Spanish coast guardsman in the Caribbean sliced off the ear of an English smuggler named Jenkins and in 1740 merged into the War of Austrian Succession. Elizabeth saw the chance to recover Parma and in 1743 dispatched Felipe to Italy with a Spanish army, under the tutelage of the marquis of la Ensenada. Felipe conquered it and by the Peace of Aix-la-Chapelle (1748) became duke of Parma.

Philip V died in 1746, and Fernando VI, his surviving son by Maria Luisa of Savoy, succeeded to the throne. Fernando retained the public servants of his father's reign and the successors to office they groomed. He gave Spain ten years of peace and prosperity. Catalonia, after a painful recovery, once more flourished economically, and the trade of Barcelona grew. Barcelona's shipping linked a lively economy that included the Balearic Islands, the thriving orchards of Valencia, and the Andalusian coast as far west as Cádiz, where it met the American trade, now opened to all Spaniards by the Bourbons. Programs of road building begun under Philip V restored wheeled carts and wagons drawn by mules and bullocks to inland commerce. La Ensenada directed a detailed census to provide data on Spain's economic strengths and weaknesses and aid in the reform of tax policy. Although conservative opposition blocked tax reform, Spain's improving economy generated more revenues, and when Fernando died, he left the treasury with a surplus that equaled a half year's ordinary income. Fernando also extended the crown's authority over the Church through the Concordat of 1753 with the pope, which clarified and amplified the king's power to nominate bishops for Spain's dioceses. Fernando and his queen, Barbara of Braganza, cultivated the arts and employed Domenico Scarlatti as their court composer. Childless but devoted to his queen, Fernando suffered a mental collapse when she died, and he died in 1759, a year after she did.

And so Elizabeth Farnese's eldest son Carlos, king of the Two Sicilies, became king of Spain as Carlos III. He abdicated the Sicilies to a younger son, Ferdinando, and embarked from Naples for Spain with his heir, now prince of Asturias and also named Carlos. Carlos III meant to continue the improvement of government and brought with him several of his best Italian ministers. Cognizant of the ideas on kingship in the eighteenth century Enlightenment, he stands prominent in the ranks of rulers called "enlightened despots" by history. According to theory, the enlightened despot should promote rational government, employ the best and brightest men available to assist him, regardless of their social status, and use his authority to support them. To Carlos this just seemed common sense. Carlos also tried to make good use of the Church in his programs and utilized the Concordat of 1753 to provide him the bishops he wanted. Traditionalists and the Jesuits, who opposed what they saw as too much government intervention in Church affairs, branded his bishops and supporters as "regalists." Regalists called their enemies "ultramontane" (people who looked "over the mountains" to Rome), suggesting they put pope over king.

While most Enlightenment intellectuals downplayed the role of religion in public life, most ordinary people believed that sovereigns ruled by the grace of God; religion remained a major prop of government alongside habit, personal loyalties, patriotism, and fear. The Catholic Church and its Inquisition enjoyed enormous influence in Spain. The clergy numbered some 200,000 men and women in a population of nearly 10 million. Huge public religious devotions remained strong, even as they waned in other parts of Europe. Throngs turned out for Holy Week processions, and every region had its pilgrimages to local shrines, such as the *romería* of El Rocío in Andalusia. Reports of miracles and apparitions were common. Carlos III was devout and once attracted cheering crowds in Madrid when he gave up his carriage to a priest carrying the Sacrament to a dying person.

The Church was also the single largest landowner in the realm. Enlightenment intellectuals thought its land management backward and preferred to put land in the hands of entrepreneurs who would make it more productive. The regime of Carlos III encouraged the spread of local economic societies of *amigos del país* (friends of the country), who discussed the improvement of agriculture as well as of industry and education. Yet any talk that threatened the place of the Church ran into opposition at once.

Carlos III not only wanted to continue the economic improvement of Spain; he also wanted Spain to play the role of a great power. He signed another Bourbon family compact with France and in 1762 belatedly entered the Seven Years War. Great Britain promptly seized Manila and Havana. To recover them at the Peace of Paris in 1763, Carlos had to make formal concession of Gibraltar, Minorca, and all of Florida to Britain, and Uruguay to Portugal. In compensation, France, stripped by Britain of Quebec, conceded New Orleans and the vast Louisiana territory to Spain.

Increased treasure from Mexico helped finance the war, as well as other reforms, but it also caused inflation. In 1766 the rising price of bread led to popular unrest and rioting that took a peculiar turn in Madrid. One of Carlos's ministers from Naples, the tactless marquis of Esquilache, had revived a ban on the broad-brimmed hats and long cloaks popular among Spanish men, on the argument that criminal elements used the hats to hide the face and the long cloaks to conceal weapons. Spaniards, he decreed, should wear tricorn hats and proper skirted coats like other Europeans. Young toughs called *majos* took to flaunting the ban by sporting the forbidden hats and cloaks. Clashes broke out with soldiers ordered to enforce the decree and quickly led to widespread violence. For two days riots continued unabated until, with the aid of Madrid's clergy, Carlos began the restoration of order by revoking the decree, sacking Esquilache, and promising to deal with the high price of bread. He appointed the count of Aranda to head the government.

While Carlos and the government in Madrid followed the latest European fashions, and Spain's army and navy looked imposing, foreign travelers increasingly remarked on the differences between Spain and other parts of western Europe and northern Italy. They found many of the nobility ill-informed about the world and indifferent to the new ideas spawned by the Enlightenment. They described the larger population as priestridden, ignorant, superstitious, lazy, and unclean. Their belief that Spaniards were lazy likely grew from what they saw of the indolence of too many of the well-to-do. Most Spaniards worked hard to make a living, although the rhythm of the seasons in the countryside required more work at some times than at others. To be sure, the extreme heat of summer could be paralyzing. Spanish cities probably had no more idlers than most other metropolises of the times, but the better weather of Spain, as of southern Italy, made idlers more conspicuous.

The apparent indifference of many of the top people of Spain to the arts and sciences is reflected in the scant production of much that was memorable. Valencia's university, long strong in science, benefited from Philip V's temporary closure of Catalan universities. The medical research of Andrés Piquer added to Valencia's renown and led to improvement in Spanish medical practice. The best known literary figure was a Benedictine professor in Galicia, Padre Benito Feijóo (1676–1764), who wrote critical works about the shortcomings of his countrymen. In music, the Catalan composer Antonio Soler (1729–1783) worked with Domenico Scarlatti in Madrid and headed the choir at the Escorial, where the Bourbons established new royal apartments. The Bourbons also brought opera to Spain, and Spanish composers wrote operas. Architecture had a late Baroque fling with a style named after the brothers Churiguerra, who did the elegant Plaza Mayor of Salamanca. It soon settled into the respectable classicism of the era, as evidenced by the Royal Palace of Madrid. Carlos III imported his chief painters, but he also gave work to a rising Spanish painter, Francisco de Goya, who would prove to be one of the great artists of all time. Under Carlos, Goya began for the royal tapestry factory the Bourbons established in Madrid a series of cartoons that depict scenes of Spanish popular life. The tapestries graced royal apartments; Goya's cartoons are now in Madrid's Prado Museum. Commissions from the king introduced Goya to high society, and he painted splendid portraits of the rich, titled, and famous, as well as of the royal family, and circulated in their company.

Beneath a colorful veneer the clash of Enlightenment and Church simmered and took its most dramatic turn with the expulsion and suppression of the Jesuits. In control of secondary education, the Jesuits remained current with developments in philosophy and science but kept them in a religious framework. The Jesuits' successes earned them the hostility of rival Catholic religious orders and people who believed that Jesuits compromised morality with worldliness. The Jesuits tended to smear any Catholic opponent, including regalists, as "Jansenists." The papacy had condemned Jansenism, derived from the austere theology of Cornelius Jansen, a seventeenth-century Flemish bishop, and by mideighteenth century, it had become largely confused in politics.

The Jesuits also dominated the Inquisition, which many enlightened ministers found an embarrassment, and they opposed the spread into Spain of freemasonry, which many enlightened ministers found attractive. Freemasonry on the European continent had a decidedly political dimension. In Masonic lodges, differences of creed and social class were suspended, and members talked of the brotherhood of mankind. While Freemasons admitted a Supreme Being, they accepted the validity of many religions. The papacy lost no time in condemning freemasonry for Deism (a belief in God but no single church), immorality, and intent to subvert the true Catholic faith. Among secular rulers, reaction to freemasonry was mixed. While instinctively suspicious of secret societies, many thought freemasonry to be a viable alternative to the power of organized religion as well as a clearinghouse for fresh ideas. In Madrid, the count of Aranda was grand master of the Masonic lodge.

The downfall of the Jesuits began in neighboring Portugal, where the enlightened chief minister, the marquis of Pombal, had them expelled in 1759. In France the Jesuits' enemies had them expelled in 1764. In Madrid, the Jesuits were made scapegoats for the Esquilache riots of 1766, and the count of Aranda proposed that they be expelled from Spain, too. Aranda had traveled widely, studied military tactics in Prussia, fought in Italy, and met the famous Voltaire, who detested the Jesuits. Aranda arranged an investigation of the Jesuits, which a panel of bishops and councillors hostile to them carried out. As a result, Carlos expelled the Jesuits from Spain in 1767. Aranda then joined with the Bourbon courts of France and the Two Sicilies to pressure the pope to suppress the Jesuit order entirely, which he did in 1773.

Without its Jesuits, the Inquisition investigated the bishops who recommended their expulsion but failed to find sufficient evidence. They also went after Aranda and his colleagues until Carlos III stopped them. Yet he and Aranda both knew that the Inquisition remained popular among ordinary Spaniards and would not abolish it. The days of burning heretics and torture waned as even inquisitors yielded to Enlightenment ideas. Still, a woman was burned as a witch in Seville in 1787, though she was strangled before the fire was lit. The most sensational case involved Pablo Olavide, royal intendant of the province of Seville. Peruvian born, Olavide, like Aranda, had met Voltaire and knew the intellectual life of the Parisian salons. In Seville he held salons to discuss new ideas and the arts in his home, which he hung with contemporary French paintings. At the same time, he made vigorous efforts to improve provincial agriculture, which aroused opposition from many landlords, including churchmen. His enemies had him hauled before the Inquisition for the possession of pornographic pictures and forbidden books, for unorthodox ideas, and for interfering with the Church in the management of its lands. The number of witnesses ready to testify against Olavide convinced even the king to let the trial proceed. It was held behind closed doors and resulted in his conviction. Humiliated, forced to wear the sanbenito and dunce cap, Olavide protested that he had not lost his Catholic faith. He was stripped of his offices and confined to a monastery for reeducation. He escaped to France and was lionized by the intellectual set. Not until 1798 was he allowed, at age seventy-three, to return to Spain.

The cases of Olavide and several other intellectuals convicted by the Inquisition chilled but did not stop the spread of the Enlightenment among its small Spanish following. Not only public servants and some of the better educated clergy but also many members of the prosperous middle class continued to seek the latest ideas in the press and periodicals, although they remained wary. Even though religious censorship prevented the publication of Denis Diderot's French *Encyclopedia*, lesser encyclopedias that emphasized science and technology and avoided criticism of religion and the Church did appear. However, the prosperity that permitted a few to keep up with new ideas and developments did not extend to the many, whose incomes failed to keep pace with inflation. Envious of the few whose lives seemed ever more dedicated to private fulfillment and pleasure, the many clung to Spain's old traditions and considered the new ideas disturbing, foreign, atheistic, and potentially dangerous to the God-given order of society.

However disturbing some of their ideas and reforms seemed to many, Carlos and his ministers persisted in what they believed best for Spain. After Aranda went to Paris as ambassador, the counts of Campomanes and

Floridablanca and Asturian legal expert Gaspar Melchór de Jovellanos emerged as the ministers with the greatest influence over policy. Floridablanca provides a good example of the kind of men who served the eighteenth-century Bourbon kings. Born José Moñino to a hidalgo family of Murcia, he studied law at Salamanca, proved a successful lawyer, and was brought into government by Esquilache. Jovellanos was arguably the most brilliant of Carlos's ministers, with the broadest range of knowledge. Though his father wanted him to be a priest, he pursued the study of law with the support of his uncle, a duke. He wrote essays, poetry, dramas, and histories and was active in the royal academies of language and history, founded by the Bourbons to promote scholarship.

Carlos III remained interested in foreign policy and kept Spain in the company of the great powers when he joined France in 1778 against Great Britain during the War of American Independence. In Paris, Aranda met Benjamin Franklin and John Jay and favored the American cause, though he acknowledged the differences between Spain and the infant republic over Florida and the Mississippi Valley. Unlike Louis XVI of France, Carlos did not recognize or directly ally with the new United States, because of territorial issues and because he did not wish to encourage his own American colonies to seek independence. In Spain there was talk that Spanish America should be divided into three independent kingdoms, each under a younger son of the king, but the most obvious candidates all died young.

In the war the Spanish army and navy failed to recover Gibraltar, despite a bitter siege. The Spaniards did combine with the French to take Minorca, and in the Atlantic the Spanish and French fleets joined to threaten England with invasion, which prevented the English from sending General Charles Cornwallis needed reinforcements and led to his surrender in 1781 at Yorktown. The Spanish navy also found time to bombard Algiers and force its corsairs to forgo further raiding of Spanish commerce and coasts. The Spanish governor of New Orleans defeated the British in the Mississippi Valley, then took Mobile, and proceeded to reconquer Florida. The 1783 Peace of Paris, which recognized the independence of the United States, conceded Florida and Minorca to Spain, although Britain kept Gibraltar. Carlos earlier recovered Uruguay from Portugal but failed to get the Falkland Islands back. Disputes between Spain and the United States over Florida and the Mississippi, valley remained unsettled, despite negotiations in 1785–1786 between Spain's emissary, Diego de Gardoqui, and John Jay, appointed by Congress to deal with him.

Under Carlos III Spain's overseas empire reached its greatest extent. In distant Alta, California, Franciscan friars established missions as far north as San Francisco, where a statue of Carlos III, a recent gift from Spain, graces the Embarcadero. To defend California the Spaniards had fewer than 200 soldiers, scattered among the presidios of San Diego, Santa Barbara, Monterey, and San Francisco and doing sentry duty at the missions. Unruly California Indians were their chief concern. Only three cannons defended the Golden Gate, although both Great Britain and Russia had interests in the Pacific that potentially menaced California and New Spain.

Aged seventy-two, Carlos III died in December 1788. To Spaniards, his reign in retrospect seemed a second golden age, at least in international prestige, prosperity, and domestic tranquility, if not in literature and the arts. While the reign of his son, Carlos IV, began with good reason for hope, it would end in national calamity and the terrible war that gave the world the word *guerrilla*.

Carlos IV kept his father's principal ministers of state, with Floridablanca as chief. Yet during the first year of his reign, revolution erupted in France and threatened the throne of his Bourbon cousin, Louis XVI. News of developments in France caused great stir in Spain and alarmed Floridablanca. Though he favored reform, it was reform from the top directed by an absolute sovereign, not reform promoted by an unruly constitutional legislature. Alarmed by the irreligion of many French revolutionary leaders, the Spanish Church shared Floridablanca's fears. The French Civil Constitution of the Clergy of 1790 caused many French clergymen to seek refuge in Spain, where they spread horror stories about the revolution. Floridablanca put the Inquisition to the vain task of keeping news of French developments from Spain. Enemies of enlightened reform in Spain linked reformist ideas with revolution, and leading ministers began to waffle. Floridablanca censored new ideas in Spanish periodicals. Campomanes refused to support a minister under attack from the Inquisition, and Jovellanos, who defended the minister, was ordered home to Asturias.

In February 1792, Carlos IV replaced Floridablanca with Aranda, whose connections in Paris seemed helpful to Louis XVI. Aranda restructured Spain's government around the Council of State, which unfortunately put more power into the hands of the weak-willed king and allowed less independence to ministers. Aranda pursued a friendly policy toward France until events overwhelmed him. In September 1792, France became a republic and put Louis XVI on trial. War had broken out between France and a coalition headed by Austria and Prussia. Carlos IV intervened on behalf of Louis XVI, who was guillotined in January 1793. French propaganda aimed at Spain called for the Cortes to arise, overthrow the Bourbon dynasty, and end the Inquisition. In Spain the most effective response came from the pulpit. Inspired by their priests, most Spaniards saw the brewing conflict as a struggle on behalf of God, fatherland, and king, against a nation of regicides leagued to the devil. Even enlightened Spaniards like Jovellanos were appalled by the spectacle of the Reign of Terror in France. Lingering sympathy for the ideals of the French revolution was reduced to university students, whom the Inquisition hounded.

In March 1793, France declared war on Spain. Spanish troops invaded Languedoc, while French troops occupied two enclaves in the Pyrenees. In 1794 the death of Spanish General Antonio Ricardos and the appearance of more aggressive French commanders led to a French invasion of Catalonia. While French officers spread revolutionary propaganda, French soldiers plundered the countryside and aggravated the hatred already incited by the clergy. French promises of Catalan independence fell on deaf ears. The French invasion of Navarre and the Basque Country met similar popular resistance.

The cost of war was stiff, and in early 1794 Aranda proposed that Spain seek peace. By then Aranda had been supplanted as chief minister by Manuel de Godoy, newly made duke of Alcudia. A handsome, twenty-five-year-old guards officer of rough charm, from a poor but proud hidalgo family of Extremadura, Godoy had become the favorite of the queen, Maria Luisa of Parma, sixteen years his senior. They met when she was still princess of Asturias, her looks not yet faded, and became constant companions and perhaps lovers. The king accepted and genuinely liked Godoy, which caused people to call him "the royal cuckold." In Godoy's explanation, Carlos IV and Maria Luisa knew that he was utterly loyal to them. They promoted him to ever higher posts and gradually demoted or eliminated the ministers who had served Carlos III. When Carlos IV rejected Aranda's proposed peace with France and dismissed him, an uproar followed. Almost everybody—nobles, intellectuals, clergymen, and commoners—clamored for Godoy's removal.

Peace did not come until the regicide government in Paris fell. By the Treaty of Basel made with the new French government in July 1795, Spain recovered the Pyrenean regions lost but ceded Santo Domingo on Hispaniola, where France already possessed what is today's Haiti. Carlos bestowed on Godoy the title prince of the Peace and elevated him above all other grandees of Spain. In October, Spain signed the Treaty of San Lorenzo with the United States, represented by minister-extraordinary Thomas Pinckney, that settled differences over Florida and the Mississippi Valley. Spanish Florida's border was adjusted roughly along the line of the thirty-first parallel. Spain accepted the Mississippi as the western boundary of the United States and permitted Americans free navigation through New Orleans.

The restoration of peace stifled the opposition to Godoy, who now opened negotiations with the French for an alliance. Spain had too many outstanding differences with Great Britain and feared for the future of Bourbon Parma when Napoleon Bonaparte invaded northern Italy. In August 1796, Spain and the French Republic became allies through the Treaty of San Idlefonso. Spain declared war on Britain, for which the price proved to be not only higher taxes but a British blockade of Spanish commerce. In February 1797, off Cape St. Vincent, the Spanish battle fleet was beaten by a British squadron and the heroics of its Rear Admiral, Horatio Nelson. The English captured Trinidad and in 1798 again seized Minorca. The combined fleets of Spain and France could not match Britain's, and Spain's century-long effort to recover the Spanish-American market for Spanish shipping and manufactures collapsed. Under pressure, Carlos IV allowed his colonists to trade legally with neutrals, which benefited the merchant marine of the United States. Great Britain came to dominate the Spanish-American market and encouraged the tendencies of Spain's colonies to seek independence.

Finding Spain pressed by war and its costs, Godoy sought the assistance of experienced ministers who had served Carlos III, including Jovellanos and his associate Mariano Luis de Urquijo. Jovellanos had refined his economic theories by reading Adam Smith and the French physiocrats, who favored the combination of free enterprise and private property. Smith emphasized commerce and manufacture, whereas the physiocrats held that all wealth came from the soil. Jovellanos drafted a detailed proposal for agrarian reform in Spain that became gospel for future reformers and anathema to the old landowning class. He believed that the system of entail, legitimized in the late Middle Ages, had resulted in the indifferent management of land, since the great clerical and noble landowners ran no risk of losing their estates, however encumbered they became with debt. Jovellanos argued that independent farmers with smaller estates, operating in a free market with its risks and profits, would prove more productive, and all Spain would benefit. Despite stubborn opposition, the needs of war forced the implementation of some of Jovellanos's ideas to pay off government bonds. The crown appropriated some 10 percent of the Church's property, sold it to private investors, and compensated the Church with low-paying annuities.

When Godoy fell victim to French intrigue and left court, Jovellanos and Urquijo carried on but were soon overwhelmed by religious issues thought dormant. When the French occupied Rome, in a gesture of charity Carlos IV allowed exiled Spanish Jesuits to return on an individual basis to Spain. They returned with a vengeance, leagued with the Inquisition, and pursued their enemies. They reached the ear of Carlos, who caved in to their demands. In 1798, he forced Jovellanos to resign and retire to Asturias. To placate Pope Pius VII, who negotiated with Napoleon Bonaparte a concordat that restored harmony between France and Rome, Carlos sacrificed Urquijo. Urquijo went to jail, and Jovellanos was sent to prison on Majorca. Rome and the Spanish Church had the upper hand over regalists and reformers.

Carlos recalled Godoy to power. Although his youthful instincts favored reform, Godoy cannily steered a cautious course between reformers and traditionalists. He won a bit of military glory in the brief War of the Oranges (1800–1801) against Portugal, when Carlos made him *generalísimo* of Spain's army and began to see himself as Spain's Napoleon. The war netted Spain the border district of Olivenza, although Carlos refused to annex Portugal from his son-in-law, the prince-regent, as Napoleon urged him to do.

In 1800 concern for another son-in-law, the duke of Parma, caused Carlos to cede Louisiana back to France. Bonaparte had annexed Parma to France but promised to establish an Italian kingdom of Etruria for the duke. Although Bonaparte agreed not to surrender Louisiana to a third party, in 1803 he sold it for hard cash to President Thomas Jefferson of the United States.

In March 1802, Spain and France made peace with Great Britain at Amiens. Spain recovered Minorca but not Trinidad. Peace did not last, and Spain's renewal of war in December 1804 put an end to a brief recovery of prosperity and resumption of trade with Spanish America. In war, all the conflicting currents that developed during the eighteenth century would come to a violent head.

7

Six Turbulent Decades

When France and Great Britain went to war in May 1803, Carlos IV and Godoy hoped to remain neutral despite treaties with Napoleon. Great Britain, however, became suspicious of a Spanish naval buildup, accused Spain of providing haven to French warships, and imposed restrictions on Spanish maritime commerce. In October 1804 a British squadron intercepted the Spanish treasure flotilla off Cádiz, sank one of its four ships, and captured the treasure. Spain called it piracy and in December declared war on Britain. In October 1805, off Cape Trafalgar, British Admiral Horatio Nelson shattered a combined French-Spanish battle fleet, ending Spain's long history as a naval power. Shocked, Godoy considered switching sides to save Spain's overseas empire.

Opposition to Godoy took shape around Fernando, prince of Asturias and heir to the throne, who turned twenty in 1805. Insinuations about the relationship of his parents and Godoy made Fernando an implacable enemy of the favorite. Many saw him as Spain's only hope for the future, and Napoleon began to use Fernando against Godoy when he learned of Godoy's double-dealing with Britain.

To Napoleon Fernando revealed his contempt for his parents and Godoy. Recently widowed, he sought a Bonaparte bride. Carlos got wind of Fernando's dealings in late 1807 and had him arrested on charges of plotting to seize the throne. Facing his parents at the Escorial, Fernando groveled and begged their forgiveness. Napoleon denied that there had been any plot.

Stuck to dealing with Godoy, Napoleon whetted his ambitions. Following victories over Austria, Prussia, and Russia, Napoleon asked that Spain assist him against Portugal. Portugal refused to subscribe to his continental system, by which no European state would do business with Great Britain. In the 1807 Treaty of Fontainebleau, Napoleon and Spain agreed to divide Portugal into a sovereign principality of the Algarve for Godoy, already rich and well married, and a kingdom of Lusitania for the Bourbons of Parma.

Spain gave safe passage to a French army, which marched into Portugal. The Portuguese royal family fled to Brazil. During the winter, French reinforcements entered Spain and took up quarters. By March 1808, 100,000 French troops were in the peninsula. Despite the inevitable incidents between soldiers and civilians, many Spaniards hoped that Napoleon intended to give a Bonaparte bride to Prince Fernando and rid Spain of Godoy. When French troops garrisoned Spanish citadels, such as San Sebastián, Pamplona, and Montjuich (which dominates Barcelona), they had second thoughts. Then Napoleon made new demands on Spain, including the cession of the provinces north of the Ebro in exchange for Portugal. Alarmed, Godoy ordered the Royal Guard and Madrid garrison to Aranjuez, where the king and queen were in residence. Napoleon feared the king and queen might flee to Spanish America, and he commanded his warships bottled up at Cádiz after Trafalgar to stop them. He rushed Marshal Joachim Murat into Spain at the head of a large force, instructing him to keep his men in line and not antagonize the Spanish population.

At Aranjuez rumors spread that the royal family would leave for America and that Fernando would not go willingly. Ugly crowds, egged on by hostile courtiers, gathered round the royal palace and on the night of March 17–18 exploded into violence. Mobs stormed Godoy's residence. Godoy barely escaped. Found by guardsmen, he was battered and locked up. The terrified king dismissed him from office. Prince Fernando took charge. On March 19, Carlos IV abdicated, and the mob acclaimed the prince as King Fernando VII. The people had spoken. A riot became a popular revolution.

On March 23, Murat entered Madrid. Fernando VII made his entry the next day. He established a new government with his supporters and ordered Jovellanos freed from prison. At the same time, he suspended the sale of Church property, which the pope had reluctantly sanctioned, to the delight of the clergy and ordinary folk. But Murat would not recognize Fernando as king until he heard from Napoleon.

Napoleon decided to remove the Spanish Bourbons and place his older brother, Joseph Bonaparte, on the Spanish throne. Unaware of Napoleon's design, the abdicated king and queen of Spain begged Napoleon's mercy and asked him to free Godoy. They would concede Spain to Fernando but said nothing nice about him. Napoleon summoned them and Fernando to meet with him at Bayonne. Leaving a Regency Council in Madrid, Fernando journeyed north and found that he had become a popular hero. He also noticed the presence of French troops everywhere. Many warned him not to continue, but sweet words and veiled threats from Napoleon had him in Bayonne by April 21. Napoleon greeted Fernando, but that night Fernando learned that Napoleon wanted him to abdicate. Pressured by Napoleon, Fernando yielded the throne back to his father. Carlos had already agreed that for the good of Spain the throne would go to Joseph Bonaparte, who thus became King Joseph of Spain. Napoleon settled pensions and residences in France on the Spanish Bourbon family. Freed, Godoy joined his benefactors. Carlos and Maria Luisa eventually retired to Italy, where they died in 1819. Godoy would die in Paris in 1851. Fernando, a captive in France, bided his time and kept all his resentments alive.

With the news from Bayonne and the presence of French troops everywhere, the Spanish population grew restless. Riots erupted here and there, despite the admonitions of nervous authorities to maintain order. On May 2, a serious riot broke out in Madrid and reached its climax when French cavalry charged a mob in the Puerta de Sol, which Francisco de Goya, in Madrid at the time, later immortalized on canvas. Murat punished the rioters with wholesale executions on May 3, an event Goya immortalized with terrifying power on a second canvas. Both are in Madrid's Prado Museum.

A month after the executions, Napoleon proclaimed Joseph king of Spain and the Indies and summoned an assembly of Spanish notables to Bayonne to draft a constitution. Joseph managed to collect a cabinet headed by Urquijo. Many well-intended or duty-bound civil servants and a few grandees and nobles accepted Joseph. Some were reformers who hoped that Joseph would provide the enlightened leadership they found in neither Carlos IV nor Fernando VII. Some were rank opportunists. All would be branded *afrancescados* (frenchified).

But many reform-minded Spaniards refused service under Joseph. Men coerced to support the new regime or journey to Bayonne defected as soon as they had the chance. Jovellanos claimed poor health. If people at the top, who knew the vapidity and ineptitude of the royal family, wavered over whether or not to accept Joseph as king, the larger population did not. Within weeks most of Spain was in a state of armed insurrection against the French. In each province or region, local authorities, leaders, and clergymen assembled in juntas to proclaim their loyalty to Fernando VII and defy the French. They ordered troops raised, and units of the regular army rallied to them. Mobs lynched officials who supported Joseph or did not oppose him. The clergy harangued against the atheistic French and called on their flocks to rebel for God, Spain, and king. The junta of Seville, headed by former royal minister Francisco de Saavedra, proclaimed itself the supreme junta for Spain and the Indies. The junta of Asturias sent a delegation to their old enemy, Great Britain, in search of help. On June 15, Great Britain announced that it would aid "Spanish patriots."

The French army controlled the road to Madrid, along which the "intruder king" Joseph proceeded with a military escort. He arrived to a sullen welcome and was solemnly proclaimed king on July 25, the feast of Santiago. Before the month ended, he was on the road again, retreating north. In Andalusia, a French force of 20,000 men had been surrounded at Bailén by Spanish regulars and angry peasants and forced to surrender. The French had brutally sacked Córdoba, and the Spaniards paid them back in kind. The savage war without quarter had begun, involving men, women and children, civilians and soldiers, mutilation and butchery, which Goya would depict in gruesome detail in his etchings *The Disasters of War* (*Desastres de la guerra*).

As the Spanish army of Andalusia marched on Madrid, another French army was repulsed at Valencia. Zaragoza and Gerona heroically resisted terrible sieges, with local men and women fighting alongside soldiers. The French warships bottled up at Cádiz were forced to surrender. The local juntas agreed to a national Central Junta, headed by Floridablanca and assisted by Jovellanos, who proclaimed their loyalty to Fernando VII.

Napoleon summoned his veterans and in November stormed into Spain at the head of 300,000 men. He and his marshals swept the outnumbered and disorganized Spanish armies, and an allied British army, from the battlefields. At the beginning of December, he entered Madrid and restored his brother Joseph to the throne of Spain. The Spanish armies, beaten in the field, withdrew to remote areas and joined with local patriots as *guerrilleros* to wage the little war, the guerrilla, that would prove Napoleon's undoing.

In early 1809 Napoleon turned the war in Spain over to his marshals and returned to Paris to face war with the Austrian Empire. The marshals completed the conquest of Andalusia and confined the Central Junta to Cádiz, protected by the guns of the British navy as well as Spanish troops and ships. The French held Barcelona and took Zaragoza and Valencia, but the countryside remained hostile. The government of King Joseph held sway over little more than central Castile. He abolished the Inquisition, limited the power of the Church, and talked reform. The overwhelming majority of Spaniards rejected him, calling him "Pepe Botellas" (Joe Bottles, for his drinking) or simply "Pepito" (Little Joe).

What seems decisive in the struggle between the Spanish people and a French army of occupation that numbered more than 200,000 men was the activity of the Anglo-Portuguese army that recovered Lisbon. Commanded by the duke of Wellington, it prevented the French marshals from cowing the civilian population into submission. In 1810 Wellington invaded Spain with 50,000 men, which rallied the scattered Spanish armies. When the French concentrated their more numerous forces to meet Wellington and Spanish regulars, the *guerrilleros* struck. The French marshals lacked enough men to meet the threat of an invading army and at the same time post small units everywhere to deal with guerrilla warfare. For them communication remained ever precarious. The *guerrilleros* butchered stragglers and ambushed small detachments and supply columns. Napoleon later referred to the situation as his "Spanish ulcer" that never seemed to stop hemorrhaging. Spain bled, too, and while it battled Napoleon, it began to lose control of its overseas empire. Great Britain, which supplied Spain's armies and *guerrilleros* with munitions, also sent arms to those in Spanish America who advocated independence.

With Fernando VII in captivity, the lines of government became blurred. Many called for the Cortes to be summoned. Several eighteenth-century Spanish historians, following the lead of French political theorist Montesquieu, came to see the Cortes as the embodiment of the sovereignty of the Spanish nation and regarded absolute monarchy as a usurpation of power by kings. Spain had developed its representative Cortes in the Middle Ages and achieved its pinnacle of historic glory during the constitutional reign of Ferdinand and Isabella. According to these historians, the defeat of the comuneros in 1521 by Charles V proved the death knell of Spanish liberty. The Habsburg and Bourbon kings imposed absolute monarchy on Spain and started the decline that led to the tyranny of Godoy, the disgraceful spectacle at Bayonne, and the Napoleonic conquest. The Cortes should draft a suitable constitution for Spain. To legitimize the summoning of the Cortes, the Central Junta ceded its authority to the Regency Council appointed by Fernando. The Cortes that assembled at Cádiz to draft a constitution proved to be reformist in line with Cádiz itself, a seaport open to the world and dominated by middle-class merchants. Of 303 delegates, almost a third were clergymen, and another third were civil servants or soldiers. Some 60 were lawyers, and only 14 were titled noblemen. For provinces unable to elect delegates because of the French occupation, substitutes were appointed by authorities in Cádiz. Substitutes were also appointed for the American colonies. The majority of the delegates who gathered in the besieged and crowded city, with enemy forces arrayed across the bay, were what we would call intellectuals and activists, men with big ideas not always shared by others. Spain enriched our political vocabulary with the word *liberals* to describe them. The liberals in turn branded their opponents as *serviles*, servile supporters of the old order.

The assembled Cortes rejected seating by estates, clergy, nobles, and commoners and sat as a single chamber, like the French National Assembly of 1789. Only one nation in the world had a written constitution at the time, the United States. Spain would become the second, the first in Europe. The Constitution, completed in 1812, embodied the pet schemes of reformers. It placed sovereignty in the Spanish nation, not the king, and provided for a unicameral legislature. The crown retained only limited veto power. It provided for virtually universal manhood suffrage, limited by a process of indirect elections. Crown ministers, while needing the confirmation of Cortes, could not sit in it. Central direction and uniform regulations were stipulated for municipalities, although provincial councils could advise on local affairs. The old guilds and special privileges for nobles were abolished, along with the seigneurial jurisdictions and noble and Church entails. While Catholicism remained the state religion, and heresy a crime, the Inquisition was abolished. Rights of expression and assembly were recognized. Subsequent regulations overhauled the old tax structure and established direct levies on business and property. Outvoted conservative and traditionalist members of Cortes were not happy with the new Constitution. Many clergymen wondered if things had gone too far.

In 1812, Wellington defeated the French at Salamanca and briefly occupied Madrid. That year Napoleon met defeat in Russia. Needing men to make up his losses, he recalled troops from Spain. In 1813 Wellington's army and Spanish forces pushed the French north. At the end of May, King Joseph and his court abandoned Madrid. They were overtaken by Wellington in June at Vitoria and thrashed. Joseph fled to France. What Spaniards call the War of Independence came to an end.

Fernando VII had spent the war in comfortable captivity. With his uncle and younger brother Don Carlos, he whiled away the time playing cards. Until the end he hoped for a Bonaparte marriage, expressed adulation of Napoleon, and addressed Joseph Bonaparte as king of Spain. Though aware of the insurrection on his behalf in Spain, he remained noncommittal. In March 1814, Fernando returned to Spain to be welcomed as the "desired one" (*el deseado*) and conquering hero. After nearly six years of savage war, Spain was economically destitute and its government bankrupt. With its American colonies asserting their independence, the treasure of the New World that had provided the eighteenth-century monarchy with a fourth of its income no longer crossed the Atlantic to Spain. The lucrative American market was also largely lost.

Surrounded by an entourage of traditionalists, many of whom like himself had spent the war in French confinement, Fernando avoided accepting the Constitution of 1812, which seemed too full of revolutionary ideas. The regular elections for the Cortes of 1813 returned many delegates opposed to it, who voiced their objections. As Fernando progressed from Gerona to Barcelona, he heard crowds of ordinary people cheer, "Long live the absolute king!" "Restore the Inquisition!" and "Down with frenchified liberals!" Persuaded by their priests, they identified the misery and suffering of the wars years with the new ideas spawned in the Enlightenment, realized by the French Revolution, and brought to Spain by Napoleon. When Fernando visited devastated Zaragoza, only General José Rebolledo de Palafox, the hero of its two sieges, spoke in favor of the Constitution. All others had reservations. Near Valencia, Fernando received a delegation of conservative members of the Cortes assembled in Madrid who equated the Constitution with anarchy. They favored a return to absolute monarchy, with a traditional Cortes based on the three estates, whose purpose would be only to ensure that the monarch ruled justly. When the president of the Regency Council, Luis de Borbón, archbishop of Toledo, formally presented the Constitution to his cousin Fernando, Fernando refused to swear to it. The captain general of Valencia, Francisco Elío, who had battled independence movements in South America, cheered Fernando as absolute monarch and publically denounced the Constitution.

Fernando needed no more prodding. By the declaration of Valencia of May 4, 1814, he labeled the Constitution of 1812 as the work of a subversive minority and declared it null and void. All who continued to support it would be guilty of lese majesty. He promised he would not be a despot and would summon an old-fashioned Cortes. He soon resurrected the Inquisition and restored the economic privileges and right of entail of the great landowners, though not their juridical powers over their domains. In Madrid the captain general of Castile put leading liberals under arrest before the king arrived to the wild welcome of the mob. If Fernando's vulgar personal style alienated the serious-minded, it endeared him to ordinary folk. Once in his capital, Fernando purged the government not only of *afrancesados* who had served Joseph but also of liberals, often under the guise of saving money. Junior army officers, many of them heroes of the War of Independence, found their careers threatened as financial straits forced the reduction of the swollen army. Many were demoted and others put on half pay. The pay of both the bureaucracy and armed forces was often in arrears.

At the Congress of Vienna, where Europe's great powers made peace after years of war, Spain was virtually ignored, despite its valiant role in the defeat of Napoleon. Statesmen wrote it off as a bankrupt third-rate power in the process of losing its empire. To save his empire, Fernando mobilized what forces he could to suppress the independence movements that engulfed Spanish America. The Constitution of 1812 put the colonies on equal footing with the mother country, though it still envisioned a centralized regime based on Spain and a closed commercial system on the old mercantilist model. But the colonial leaders of each of the viceroyalties, presidencies, and captaincies-general of Spanish America had seized control of their own destinies, aided and abetted by British commercial interests and the ideals and interests of the United States. The reduced Spanish navy ferried reluctant army units across the Atlantic in vain. By 1825, all that remained to Fernando were Cuba, Puerto Rico, the Philippines, and Guam.

The effort to prevent Spanish-American independence demanded more resources and manpower than war-ravaged and depressed Spain could provide. Too many army officers had been demoralized by Fernando's purges and embittered by arrears in pay and shortages of equipment. Employing the rhetoric of European Romanticism, they postured as forgotten war heroes, talked of government ineptitude, and dreamed of a more liberal regime. Among the men under their command, few wanted to be shipped across the Atlantic, to fight and die in malarial jungles. In 1820, a disgruntled expeditionary force refused to embark at Cádiz and, led by its officers, marched on Madrid. Major Rafael Riego spoke for the mutineers through a pronunciamento, a proclamation against the corruption of government and for the restoration of the Constitution of 1812. Other garrisons, along with urban militia units made up of former guerrilla fighters, quickly joined in the pronunciamento, and Fernando caved in. Liberals returned to government, though many had become more moderate since 1812 and wished to modify the Constitution. Fernando would not cooperate and referred to liberal ministers as "jail-birds," as he had imprisoned many of them in 1814. Through his agents he furtively searched for support both in Spain and abroad.

The liberal government again abolished seigneurial rights and the Inquisition and brought religious orders under closer state regulation. Church lands owned by monasteries were put up for sale, and efforts were made to get the huge government debt under control. Finally implemented was the reorganization of Spain into fifty-two provinces, including the Balearics and Canary Islands. The new government also faced peasant unrest over the enclosure and sale of common lands and a strike by textile workers against the introduction of new machinery. Nineteenth-century liberal economics, with its stress on free markets, proved at odds with peasants' desires to keep much land in common pastures and woods and craftsmen's fears of competition by machines.

Liberals who had not become moderate thought the government too cautious and demanded further reforms. Called *exaltados*, they met in the Masonic lodges of provincial capitals and won local support by protesting against recruiting and further prosecution of the war in America. The *exaltados* wanted further tax reform, universal manhood suffrage, greater regulation of religious orders, and the expropriation of the Church's remaining lands. As jobs were scarce, political patronage and promotion in the armed forces became part of the game. *Exaltado* influence was strong with the urban militias, whose members came mainly from the ranks of shopkeepers, artisans, and low-paid professionals. In the elections of 1822 the *exaltados* won control of the government and promptly moved against the Church, beginning by throwing the restored Jesuits out. Moderates became alarmed and serviles talked of taking up arms, winning strong support among the devout peasants of northern Spain. Incipient civil war began to spread in the northern countryside, and violence and murder marred urban political life. In regard to the Church, the urban mob was volatile, sometimes for the clergy, sometimes against. In July, the Guards Regiment in Madrid defied the government and rallied to the king. Though pleased, Fernando failed to act. Loyal regulars and the Madrid militia crushed the Guards' rising. Their chief, Colonel Evaristo de San Miguel, formed a yet more radical and anticlerical government.

Developments in Spain inspired liberal unrest in the Italian peninsula, Portugal, and elsewhere, and the conservative statesmen of Europe took notice. The Russian Empire, the Austrian Empire, the kingdom of Prussia, and the kingdom of France, with its restored Bourbon king Louis XVIII, formed a Quadruple Alliance to uphold the old order. Louis XVIII mobilized an army, the Hundred Thousand Sons of St. Louis, about 60,000 veteran French soldiers, and prepared to intervene. Attempts to work out an agreeable compromise with San Miguel failed. Disgusted moderates abandoned him, while the royalist cause grew ever stronger in the north. As Madrid became unruly, the government withdrew to Seville, dragging Fernando with it. In April 1823, the French marched into Spain. They maintained discipline and paid for their supplies. The royalist north welcomed them, and Spanish regional captains general who, as General Pablo Morillo put it, preferred a government based on men of property rather than a "hallucinated minority," came to terms with the invaders. San Miguel's government retreated to Cádiz, the king in tow, and the French followed. In September, the government surrendered in return for amnesty.

Restored to authority, Fernando established a traditionalist authoritarian regime. Supported from the pulpit, it restored order and proved popular with most. Despite the pledge of amnesty, repression proved brutal. The government was purified of liberals, and the army, under French supervision, was reorganized. Yet ridding the government and army of liberals was easier said than done, since too many civil servants and junior officers were at least moderate liberals. The chief stumbling block to liberal reform had been its anticlericalism, which made enemies of even liberal churchmen. The promotion of liberal ideas through the periodical press could not compete with thunder from the pulpit in reaching a population of whom three-fourths were illiterate.

Fernando persisted in his pragmatic absolutism, which proved most effective in fiscal reform, and the increased taxation of the rich to pay government debts. The survival of moderates and liberals in government posts, because of their competence, bothered extreme royalists, who increasingly gathered around the childless king's brother, Don Carlos. Royalist irregulars called Volunteers, who rallied to Fernando in 1823, wanted places in the army that had been denied them by the professionals, whether conservative or liberal. In 1827 "aggrieved" royalists rebelled in Catalonia and were crushed.

The revolution of 1830 that brought Louis Philippe of Orleans to the French throne as the "bourgeois king" triggered several abortive liberal risings in Spain that served chiefly to provide the liberal cause with martyrs. Spanish clericals and conservatives grew more attached to Don Carlos, whereas their opponents put their hope in the new queen, María Cristina of Naples. Aged twenty-three, she had won the heart of the older king. After some wavering, Fernando issued a Pragmatic which declared that her child, whether daughter or son, would succeed to the throne. The tradition of the House of Bourbon was the Salic law—that only a son could succeed to the throne. María Cristina had two daughters, Isabel and Luisa. When Fernando VII died in 1833, Isabel, aged three, became Queen Isabel II, and her mother, María Cristina, regent. In opposition, Isabel's uncle. Don Carlos declared himself to be King Carlos V.

The regent soon replaced Fernando's last chief minister, conservative Francisco Cea Bermúdez, with moderate Francisco Martínez de la Rosa, a onetime "jailbird." He presided over the drafting of the Royal Statute of 1834, a sort of constitution bestowed by the crown. It provided for a two-chamber Cortes, with an upper house that resembled the English House of Lords with archbishops, bishops, grandees, and titled nobles, plus designated appointees; and a lower chamber of deputies, to be elected indirectly by a restricted electorate. Its functions were consultative, and the ministers remained responsible to the crown. No bill of rights was included. The liberal direction of Spain was paralleled in Portugal and encouraged by Britain and France. They joined with Spain and Portugal in a new Quadruple Alliance to preclude foreign interference. Whereas many moderate liberals were satisfied, other liberals were not, and in the provincial capitals the Progressives, the heirs of the *exaltados*, began to dominate the political debate. The differences of Moderates and Progressives would be played out against the background of the Carlist Wars.

Don Carlos, a vain, closed-minded man, soon had followers in arms, chiefly in the Basque Country, Navarre, Aragón, and rural Catalonia. These were regions where the Church was strong and with significant populations of poor but proud smallholders, regions that enjoyed historic privileges which seemed threatened by the centralizing policies of impatient liberals. Their battle cry proclaimed God, king, fatherland, and regional privileges (*fueros*). Conservative soldiers, former *guerrilleros*, and sometime bandits formed the core of the Carlist forces. While Don Carlos announced that their commander in chief was the Virgin of Sorrows, their best general was a professional soldier and hero of the War of Independence, "Uncle" Tomás Zumalacárregui. He drove government forces from the countryside of Navarre and the Basque Country but lacked the heavy equipment necessary to conquer the well-garrisoned and liberal capitals of Bilbao, San Sebastián, and Pamplona. When Don Carlos arrived in Spain in 1835, he pressured Zumalacárregui to assault Bilbao. The assault failed, and Zumalacárregui died of wounds. The First Carlist War sputtered on until 1840. Both sides massacred prisoners and terrorized civilians. Attempts at compromise based on the betrothal of Queen Isabel II to Don Carlos's son, Carlos Luis, count of Montemolín, foundered on Don Carlos's intransigence. In 1837 the Carlists paraded to the outskirts of Madrid, but found no popular support and withdrew. By 1839, on the northern front the government arrayed 100,000 men and 700 guns, under General Baldomero Espartero, against the Carlists' 32,000 men and 50 guns, under Rafael Maroto. A professional officer, Maroto knew his side had no chance; so with Espartero he signed the compromise of Vergara, which allowed the Carlists to lay down their arms, and the regular officers who had served Don Carlos to return to the army without loss of rank. This gave the Spanish army a notoriously high ratio of officers to men. By 1840 the war was over. Don Carlos fled to France, where he settled at Bourges, under the gaze of an unfriendly French government.

While their future depended on the defeat of the Carlists, the politicians in Madrid wrangled over revenues and constitutional questions. The task of finding money to meet war costs went to an energetic banker of Cádiz and London, Juan Álvarez Mendizábal. His enemies noted that he was both a Jew and a Freemason. Early in 1836 he rammed through a measure that had profound consequences: the disamortization (release from mortmain, a kind of entail), appropriation, and sale of all Church lands that did not directly support parishes, hospitals, or schools. For an idea long around, the moment had come. Mendizábal and his allies hoped that the chief beneficiaries of disamortization would be members of the middle class, who would purchase Church lands and become wedded to the liberal cause in order to keep them. For the Church hierarchy it was the last straw. The bishops broke irrevocably with liberalism and privately put their hopes on the Carlist side. Rome refused to confirm many of the Spanish crown's episcopal nominees, and half of Spain's dioceses were soon without bishops. As Church wealth dwindled, perhaps one-third of Spain's clergy renounced their vows and quit.

The disamortization of Church lands formed part of the liberal economic program to encourage increased agricultural productivity through greater private entrepreneurial activity. The common lands of the former Church domains were also privatized, which led to more peasant unrest and several violent insurrections over the following thirty years. The same environmental and technological constraints that had always affected Spanish agriculture persisted, and the new patterns of ownership led to no marked increase in productivity.

In elections under the Royal Statute of 1834, the Progressives got the edge in the municipalities, and the unruly urban militias they dominated demanded the restoration of the Constitution of 1812. Demonstrations in Madrid in August 1836 caused the sergeants of the Royal Guards at the summer palace at La Granja to confront the regent over the matter. Faced with the "Sergeants' Revolt," she agreed to accept it and made it the business of the Cortes to undertake the necessary revisions. In 1837 she promulgated a new Constitution that provided a Cortes with a senate, appointed by the crown from lists submitted by designated provincial electors, and a Congress of Deputies, for which 4 percent of the male population could vote.

Dominated by Moderates, the Cortes gave the central government tighter control over Spain's municipalities in 1840. Progressives took to the streets and rioted. Much of the tinder for riot and unrest was provided by office seekers. In Spain, as in the United States at the time, the spoils system reigned. The party that won power dismissed officeholders of the losing party and rewarded its own followers with their jobs. Government jobs had long been the chief aspiration of ambitious university graduates in a Spain that produced more lawyers than engineers, physicians, or scientists. Called *pretendientes*, those out of office became a fixture on the Spanish scene. Depending on family support to eat, they conspired and agitated to restore their party to power. With the transfer in 1836 of the University of Alcalá to Madrid, as the Universidad Central, university students joined the politically restless elements of the capital.

To restore order, the regent in desperation appointed General Espartero as prime minister. The first of the political generals who dominated Spanish politics for the next two dozen years, he was the son of a carter of La Mancha and identified with the Progressives. Given his humble origins, he also made clear that the army provided a career open to talent. When Espartero and the regent differed, he used the need to end disorder to coerce her into yielding the regency to him. María Cristina's position was already compromised by her marriage, soon after Fernando's death, to Augustín Muñoz, a sergeant of the Guards, whom she had her daughter make a duke and grandee. María Cristina and Muñoz departed for France.

With Espartero regent and Progressives once more in control of the Cortes, the number of men enjoying the franchise was doubled. A pronunciamento by Moderates in the Basque Country was quickly squelched, and Basque privileges were curtailed. Concern over a swing to the right in Barcelona led to a more radical Progressive rising and the establishment of a popular junta, with budding labor unions involved. Unruly mobs dismantled part of the royal citadel erected by Philip V, and the Barcelona junta challenged the liberal doctrine of free trade and called for protectionism. Then tax riots broke out, and by the end of 1842, order had collapsed. Angry, Espartero refused to compromise with Barcelona, turned his artillery on the city, then stormed it.

Many Progressives abandoned Espartero in disgust and joined the Moderates. When their coalition won control of the Cortes, Espartero dissolved it. All over Spain disgruntled garrisons and municipalities pronounced against him. Moderate General Ramón Narváez returned from exile in France and engineered Espartero's fall. Rather than make Narváez regent, his rivals had the Cortes declare Queen Isabel II to be of age, a year early since she was only thirteen. But Narváez would dominate the government for most of the next ten years.

Spain's economy began a slow expansion with the restoration of order in most of the country, which was maintained by the newly established paramilitary Civil Guard. Growth was more pronounced on the periphery: Catalonia and Valencia on the Mediterranean, western Andalusia, and the Basque Country. Old and New Castile remained poor, and Madrid seemed bloated by contrast. Also poor were Aragón and Galicia; Extremadura and rural Andalusia were the poorest of all. By midcentury, Spain's population neared 15 million, an increase of more than 3 million since 1800.

Spain's political elite, centered on Madrid and including the court, the politicians, the army, the bureaucracy, and the press, now fussed about the queen's marriage. The Church hierarchy was not out of the picture, though it was still offended by its loss of landed wealth and the restrictions placed on religious orders. Great Britain and France also had ideas. Isabel II, with her mother remarried and exiled to France, grew up spoiled, indulged, overweight, and sensual. To every candidate for her hand objections sprouted. What seemed most logical, her marriage to the Carlist heir, Montemolín, foundered on his claim that he was already King Carlos VI. In the end she married the least objectionable candidate, her first cousin Don Francisco de Asís, son of her uncle, the duke of Cádiz. Aged twenty-four, Don Francisco de Asís was a fastidious army officer whose sexual relations with the queen derived from his sense of duty. Many attributed her unhappy situation to duplicitous French diplomacy. When Britain objected to a French proposal that she marry a son of King Louis Philippe, his son, the manly duke of Montpensier, married her sister, the Infanta Luisa. Suspicion grew that the French hoped Isabel and her ascetic consort would be childless and that Montpensier's offspring would succeed to the Spanish throne. Isabel II and Don Francisco de Asís soon lived in separate quarters, but she bore four daughters and a son who survived early childhood and, despite questions regarding their paternity, were accepted as legitimate. Notoriously she took many lovers, mostly macho army officers. Although most regarded her behavior as scandalous, they admitted her marriage was unhappy.

Following Isabel's marriage in 1846, a Carlist rising surfaced in Catalonia on behalf of Montemolín. Called the Second Carlist War and fueled by peasant unrest, it peaked in 1848 but was quelled by 1849. Coping with it brought Narváez back to power in late 1847. In 1848, a year of revolution in much of Europe (which cost King Louis Philippe his throne in France), he kept a firm grip on the political life of Spain and sent an expeditionary force to Rome in 1849 to support the pope against revolutionaries there. In 1851 a coalition of disgruntled Moderates and ultraconservatives forced him from office once more. They were aided by court cabals that included Francisco de Asís, who found his niche in government through intrigue. The new government of Antonio Bravo Murillo dismissed the Cortes, which had a splendid new palace, and attempted to rule by decree, influenced by developments in France where Napoleon III seized power.

The more liberal Moderates joined with the Progressives in opposition. Financial scandals associated with the building of Spain's first railroads and involving much foreign capital touched the court and engulfed the queen mother and Muñoz, whom Isabel had allowed back to Spain. As the government fell into confusion, unrest spread. On June 30, 1854, General Leopoldo O'Donnell, at the head of an army column at Vicálvaro outside Madrid, pronounced against the government. In Madrid rioting erupted and raged for four days. In desperation, Isabel called the popular Espartero from retirement. He revived the urban militias, a mainstay for the Progressives, and restored order. An election in which 700,000 Spaniards cast votes returned a Cortes dominated by Progressives, who drew up the Constitution of 1855. Sovereignty was, as in 1812, placed in the nation, which would be a constitutional monarchy with a two-chamber Cortes. It broadened civil liberties, although it slightly narrowed the franchise and reserved the Senate for the well-to-do. The new Cortes passed legislation that privatized yet more Church lands and favored free trade. Although it addressed complaints of the poor over taxes, in particular the *consumos* levied on basic consumer goods, it continued to restrict labor union activity.

Anxieties about Espartero's Progressive regime caused the queen to replace him arbitrarily with General O'Donnell, a Moderate who embraced the politics of reconciliation developed by journalist and historian Antonio Cánovas del Castillo. While most Progressives went along, riots in Madrid and Barcelona required the use of armed force. When O'Donnell suspended the Constitution, popular clamor forced the queen to bring Narváez back to power. In 1858, differences with her brought Narváez's resignation. O'Donnell returned and, through a blatantly rigged election, brought his party of reconciliation, dubbed the Liberal Union, into control of the Cortes. Elections were often dominated by the rich and influential of each region, eager for government patronage and favor, but no one had previously so successfully orchestrated the outcome. It was no mean feat for local political bosses, called *caciques* (a term for a Caribbean Indian chief), to deliver the votes of a relatively extensive electorate, which required a wide range of controls that ran from bribery to intimidation.

Secure with the Cortes, O'Donnell dazzled Spain with military successes abroad. A short, triumphant war in Morocco in 1859–1860 brought Tetuán and its vicinity under Spanish control. Spanish and Filipino troops fought alongside the French in Viet Nam in 1859–1863 to prevent the repression of Christianity, although they left the colonization of Viet Nam to France. In 1862 Spanish troops joined the French in Mexico to force the repayment of debt claims. However, General Juan Prim, commander of the Spanish expeditionary force, refused to participate in the French overthrow of President Benito Juarez and their installation of Maximilian of Austria as emperor. Over petty incidents the revived Spanish navy fought the War of the Pacific (1865–1866) against Chile and Peru and bombarded Callao and Valparaiso.

In Spain, O'Donnell's virtual one-party rule bred too much opposition from all sides and led between 1863 and 1865 to his replacement by others, lastly Narváez. Student demonstrations and clashes with soldiers in 1865 brought Narváez down and O'Donnell back to power. Constitutional issues, sniping by an unrestrained press, and the alienation of devout Catholics after O'Donnell extended diplomatic recognition to the new kingdom of Italy, which the pope opposed, kept unrest alive. He tried to placate the Progressives, who found a new hero in General Prim, by enlarging the electorate. He posted Prim to distant Asturias. However, in June 1866, a military conspiracy inspired by Prim came to a head at the San Gil Barracks near Madrid's Royal Palace, when officer conspirators lost control of the ranks. Several officers were shot and mutineers took to the streets. Bloody fighting ensued against forces loyal to O'Donnell. After losing over 200 dead and wounded, some 500 mutineers surrendered. Seventy-six were executed by firing squad. When O'Donnell refused to execute more, the queen summoned Narváez to power. O'Donnell died the next year, a bitter exile in Biarritz.

An economic downturn in 1866–1868 kept all the currents of unrest alive. Narváez struggled to maintain order but died in April 1868. Faced with a budget crisis, the new prime minister, Luis González Brabo, a civilian who had been Narváez's right-hand man, trimmed military expenditures, which turned both army and navy against him. He ordered the more political generals to the Canaries and Balearics. In defiance, Admiral Juan Topete, hero of the Pacific War and naval commandant at Cádiz, sent warships to return the generals. Joined by Prim and General Francisco Serrano, Topete then issued a pronunciamento. The main opposition parties—the Liberal Unionists, Progressives, and Democrats (formed from the ranks of the Progressive left) banded together, while Serrano led mutinous troops north from Andalusia and Prim raised the banners of revolt in the Levant and Catalonia. As government forces marched against the rebels, Queen Isabel II and her court undertook a trip from La Granja to San Sebastián. At Alcocea, near Córdoba, Serrano defeated the government's army and marched into Madrid. There he and Prim proclaimed the overthrow of the Bourbon monarchy to cheering throngs. Receiving the news at San Sebastián, Queen Isabel II fled with her husband, her children, and her current lover to France, where her onetime lady-in-waiting, Eugénie de Montijo, was empress of the French, as wife of Napoleon III.

The revolution of 1868 brought Spain to a seeming crossroads.

8

A Search for Stability

The generals and their civilian allies who overthrew the queen established a provisional government, headed by General Serrano and dominated by General Prim. Whereas some favored a republic, most were habitual monarchists but wanted a new sovereign to replace Isabel II, "that impossible woman." They arranged for the election of a Constituent Cortes to draft another constitution but differed over what it should provide. Most generals and bureaucrats wanted power to remain centralized, but others, mainly leaders of the provincial juntas that sprang up during the revolution, wanted a federal regime and regional autonomy. Despite objections by Cánovas del Castillo and Liberal Unionists on the right and radical Democrats, federalists, and republicans on the left, the Progressives and conservative Democrats rammed through the Cortes the constitution they wanted. Promulgated in June 1869, it declared Spain a constitutional monarchy, established a bicameral legislature elected by universal manhood suffrage, and provided extensive civil rights. Government remained centralized in Madrid, and the Catholic Church was officially sanctioned, although toleration was extended to other religions over its furious protests.

As the politicians voted in Madrid, unrest troubled the provinces, where troops suppressed widespread federalist and republican uprisings, fed by a variety of discontents. More ominous was the eruption in Cuba of the First

War of Cuban Independence or Ten Years War (1868–1878). Because of threats from Mexico and Colombia following their independence, Spain had endowed the captain general of Cuba with dictatorial authority. Appointed by Madrid, the captains general habitually favored peninsular Spaniards in the Havana government. The Creoles, the old-time colonials of Cuba, resented the favor shown peninsulars, but the big Creole landowners took no risks and provided no leadership. Agitation against the Spanish government was left to middle-class lawyers, teachers, and the like, who could be isolated and intimidated. While many Cubans were willing to settle for reforms that would give Cuba greater autonomy, many aspired for full independence. Slavery was part of the problem. The landowners, whose plantations provided one-third of the world's sugar, employed African slave labor and connived for the continuation of the slave trade, even after Spain accepted British demands to outlaw it. Many had considered annexation to the United States until slavery was abolished after the U.S. Civil War, leaving a choice of greater autonomy or full independence. The revolution in Spain led to expectations that Madrid would concede Cuba greater autonomy but the Spanish captain general and his supporters in Havana proved intransigent. Revolt had erupted before a new captain general arrived, ready to make concessions, although Madrid still insisted that Cuba remain part of an empire centered on Spain. Budding Spanish industry did not wish to yield its favored place in Cuba's commerce to British and North American competition. Spain would still permit slavery in both Cuba and Puerto Rico.

Prim even considered selling Cuba to the United States. Willing to grant it autonomy, he felt trapped by peninsular interests in Havana, Spanish business interests at home, and the dogged pride of many Spaniards in the empire. To maintain fighting forces in Cuba cost money the treasury did not have and required continued conscription, which the government had hoped to end in the face its of unpopularity. While officers might see in Cuba a chance for glory and promotion, unlucky conscripts too poor to buy exemption saw only the prospect of guerrilla warfare and tropical disease. Conscripts' wailing mothers and angry fathers and kin became a part of the Spanish landscape. In Cuba, matters became ugly, bloody, and bitter, and Spanish policy seemed hostage to stubborn loyalist interests in Havana.

Reluctantly waging war in Cuba, Prim sought an acceptable king for Spain. Both he and most conservative politicians favored the duke of Montpensier, husband of Infanta Luisa, but Napoleon III did not want a member of the House of Orleans on the Spanish throne. Montpensier put himself out of the running when he killed a rival candidate in a duel. The Carlists had already proclaimed Don Carlos María as king. Progressives and radical

Democrats demanded a liberal king. After a failed search in Portugal, they promoted Amadeo, an Italian prince of the House of Savoy. But the Church opposed Amadeo, whose father, King Victor Emmanuel II, had annexed all the lands of the papacy, save Rome, to his new kingdom of Italy.

Seeking an alternative candidate, Prim heeded the suggestion of the Prussian ambassador that he consider Prince Leopold of Hohenzollern-Sigmaringen, a south German Catholic married to a Portuguese princess, and, most significantly, a kinsman of King William I of Prussia. Spain's generals, like generals everywhere, admired the triumph of Prussian arms in the wars of German unification and favored friendly relations with Prussia. Prim offered Leopold the Spanish crown and hoped to have him acclaimed by the Cortes before any foreign power might object. But the news got out and Napoleon III objected strenuously. France did not want a German king on the Spanish throne, for reasons of grand strategy and because one-third of France's foreign capital investments were in Spain. Although Prussian Chancellor Otto von Bismarck wanted a war with France to complete the unification of Germany, King William convinced Leopold to refuse the Spanish offer. Napoleon pressed King William too far, and Bismarck got his war. Prussia quickly defeated France, which deposed Napoleon III and proclaimed a republic. Prim was left with no one but Amadeo, whose standing with the Church plummeted yet further when the Italian government occupied Rome and left the pope the "prisoner of the Vatican."

The day in December 1870 that Amadeo arrived in Spain, an assassin shot Prim in the streets of Madrid. Three days later Prim died. Though suspects range from the duke of Montpensier to Cuban slaver dealers, who shot Prim remains a mystery. Aged twenty-five, Amadeo had already proved himself as a soldier in Italy's 1866 war against Austria. Although politically naive, he was determined to reign as a conscientious constitutional monarch. However, without the talents of Prim to hold them together, the uneasy coalition of Progressives, Unionists, and moderate Democrats that put him on the throne began to unravel. As Serrano moved closer to the Unionists, Práxedes Sagasta emerged to lead the moderate Progressives, while Manuel Rúiz Zorilla rallied the more radical wing of the party and allied with Democrats and even Republicans. Sagasta and Zorilla, hitherto allies, became bitter rivals. Sagasta was the more pragmatic, opportunistic, his enemies would claim, and Zorilla, the more doctrinaire. A succession of governments rapidly alternated in office, with Serrano, Sagasta, and Zorilla taking turns as prime minister. Sagasta developed a keen skill in rigging elections through local caciques, but after he made a majority in the Cortes in early 1873, protests and threats from defeated Radicals and Republican unruliness in the provinces forced his resignation as prime minister. Serrano, who succeeded him, asked King Amadeo to suspend the Constitution to permit a crackdown on republicans and the Carlist threat, but Amadeo refused and Serrano resigned. As no other leader of the majority coalition would serve, Amadeo summoned Zorilla to take office. In disgust, Serrano quit the army, returned his medals to the king, and headed a mass resignation of generals and a withdrawal of conservatives and moderates from the government. The election of August 1873 brought a Radical majority to the Cortes, which once more went after the Church, reduced the wages of the clergy, and abolished slavery in Puerto Rico. The persistence of republican unrest in the provinces embarrassed Zorilla, while Carlists took to arms in Navarre and the Basque Country. To deal with the Carlists, Zorilla appointed General Baltasar Hidalgo de Quintana. A Radical in politics and formerly of the Artillery Corps, Hidalgo had been unjustly implicated in the San Gil mutiny. His appointment by Zorilla led to the mass resignation of artillery officers. Zorilla rammed a reorganization of the Artillery Corps through the Cortes, and Amadeo dutifully authorized it. Amadeo then submitted his abdication. He despaired of the infighting among the coalition leaders who made him king and opted out. Privately he remarked, "We are in a cage of madmen."

Zorilla and his Radicals aligned with the Republicans, and the Cortes proclaimed Spain a republic. Estanislao Figueras, a Catalan, became its first president, and another Catalan, Francisco Pi y Margall, its leading minister. In no time, tensions came into the open between those Republicans who, along with the Radicals, favored a centralized government and those who, with their Federalist allies, wanted a Spain of autonomous regions. The Republican leadership urged all to await the election of a Constituent Cortes, but matters in the provinces got out of hand. As Figueras and Pi tried to forestall the creation of regional autonomy, Carlist insurrection spread across northern Spain from Catalonia to the Basque Country.

New class-rooted elements added to the unrest. In 1869, an Italian anarchist named Giuseppe Fanelli, representing Mikhail Bakunin, Europe's chief promoter of anarchism, met in Madrid with eager Spanish disciples. Bakunin had already parted ways with Karl Marx and Friedrich Engels, who dominated the Socialist International. In Spain, Bakunin's Anarchist International appeared first. His anarchism had a mystical quality and stressed spontaneous collectivism as natural to mankind, hindered only by the greed and selfishness of the ruling classes, who must be eliminated. Bakunin, an atheist, saw religion as a tool of oppression. He rejected Marx's stress on disciplined organization. People banded together naturally, and leadership derived from popular recognition. His ideas found their most intense response among the downtrodden poor of rural Andalusia, who dreamed of agrarian collectives to replace oppressive latifundios. They saw their priests cozy with landowners and the rich and felt abandoned by the Church. They quickly turned to violence and political assassination. Against rural anarchists in Andalusia and Extremadura the Civil Guard moved quickly and brutally but only drove them underground.

Fanelli also recruited disciples in Barcelona, who preached the anarchist creed to craftsmen and factory workers and set up a study center. While anarchist workers imagined a world of democratically owned and managed industries, cooperating for the common good, in practice they most often tended to function as trade unionists, seeking better wages and working conditions. At the end of 1872, Spain's anarchist leaders assembled at Córdoba and agreed on a gradualist program of recruitment, education, and limited action. They also agreed to violent action when the chance arose.

The chance arose quickly. While Figueras and Pi waited for the Constituent Cortes to enact a federal republic, whole regions ceased drafting recruits for the army. Discipline collapsed, leaving officers with little control of their men. Over the protests of the generals, the government abolished the death penalty. In Barcelona the ruling junta refused to proceed against soldiers who had murdered their colonel. Political factions vied for control of the local militias, which became the instruments of this or that agenda. In many localities a cantonalist movement appeared, an extreme form of federalism that asserted municipal autonomy within the proposed federal regions. A Spanish confederacy rather than a federal Spain became the rallying cry of many: Málaga, Cartagena, and Seville asserted local self-government, and in Barcelona, a Committee of Public Safety took control. In July 1873, in the paper-manufacturing town of Alcoy, not far from Valencia, workers proclaimed a general strike. It turned violent. They won a skirmish with police, murdered the mayor and several policemen, and paraded their heads through the streets. They burned churches and assaulted members of the clergy. Horror stories soon appeared in the papers of nuns raped and priests crucified.

Conservatives and Moderates, old Progressives and even Radicals, joined by army brass and the Church, were aghast at developments and feared a Spanish version of the 1871 Paris Commune. Cánovas del Castillo, who had withdrawn from public life to pursue historical studies, emerged to rally them. Using the press and the rostrum of the Ateneo, Madrid's club for intellectuals, he worked to persuade them to bury their differences for the good of Spain and accept as king the son of Isabel II, Alfonso, an eighteen-year-old cadet at Sandhurst in Britain. He envisioned a British-type monarchy for Spain, with a two-party system in place of the multiparty system that had plagued Spanish politics, each party an extension of its chief's ego. Isabel agreed to step aside, and Cánovas hoped that the Cortes would see the light and put Alfonso on the throne.

As Cánovas labored to restore the Bourbon dynasty, Pi saw his dream of a federal republic, with some of the most enlightened legislation of the period, evaporate. Amid the bickering of Republicans and Federalists, the presidency passed from Pi to Nicolás Salmerón and then to Emilio Castelar, a yet more conservative Republican and a historian by training. Salmerón and Castelar turned the generals to restore order and revived the death penalty in martial law. The generals marched their ill-disciplined troops against even more unruly militias and rioters and soon broke up the cantonalist risings. Last to fall was the naval base of Cartagena, where mutinous sailors joined the urban militia and used their ships to engage in acts of piracy, which brought foreign warships against them.

Resort to court martial and firing squad in the restoration of order cost Castelar the confidence of the Cortes, and when he resigned in early January 1874, Captain General Manuel Pavía marched his troops into the palace of the Cortes, fired a few shots in the air, and sent the delegates packing. General Serrano reemerged to assume the presidency and formed a government that included members of all parties but the Federalist, Cantonalist, and Carlist. His government generated little enthusiasm, unruliness persisted, and the Carlist War intensified.

A few days after Christmas 1874, Brigadier General Arsenio Martínez Campos, who had won laurels in Cuba and crushed Cantonalist risings at Alicante and Cartagena, assembled his ragtag force of several battalions at Sagunto, near Valencia, and issued a pronunciamento on behalf of Alfonso XII, whom he had sounded out. The other captains general quickly joined or acquiesced in the pronunciamento, and in Madrid Serrano stepped down, replaced by a provisional regency government headed by Cánovas. Unwilling to stir up new disorder, the moderate Progressive leader Sagasta went along. Without waiting for Cánovas's hoped-for tide of monarchist sentiment to restore the king, the army had acted. Alfonso, in Paris with his mother for the holidays, hurried to Marseilles and in a Spanish warship embarked for Spain. After touching at Barcelona, he landed at Valencia on January 11 and three days later entered Madrid.

The teenaged king, trained to be a soldier, soon departed Madrid for the Carlist front, where at some risk he surveyed the field and gave encouragement to his generals and men. His opponent, the Carlist pretender Carlos María, self-styled duke of Madrid, grandson of the first Don Carlos and nephew of Montemolín, was twenty-nine and the most attractive of his lot, although he was thought by some diehards to be too liberal. His forces controlled most of Navarre and the Basque Country and much of the rural Catalonia and upper Aragón. Bilbao, held by government forces, was under close siege. With renewed purpose, Alfonso's armies took the offensive. Martínez Campos cleared Catalonia and Alfonso led the forces that recovered Navarre. Through the summer of 1875, government forces numbering over 150,000 men, against perhaps 35,000 Carlists, cleared the Basque Country and in February 1876, Don Carlos María abandoned Spain for France. Until his death in 1909, he promoted his vain cause. With the Carlists defeated, the regional privileges of the Basque Country were liquidated, and it was subjected to direct rule by a vindictive Madrid. Martínez Campos took reinforcements freed by the end of the Carlist War to Cuba and soon had the rebels confined to the eastern part of the island.

Alfonso XII ratified the new Constitution in June. The work of Cánovas, it was drafted by a Constituent Cortes dominated by his people, thanks to the electoral machinations of his interior Minister, Francisco Romero Robledo. Only some 45 percent of the voters voted, although the 1869 provision for universal manhood suffrage remained in effect. Many voters were purged from the rolls or otherwise disqualified for a host of reasons, and the opposition press was muzzled. Many voters abstained. The Constitution of 1876 reestablished a constitutional monarchy, with sovereignty placed in the king and the Cortes, and once more limited the franchise to substantial taxpayers and educated professionals, some 5 percent of the population. The Cortes consisted of a Senate and Congress of Deputies. The Senate resembled England's House of Lords, with hereditary and appointed members, including senior bureaucrats, army and navy officers, and churchmen, along with persons chosen by designated corporate bodies. The Congress of Deputies was elected by district. Cánovas departed from his English model regarding trial by jury, introduced in 1869, and restored justice to judges and professional jurors in line with the European mainstream. Although the Constitution proclaimed Spain to be Roman Catholic and restored many Church privileges, it continued to allow limited toleration of other religious creeds.

Convinced that stability had come to Spanish political life, Cánovas stepped down after three years in power, and Martínez Campos succeeded him. In 1878 Martínez Campos had patched up a peace with the Cuban revolutionaries, which made him a public hero, provided significant relief for the treasury, and allowed a reduction in the army and the unpopular draft. Martínez Campos called for a new election, which his interior minister, the scrupulous Francisco Silvela, conducted in a relatively fair manner. The opposition coalition of Democrats and Radicals, headed by Sagasta, increased its representation, but the united Conservatives retained a solid majority. Cánovas again became prime minister and in 1880 abolished slavery

110   The History of Spain

in Cuba. His clear opposition to generals in politics caused some of the more liberal among them, such as Martínez Campos and Serrano, to drift into opposition and join Sagasta in a Liberal Fusionist Party. Seeing the two-party system he wanted taking shape, Cánovas resigned in 1881 over minor differences with the king, who summoned Sagasta to form a government. In office, Sagasta played the electoral system to get a Liberal Fusionist majority. He tackled the public debt with some success; proceeded to act in the area of education, long talked about; and seriously began to build a public school system and attack the problem of illiteracy. Two-thirds of Spaniards were still illiterate, which had a detrimental effect on both efforts to build a democratic public life and a modern economy. He also liberalized the laws regarding workers associations, which allowed the labor movement to grow.

At twenty-one, Alfonso married a daughter of the duke of Montpensier, but she soon died. His government favored a more ambitious match, and in 1879, he married María Christina of Habsburg, a cousin of Austrian Emperor Franz Josef. With peace in Cuba, Alfonso and his government sought a more important role in Europe and elevated Spain's envoys to the great courts to the rank of ambassador. Like his generals, Alfonso admired the Prussians and visited Kaiser William I in Berlin, which hardly endeared him to the French when he visited his exiled mother in Paris. Cánovas made it clear that she would not be welcome back in Madrid. German Crown Prince Friedrich visited Alfonso in Madrid, although his visit was marred by difficulties over German encroachment on the Caroline and Mariana Islands in the Pacific, which Spain long claimed but, apart from Guam, did not control.

In private Alfonso sought romantic affairs, though his health was not the best. Afflicted with tuberculosis, he began to weaken, and when he visited Granada after a devastating earthquake in 1884, people took notice. Cánovas, once again prime minister after a handful of republican uprisings embarrassed the Liberals (as the Liberal Fusionists had become), tried to suppress all news about the king's health. In November 1885, Alfonso died. Not yet thirty, he had been a model constitutional monarch, and Cánovas was determined that constitutional monarchy survive. He met with Sagasta and Martínez Campos and, after the king's death, with Queen-Regent María Christina. Cánovas agreed to resign and let Sagasta form a government, on the understanding that in due time Sagasta would resign and Cánovas would form a government, and so on. The scheme soon became apparent and something of a joke, but it would work and give Spain a dozen more years of parliamentary stability.

Because María Christina was pregnant, the succession to the throne was held in abeyance in case she had a son. She already had two daughters and the older bore the title princess of Asturias, but the law of succession favored a male heir. In May 1886 she delivered a son, who upon birth became King Alfonso XIII. Pope Leo XIII agreed to be the baby king's godfather, which kept the Spanish Church in line, to the chagrin of the Carlists. The regency government in turn favored the Church, in which Leo inspired a reconciliation with modernity that promoted a significant Catholic revival in Spain and other parts of the world.

In office, Sagasta restored universal suffrage and Cánovas played loyal opposition, although he was unable to resolve differences in his party between unscrupulous Romero Robledo and scrupulous Silvela. Civil rights were again extended and jury trials restored. When Cánovas returned to office he reversed the Liberals' policy of free trade and erected protective tariffs demanded by manufacturing interests and many labor unions. Agriculture, rich from exports, was not happy, and divisions among Conservatives brought Sagasta to power again.

Beneath the mildly contentious surface of the parliamentary charade, Spain was modernizing and not always peacefully. In January 1892 some 500 grape pickers led by anarchists marched into Jerez de la Frontera calling for revolution and shouting "Death to the bourgeoisie." The Civil Guard routed them, and the courts sent dozens to prison. Four ringleaders were publicly garotted. To avenge them a young anarchist in Barcelona tried to blow up Martínez Campos in 1893 but missed him and killed a soldier. A firing squad shot him, and in revenge, a companion lobbed a bomb into the glittering crowd at Barcelona's Gran Teatre del Liceu for the opening of the opera season, killing twenty-two and wounding fifty. More anarchists were rounded up, and hangmen and firing squads were kept busy.

The chief drama came with the outbreak in 1895 of renewed revolt in Cuba. Embarrassed, Sagasta resigned and Cánovas returned to office. He sent Martínez Campos once more to Cuba but refused to agree to the terms of virtual autonomy Martínez Campos negotiated with the rebels until they laid down their arms. Revolt again flared, and Cánovas replaced Martínez Campos with General Valeriano Weyler. Dubbed "Butcher Weyler" in the yellow press of North America, Weyler had a record of ruthlessness in dealing with insurrection both in Barcelona and in the Philippines. He moved vigorously against the rebels and forced civilians into concentration camps, both for their own protection and to prevent their trafficking with rebels. From their backers in the United States the rebels received encouragement and arms, while the U.S. government sent a delegation to Madrid to find an acceptable settlement. Cánovas appreciated the urgency of the matter and submitted legislation to the Cortes for home rule in Cuba that would permit

Cuba broad latitude in its trade relations with the United States. In August 1897, before the Cortes acted, an anarchist assassinated him.

As tensions continued to mount and the press in both countries inflamed public opinion, Sagasta was soon again in power, legislation for Cuban home rule passed the Cortes, and a conciliatory captain general replaced Weyler in Cuba. But when the second-class battleship U.S.S. *Maine* blew up in Havana harbor in February 1898, events took their own course. War fever raged in the United States, where people believed that a Spanish mine had destroyed the *Maine*. The United States demanded that the Spanish army evacuate Cuba, which would in effect make Cuba independent. War fever in Madrid was equally inflamed, and in April Sagasta broke off diplomatic relations with the United States. U.S. President William McKinley responded with a blockade of Cuba, and on April 24, Spain declared war. The Spanish public believed that their larger army would be more than a match for the tiny American army, although the war minister in Madrid feared otherwise. The U.S. Navy, with three new battleships, several second-class battleships, and armored cruisers, more than outmatched Spain's cruisers and torpedo boats. On April 25 Congress declared war on Spain. In the Philippines and Cuba, where Spanish Admiral Pascual Cervera went down to gallant defeat, U.S. naval squadrons shattered Spain's outclassed flotillas. The U.S. Army, its ranks swollen by national guardsmen and volunteers, joined with Cuban insurgents to defeat Spain's isolated forces in Cuba and landed troops in the Philippines, where Filipino insurgents were also in the field.

At the end of July, Spain sued for peace; by the Peace of Paris of September, it gave up Cuba, Puerto Rico, the Philippines, and Guam. Cuba got its independence, and the United States kept Puerto Rico, the Philippines, and Guam, in return for $20 million to Spain. If the United States' days of empire had begun, Spain's were over. In 1899, Spain sold the disputed Carolines and Marianas to Germany. All that remained were Spanish Morocco and a few enclaves and islands on the African west coast.

For most Spaniards, the defeat came as a shock. Few thought that it would be so swift or so complete. Any notion that Spain had returned to the ranks of major European powers vanished. Spain seemed suddenly backward, although there were those, not happy with modernism, who thought its backwardness perhaps a good thing. Cánovas had once said in a cynical moment that a Spaniard was someone who could be nothing else.

To foreigners, if they no longer took Spain seriously as a power, Spain remained picturesque and exotic. Many Spaniards, if they thought about it at all, agreed. Even before the arrival of Queen Isabel II as an exile in France in 1868, Spain had captured the European and North American Romantic imagination. Lord Byron passed through Spain in 1806 and took up with the

Don Juan legend in his unfinished epic *Don Juan*. Richard Ford, an English-man who had gone to Spain with his wife Harriet for her health, provided readers with the local color of Spanish life in his *Hand-book for Travellers in Spain* (1845). An equally picturesque, if somewhat more jaundiced, view can be found in George Borrow's *The Bible in Spain* (1843), based on observations he made as a Protestant Bible salesman.

Romanticism, nationalism, and popular psychology made the topic of national character fashionable, and both foreigners and Spaniards became fascinated with its application to Spain. Although regional differences complicate the matter, the 1901 Karl Baedeker *Guide to Spain and Portugal* informed travelers of the "lively, cheerful and obliging tone of society, . . . the charming spontaneity of manner, and . . . somewhat exaggerated politeness" but warned against "turning the conversation on serious matters," above all religion and politics, because of "the national pride of the Spaniard and his ignorance of foreign conditions." It added that the lower-class Spaniard possessed "more common sense and a much healthier dislike of humbug than his so-called superiors." It concluded that social relations were "marked by a degree of liberty and equality which the American will find easier to understand than the European, to whom the extreme independence of the middle and lower classes . . . will often seem to border on positive incivility."

Spain's history and institutions exercised a peculiar fascination on foreign historians. Many subscribed to the "Black Legend" (*Leyenda negra*), which held that Spain, after its heroic Middle Ages, established the Inquisition, conquered the Americas through cruelty and deceit, and fomented the Wars of Religion against Protestants. In its pride, Spain became the bastion of bigotry, obscurantism, and reaction, and as pride goes before a fall, so Spain declined to the status of a weak and impoverished state. Many Spanish historians agreed, and some contributed to the legend, like former Inquisitor Juan Alonso Llorente, who in 1815–1818 published a critical study in Paris of the Spanish Inquisition. However, a growing number of professional historians tried to be objective and to study the past on its own terms, aided by archival material. New York author Washington Irving, who served as U.S. ambassador to Spain, though not a professional historian, used the archival researches of Spanish naval scholar Martín Fernández Navarette to write *Christopher Columbus* (1826), the first serious study of this explorer. He followed it with his *Chronicles of the Conquest of Granada* (1829) and popular *Tales of the Alhambra* (1832). Irving played a major role in saving the fabled but dilapidated Alhambra from ruin. Boston historian William Hickling Prescott labored most of his life on the grand age of Spanish history, which he tried to treat without prejudice. Wealthy, though losing his eyesight, Prescott accumulated rare books and acquired transcripts of manuscripts from Spain's Royal Academy of History and state archives in Madrid and Simancas. In the richly cadenced style of his time, he wrote his masterpieces: *The Reign of Ferdinand and Isabella* (1837); *The Conquest of Mexico* (1843); *The Conquest of Peru* (1847); and the unfinished *Reign of Philip II* (1855–1858). Of Spaniards who addressed Spain's past, polymath Marcelino Menéndez y Pelayo remains most impressive. Although a conservative Catholic, he ranged sympathetically through Spain's history to deal with the problems of religious orthodoxy and heterodoxy and Spanish achievements and shortcomings in the arts and sciences .

Foreign artists flocked to Madrid to visit the Prado Museum, opened by Ferdinand VII, where they discovered the Spanish masters, above all Velázquez. For French painters Eugène Delacroix and Edouard Manet, and the American John Singer Sargent, Velázquez was the ultimate painter's painter. Most nineteenth-century Spanish painters produced the kind of historical and religious paintings and realistic landscapes that were popular in other parts of Europe. Toward the end of the century, as Impressionism came into vogue, Valencian painter Joaquín Sorolla y Bastida (1863–1923) best caught its play of light and shadow, especially in his sun-washed beach scenes.

Spanish architecture tended to reflect the prevailing French beaux arts style, as can be seen in so many public buildings and elegant apartment blocks, like those of Madrid's fashionable Salamanca district. In its International Exhibition of 1888, Barcelona proclaimed its modernity by emulating the fashionable elegance of Paris, London, and Rome. But Spanish beaux arts buildings frequently displayed a playful Baroque extravagance, as in Madrid's wedding cake main post office (1913), while the historicist dimension of the beaux arts school caused many Spanish architects to design buildings in a consciously Moorish style.

In the theater some Romantic Spanish drama played well both in and outside of Spain, and some remained uniquely Spanish. Still popular in Spain is *Don Juan Tenorio* by José Zorrilla (1817–1893), drawn from the earlier play by Tirso de Molina. *El Trovador,* by Antonio García Gutiérrez, provided Giuseppe Verdi with the book for his opera *Il Trovatore* (1853), while *Don Alvaro* by Antonio de Saavedra, duke of Rivas, became Verdi's *La Forza del Destino* (1862). After a visit to Spain, the French author Prosper Mérimée wrote *Carmen,* the novel about a gypsy girl that Georges Bizet made into the more famous opera *Carmen* (1875).

The Spanish musical themes Bizet employed had already turned up in works such as the *Jota Aragonesa* by Russian nationalist composer Mikhail Glinka, who visited Spain in 1845–1847. The folklore movement had come to Spain as to other parts of Europe, and scholars and antiquarians searched for the customs, costumes, and traditional music and dance of the folk of Spain's regions. What they found, professional composers and musicians embellished. Subsequent foreign composers who sought Spanish musical color were the Russian Nikolay Rimsky-Korsakov and Frenchmen Emmanuel Chabrier, Edouard Lalo, Jules Massenet, and Maurice Ravel. Spanish composers came into their own with the golden age of zarzuela, Spain's native musical comedy or operetta. The modern zarzuela appeared in the 1840s, grew rapidly in popularity, and persisted well into the twentieth century. Francisco Barbieri matured the form with his *Pan y Toros* (1864) and *Barberillo de Lavapiés* (1874). The great favorite of *madrileños* (natives of Madrid) was *La Gran Via* (1886), with music by Ruperto Chapí, who collaborated on close to a thousand zarzuelas. Another Madrid favorite was *La Verbena de la Paloma* (1894), by Tomás Bretón, who also ventured grand opera in *La Dolores* (1895) with its stirring *jota* (an Aragonese folk dance). Many of the *pasodobles* (double-steps) blared by brassy bands at bullfights come from zarzuelas.

While the zarzuela best reflects musical Spain at the time, foreigners were more attracted to the exotic flamenco. Derived from the *canto hondo* (deep song) of Andalusia, it was taken up by gypsies who performed in night clubs in Seville and caves in Granada and Málaga. At first an entertainment that ranged from raucous to amorous and sensual, it developed into a minor art form in the twentieth century. Its spirit was caught well in paint by John Singer Sargent, in "*El Jaleo*" (1882), while Spain's finest modern composer, Manuel de Falla, orchestrated flamenco themes brilliantly to open the second act of his opera *La Vida Breve* (1905). Falla also acknowledged the revival of Catalan literature in his unfinished scenic cantata *l'Atlantida*, a setting of the 1879 epic poem by Jacint Verderguer.

In these years Spain produced a first-rate novelist, Benito Pérez Galdós, whose works are not much known abroad. He studied in England and knew Dickens's work; he also read French and favored Balzac. He adored Cervantes. His masterpiece *Fortunata y Jacinto* (1887) depicts the life of midcentury Madrid on an epic scale. Over forty volumes comprise the series *Episodios Nacionales*, which blend fact and fiction to trace the history of Spain from 1805, with the first, *Trafalgar* (1873), to the 1880s dominated by *Cánovas* (1912). They range through the whole spectrum of Spanish life, with memorable characterizations and vivid detail. By the time Pérez Galdós died in 1920, Spain was much changed from the Spain of Cánovas. After the debacle of 1898, all kinds of significant and troublesome developments obscured by Spain's parliamentary charade became patently clear.

9

A Troubled New Century

Defeat in 1898 brought Sagasta down, and Francisco Silvela formed a government. While Finance Minister Raimundo Fernández Villaverde tackled the problem of colonial and war debts through tax reform, Silvela made new arrangements with the Vatican over the religious orders that outraged liberal opinion. The 1851 Concordat with the papacy specifically allowed two orders, the Oratorians, who were preachers, and the Salesians, who were educators, and permitted a third agreeable to Rome and Spanish bishops. Each bishop selected an order, and religious orders proliferated. Deprived of their former domains, both bishops and orders invested their money in stocks, bonds, and urban real estate. The Jesuits, who ran elite secondary schools and were fashionable with the pious rich, seemed to thrive. Popular opinion regarded them as immensely wealthy.

It was the tax reform that brought Silvela down. Because he insisted on fair elections in 1899, his majority was slim and soon vanished. After two short-lived regimes, Sagasta came to office in 1902. Tired and disillusioned, he did not last. The religious issue split his party as he tried to find a solution to the problem of the orders. In 1903, he died and his party broke up. In 1902, Alfonso XIII had come of age, and with Sagasta's death, he felt free to exercise the royal prerogative as defined in the 1876 Constitution. He summoned a Conservative government under Fernández Villaverde, soon replaced by the dynamic and imperious Antonio Maura, a former Liberal. The traditional Liberals divided into factions headed by Segismundo Moret and Eugenio Montero Ríos, while the more democratic of them broke to follow José Canalejas.

The coalitions of assorted Conservatives, Liberals, and Democrats who alternated in power faced mounting social unrest generated by the growth of industry and commerce and the related spread of socialist and anarchist ideas. Strikes erupted in Barcelona, Zaragoza, and Valencia, unrest gripped rural Andalusia and Extremadura, and small farmers protested in Castile and León. Few politicians, most of them middle-class lawyers or conscientious aristocrats, few bureaucrats, and few army generals seemed either to grasp what was happening in Spain or to show much patience with it. Caught up in the whirl of Madrid, they strutted their egos and contentiously clung to narrow ideologies. Politics revolved around personalities and the fine points of factious party agendas. What to do about the place of the Church in Spanish life seemed the chief focal point of their harangues. When it came to the problems of regionalism, land, its ownership and use, the conflict of labor and capital, or the costs of a bloated army and bureaucracy, most politicians mouthed timeworn platitudes and seemed at a loss for deeds.

By 1900 Spain was in the full throes of economic modernization. A national network of railroads linked Spain's cities and provincial capitals, and Spain with the rest of Europe. Because for its main lines Spain used a wider gauge track than France did, at Irun and Port Bou on the frontier, passengers and goods had to change trains. Within Spain, the railroads overcame geographic barriers that had forever frustrated the development of a national economy. Steamships increased maritime commerce, both along Spain's coasts and with foreign ports. Spain exported citrus fruit, wine, olive oil, and the products of its mines, including coal and iron ore from the north and copper from the Rio Tinto. As manufacturing grew, stimulated by the spread of rails, iron ore soon headed for Spanish mills. To finance rail expansion and then its growing industry, Spain developed modern banks, beginning with the private Banco de España, formed in 1847 from two older banks.

Catalonia took the lead in industrialization and the Basque provinces of Vizcaya and Guipúzcoa followed. In Catalonia the family firm was the norm, and textiles the chief industry. With iron ore in the Basque country and coal shipped from mines in Asturias, Vizcaya's capital, Bilbao, became Spain's center for heavy industry with steel mills, factories, and modern shipyards. Looking toward England, the Basque industrialists used the corporate model of organization. To finance their enterprises, two of Spain's principal banks were established in Bilbao: the Banco de Bilbao and the

Banco de Vizcaya. The Banco de España, headquartered in Madrid, issued Spain's bank notes and handled most government business. The Catalans, with their family orientation, were slower to develop big commercial banks.

Outside the Basque provinces and Catalonia, most Spanish industry was related to agricultural activities, local construction, public works, and utilities. In a mountainous country, hydroelectric power was an obvious source of energy after the appearance in 1890 of effective transformers. A network to provide electric power sprang up, largely financed with foreign capital, as with the railroads earlier, although in the 1920s Spanish banks proceeded to gain control of most of the electrical system.

With steam and electrical power to provide energy, Spanish industry grew, and with its growing pains came labor unrest and not infrequent violence. Workers organized to seek higher wages, job security, and better conditions, as they did elsewhere in Europe and the United States. The earliest Spanish workers' unions or syndicates, established along anarchist lines, put little emphasis on national organization. In theory they remained aloof from what they regarded as bourgeois politics, although during periods of political unrest they promoted revolution. By 1910 anarchist industrial workers diverged significantly in their concerns and tactics from rural anarchists. Their movement became known as Anarchosyndicalism, and in 1910 their leaders established the National Confederation of Workers, known as the CNT (Confederación Nacional de Trabajadores). The CNT tried to keep both industrial and agricultural workers in the fold, but in 1927, anarchist purists would found an Iberian Anarchist Federation (FAI—Federación Anarquista Ibérica). Although revolution remained an espoused goal of the anarchist movement, most members concentrated on union activity for immediate gains.

Marxist socialism came slightly later than anarchism to Spain. The Spanish Worker's Socialist Party (PSOE—Partido Socialista de Obrero Español) emerged in 1879, and in 1886, its periodical, *El Socialista*, appeared. Galician-born printer Pablo Iglesias, who learned his craft at an orphanage in Madrid, was its founding hero. In 1882 he led a printers' strike and was jailed. In 1888, unions organized by him and other Socialists formed the Unión General de Trabajadores (General Union of Workers), known by its initials UGT. The tightly disciplined UGT got the edge over the CNT in Madrid but elsewhere grew at a slower pace than did the CNT. The UGT had its greatest success in organizing the miners of Asturias. In 1910 Iglesias became the first Socialist elected to the Cortes.

Spanish Catholics, inspired by the encyclicals of Pope Leo XIII, took up social work, and Catholic labor unions developed, especially in the Basque Country where the clergy remained closer to ordinary people. Labor relations in general were better in the Basque provinces than elsewhere, although strikes were hardly uncommon. But many Spanish workingmen associated the clergy with the rich and comfortable and saw them as enemies and Catholic charitable work as a sham. Radical, Socialist, and anarchist rhetoric kept the Church a prime target.

Spain's regional problems were rooted both in its historic and cultural past and in the persistence of regional economies, which railroads only began to link. Nineteenth-century Romanticism had a fascination with traditional folkways and study of them made clear their rich regional variety. Catalan literary scholars found a trove of medieval and renaissance romances, such as *Tirant lo Blanch* (1460), in the Catalan language. Beginning in 1859, an annual poetry contest in Catalan, the *Jocs Florals* (Floral Games), was held. In Barcelona newspapers began to appear in Catalan, and novels and historical studies in Catalan soon followed. In Galicia antiquarians and enthusiastic university students revived the Galician language, which is rich in medieval poetry. Basque scholars began the serious study of their native language and customs, though Basque lacked a significant literary heritage. Students of dance found that Castile has its stately dances and that bagpipes accompanied the dances of Galicia and the Basque Country. Aragón had its bounding *jota* and Catalonia its intense *sardanas*, danced to blaring brasses. For the Hispanic Society of New York, Sorolla depicted the colorful regional costumes of Spain, which only began to disappear from common use in the early twentieth century.

Supported by scholarship and decked out with folklore, regionalism became political, especially in Catalonia, the Basque Country, and Galicia, where the mother tongue differed from the dominant Castilian. Regional autonomy, privileging the regional language, local control over education, and a greater say about taxation and the conduct of the army in the region formed the chief demands, which invariably met objections in Madrid and the Castilian hinterland. The Catalan Pi y Margall's hope for a federal Spain that would meet regionalists' demands collapsed with the Restoration of 1875. Carlism had always extolled regional privileges, but its reactionary mystique and above all its clericalism were too much for most Spaniards to stomach.

At the turn of the century, regionalist sentiment was most vociferous in Catalonia. In 1882, Valentí Almirall, a onetime supporter of Pi, founded a Catalan Center (Centre Català) and a newspaper to promote Catalanism. In 1887, the Lliga de Catalunya appeared with a political agenda, spelled out in 1892 by the *Bases de Manresa,* drafted by Catalan intellectuals and professional men. One declared that Catalonia is the fatherland and Spain a state system hostile to the fatherland. As industrialization bred unrest and class divisions, and the army was needed to keep order, better-off members of the Lliga became ambivalent about what they really wanted. The loss of the Cuban market proved a serious shock, for which they blamed Madrid, although their own concern to monopolize the Cuban textile trade was part of the problem. The big problem was the drift of Catalan workers to the political left, which divided the Catalan Lliga into conservative and leftist camps despite the efforts of its chief, Francesc Cambó, to keep all focused on the demand for Catalan autonomy.

While Catalan workers shared the regionalist sentiments of the educated classes and intellectuals, they also sensed that their movement was more than regional or even Spanish but, rather, international. Anarchosyndicalist activity was strong, and Barcelona became the scene of Spain's worst labor unrest. By 1900 the population of Barcelona and its suburbs, where much of its industry lay, exceeded a half million. There in search of work came thousands of poor men from impoverished Murcia and Andalusia. They competed with native Catalans for jobs, creating a volatile mix. In 1902 the syndicates proclaimed a general strike. Bombs were thrown and people killed and injured. Authorities and employers blamed the strikers; the syndicates insisted that agents of the employers or government threw the bombs to implicate the strikers in murder and mayhem. Sagasta sent General Weyler to impose order, which stirred protests in the Cortes.

Like Catalan regionalism, Basque regionalism grew in an industrializing part of Spain that attracted poor men who spoke Castilian from other parts of the country. In 1895, Sabino Arana Goiri, son of a wealthy Carlist and a student of Basque history, formed the Basque Nationalist Party (PNV—Partido Nacionalista Vasco), whose first aim was to recover the regional privileges (*fueros*) lost in 1839 and 1876. The original party smacked of Carlist ideology, was strongly Catholic and was suspicious of both modern liberalism and socialism. Arana feared the strikes and unrest brought by the UGT and CNT.

Unrest in 1903 and 1904 flared in other cities, not only Barcelona, and Sagasta's successors responded as he did, using civil guards and the army. In 1906, an anarchist in Madrid hurled a bomb at Alfonso XIII on the occasion of his wedding to Victoria Eugenia, a granddaughter of Queen Victoria. A new wave of bomb throwing broke out the same year in Barcelona. Because much of the hostility was directed at the army, the government passed a Law of Jurisdictions that allowed courts martial to try people who criticized the military.

Alfonso turned to the Conservative leader Maura to maintain order. By instinct a moderate, Maura believed that a combination of sternness and fairness was the course to follow. He addressed the Catalan question and embarked on electoral reform. He legalized unions' right to strike, as well as employers' right to use lockouts. He tried to regulate agrarian rents, and he made the judiciary more independent. But continued anarchist activity demanded repressive responses, which embroiled him with the Liberals and Democrats led by Canalejas. What brought his government down were setbacks suffered early in 1909 by the army in Morocco, which led to Barcelona's "Tragic Week" of late July.

In Barcelona the failure of the 1902 general strike had cost the Anarcho-syndicalist leaders the confidence of many workers. They began to listen to the wild rhetoric of Radical Republican demagogue Alejandro Lerroux, who emphasized the role of the Church in the wrongs of the world and the need of a republic to right them. He set up in Barcelona and other cities *casas del pueblo* (Houses of the People), which provided meeting rooms and radical newspapers and books. His younger followers likened themselves to barbarians, out to destroy a decadent civilization. To counter Lerroux, the Anarcho-syndicalists quickened their efforts to organize workers in the midst of an economic slump. To undermine those efforts, several employers in the spring of 1909 responded with lockouts and layoffs. Labor unrest mounted rapidly.

In the midst of this unrest, Maura called up Catalan reservists for service in Morocco. These were young men who had served their term of active duty but were obliged to remain for another nine years in the reserves. Protests erupted from them, their families, and friends. Many had married and become family breadwinners. In sympathy, several Barcelona labor leaders met on a Saturday night and called for a general strike, while Radical demagogues urged violence. When Monday morning came, workers took to the streets. The civil and military authorities deadlocked over how to react. Without leadership, the police lost control of the crowds and were soon besieged in their station houses. Mobs roamed the streets. Many turned to anticlerical violence and desecrated, destroyed, or damaged over eighty churches, convents, and Catholic charitable institutions. A week later reliable police and army units finally restored order. Eight policemen had been killed and nearly 150 wounded, and at least two monks were murdered. Among rioters and bystanders, the official count fixed 104 dead; some participants believed the dead numbered closer to 600. Hundreds more suffered injuries. Along with suspects, the police rounded up journalists sympathetic to the workers and crammed them all into the dungeons of Montjuich. Using brutal methods, they obtained nearly 2,000 indictments, of which more than 400 went to trial. After trials that blatantly favored the prosecution and scandalized worldwide liberal opinion, five of those convicted were executed and another dozen given life imprisonment. The execution of one, Francisco Ferrer, a revolutionary intellectual not involved in the riots, evoked massive international protest. Lerroux was conveniently out of the country.

In response to Liberal and Democrat threats to boycott government and the wider European outcry, Alfonso asked for Maura's resignation. The Liberal Moret became prime minister but soon yielded to the younger and more pragmatic Canalejas. Canalejas, whose political style was open and gregarious, traveled throughout Spain drumming up support. The elections of 1910 were the most honest yet and gave Canalejas and his Liberals 219 seats to 102 for Maura's Conservatives. Smaller parties shared the remainder of seats. While conciliatory in his dealings with Maura, he pushed through significant liberal reforms. To favor the poor he lowered taxes on commodities, while he raised imposts on real estate investments by the rich. He made the military draft more equitable. He hoped to implement a program of wage arbitration, workers' disability compensation, regulation of working hours and conditions, and small land reform measures, and he developed a plan of partial autonomy for Catalonia. As usual, the Cortes became most excited when he proposed that no more religious orders be established in Spain until the matter had been sorted out and that the existing orders' investment income come under scrutiny for tax purposes. While clericals and conservatives screamed in Madrid, relations with the Vatican neared rupture.

Conservatives also noted that under Canalejas strikes continued unabated. Although he respected workers' rights to strike, he took strong measures when strikes turned violent. He used the army to run trains during a railroad strike and on several occasions declared martial law, to the irritation of the left. In November 1912, he was assassinated by an anarchist outside a bookstore on the Puerta del Sol.

When Alfonso appointed the count of Romanones (Álvaro de Figueroa y Torres) to succeed Canalejas as leader of the majority Liberal coalition, Maura exploded. He believed that power must rotate between the main parties, and if it did not, he would no longer serve. Alfonso held his ground and Romanones took up Canalejas's plan for Catalonia. Called in Catalan the *Mancomunitat*, it basically consolidated the four provincial governments of Catalonia into one. Between some who feared that it would give Catalonia more clout than other provinces and those who feared that it would lead to the breakup of Spain, it soon brought Romanones's government down, though it did become law in 1914. To form a new government, Alfonso next turned to Conservative Eduardo Dato after Maura refused to serve except on his own terms. Toward Dato, Maura proved unforgiving, and he soon had a dedicated following that splintered the Conservative Party.

   In August 1914 most of Europe went to war. Spain did not. Held in low esteem as a military and naval power, Spain was part of no alliance system, nor was there any sentiment in Spain that it should be. What international difficulties it had with France over the establishment of a French protectorate over most of Morocco had been settled in 1913 through diplomacy. Alfonso XIII used his neutrality to promote negotiations among related sovereigns, to no avail, and won some goodwill through benevolent efforts on behalf of the war's victims.

   For Spain, neutrality brought economic benefits, through an increase in exports to the belligerent Allied powers—Germany was under tight blockade—and to its own and South American markets whose needs the belligerents could not meet. During the war Spain's gold reserves more than tripled, and the government was able to liquidate much of the national debt. Employment and wages rose, though not as much as profits did, and labor continued to agitate for more. With their pay failing to keep place with inflation, junior and middle rank army officers formed juntas to demand higher salaries and protest promotion polices which they claimed favored those with friends at court or in government. In Madrid the Liberal Romanones, the Conservative Dato, and the Democrat Manuel García Prieto went in and out of office, hapless in their handling of mounting problems. Voter apathy evinced a widespread distrust of politicians and in the elections of 1916, a third of the seats for the Cortes were uncontested and less than half the voters voted.

   At the end of 1916, leaders of the Socialist UGT and the Anarchosyndicalist CNT came together and concerted a one-day general strike. In 1917 the number of strikes grew, while news of the February Revolution in Russia excited the disaffected. Many hoped that the officer juntas might turn revolutionary. The Catalan Lliga and many Catalan delegates to the Cortes met in Barcelona and called for elections for a convention to draft a new constitution. The UGT, under its rising star Francisco Largo Caballero, once a plasterer, called for a general strike in August 1917. The UGT bore the brunt of it, as the CNT failed to mobilize adequately. Labor violence alarmed the more moderate reformers, and the government imposed martial law. The army, whatever its own grievances, cracked down on the threat from the left. New elections at the beginning of 1918 returned a fractious Cortes. Of some 400 seats, Prieto's Democrats won ninety-eight, Dato's Conservatives, ninety-two, and no other party more than forty.

   The king turned to Antonio Maura, who tried to forge a national government of the mutually suspicious party leaders. The Catalan Cambó became minister of development and hatched a scheme for state capitalism, spearheaded by Catalonia. He also developed an ambitious plan of public works and got some started, before Maura resigned after eight months. The egos of the faction leaders were too big, their rivalries too intense. What seems in hindsight the last best chance of constitutional monarchy to succeed was squandered.

Romanones succeeded Maura and made a heroic effort to settle the Catalan question, which foundered on the suspicions of the Catalan right and left. The return of peace to Europe in 1918 brought economic disruption to Spain, as it did to other parts of Europe and the Americas. In Spain, Catalonia suffered worst, and the spiral of violence soared. A round of strikes against the local power and light company gained an eight-hour day and union shops. The employers, less than enthusiastic about labor's gains, got tough and turned to lockouts and firings. They also hired *pistoleros* (gunmen) to pick off agitators and union organizers. The CNT, UGT, and other organizations on the left, including an infant Communist Party inspired by the Soviet Revolution, also hired *pistoleros* to get revenge and intimidate employers and recalcitrant workers. The police joined in, on the employers' side.

A frightened middle class and alarmed rural smallholders, with the specter of red revolution before their eyes, gave Dato's Conservatives 185 seats in the election of early 1920, which allowed him to form a majority block by enlisting Conservatives of Maura's faction and others. The discontented, the unions, and the left, from Catalonia and the north coast to the latifundios of Andalusia, responded with a rash of strikes. Over 400 were counted that year and cost Spain over 7 million man-days' labor. In cities and provinces all over Spain, martial law was proclaimed to curb the violence and protect property. In March 1921 an anarchist assassinated Dato, which only heightened the repression.

All the time, the Spanish army became further mired in Spanish Morocco, the north coastal region allotted to Spain when France made the rest of Morocco a French protectorate. The army kept headquarters at Ceuta and Melilla, Spanish strongholds for some four centuries. Between them stretch the Riff Mountains, a rugged chain near 200 miles long, home to fiercely independent tribes. Despite bribes paid to tribal leaders, tribesmen harassed Spanish efforts to build a road network and operate iron mines. For Spanish soldiers, guarding the mines and roads meant hellish garrison duty, patrols under a blazing sun, and bloody skirmishes. Corpses suffered mutilation and captives risked torture and execution. Aware that deaths of conscripts in Morocco, coupled with lurid coverage of atrocities in the press, meant trouble at home, the army formed units of Moroccan regulars and in 1920 created a Foreign Legion on the French model, but it still had to rely on Spaniards for the bulk of its strength. With all the difficulties in Spain and government finances strained as usual, the troops in Morocco were poorly equipped and supplied. As ever, too much of the military budget went to pay the bloated officer corps.

In 1919, Riff leaders opted for hostility against the Spanish presence, which prompted the principal Spanish commander, Dámaso Berenguer, to open in 1921 a two-pronged offensive from Ceuta and Melilla against the Riff Mountains. His attack from Ceuta enjoyed limited success. In July 1921, from Melilla, the second prong of some 20,000 men marched out under General Fernández Silvestre to secure control of Alhucemas (Al-Hoceima) Bay and establish a base aimed at the heart of the Riff country. Advancing up the main road through a wide valley, his listless troops had neither tanks nor modern armored cars. As they turned north some fifty miles from Melilla to cross to the coast, they encountered intense opposition by well-armed tribesmen led by their chief, Abd el-Krim, a guerrilla leader of genius. The main body of Spaniards bunched up in the village of Annoual. On July 21, Abd el-Krim struck hard at the outposts, overran them, then slammed into Annoual. From nearby villages armed men, including the local police, rushed to join Abd el-Krim's Riffs. Running low on ammunition, Fernández Silvestre ordered a retreat. It became a rout. Even though some troops fought well, most ran. Many were cut down, and most who tried to surrender were slaughtered. In a fortnight the defense perimeter around Melilla collapsed as panicked troops fled to the safety of its fortifications. The dead alone numbered near 10,000 and included Fernández Silvestre.

The news hit Spain like a bombshell. Alfonso XIII was in Burgos for the reburial of El Cid's remains and hoped to announce a Spanish victory in Morocco. Many clamored for revenge; others demanded that Morocco be abandoned. Nowhere was antiwar sentiment more furious than in Catalonia, where the army imposed martial law. General José Picasso prepared a report on the disaster, while governments came and went. Prime Minister José Sánchez Guerra established a committee to act on the Picasso Report, but too much was leaked and he resigned. A liberal coalition under García Prieto eased the restrictions imposed on Barcelona, where violence at once escalated. In April 1923 elections were held. Barely 40 percent of the disillusioned electorate turned out to vote. García Prieto got a slim Liberal majority, and his foreign minister, Santiago Alba, sought to put Spanish Morocco under a civilian High Commissioner and allow Abd el-Krim and his fellow tribal leaders virtual autonomy in the Riff. Neither Abd el-Krim, who had an independent Riff republic in mind, nor the Spanish army, smarting under the criticism heaped on it in the Cortes and set on revenge, went along. In Madrid a military conspiracy took shape, without objection from an aware King Alfonso.

On September 13, two days before the Cortes' findings on the Picasso Report would become public, the captain general of Catalonia, Miguel Primo de Rivera, issued a pronunciamento on his own. He promised to save Spain from professional politicians. A gruff, hearty Andalusian with the common touch, he had never been enthusiastic about the war in Morocco and enjoyed considerable popularity, even among Catalans. When the king failed to back the government, it resigned. The army, waiting to see which way the wind blew, posed no objection, and Alfonso appointed Primo de Rivera to be prime minister and allowed him in effect dictatorial powers, such as King Victor Emanuel III in Italy allowed Benito Mussolini a year earlier. In the years after the Great War, disillusionment with liberal democracy was rife, and many thought Fascist- or Communist-style dictatorships were the wave of the future. For some years pessimistic Spanish intellectuals, such as Joaquín Costa and José Ortega y Gasset, had despaired of political factiousness and felt what Spain needed was a strongman. When after three months the king refused to authorize new elections, it was clear that the Constitution of 1876 was effectively dead.

Primo de Rivera was no Fascist and at first did not admit that he was a dictator. In his own mind he was a common soldier, a man of the people (though he had a title inherited from his uncle), and he intended no more than to "renovate" Spain. Fascism, like communism, is totalitarian. Primo was an authoritarian, who meant to rule with a strong hand and otherwise leave Spaniards to live their lives as they saw fit, in a country free of bickering and disorder. Many Spaniards felt relieved to have a strongman in command. Civil rights were curtailed, the press muzzled, and strikes were forbidden, but the indifferent majority was content to know that the crime rate dropped sharply. Many Spanish males, even those who did not agree with his politics, could identify with a dictator who enjoyed the camaraderie of cafes, the bullring, and the racetrack and the pleasures of brothels.

At first Primo appointed a cabinet of military officers to serve him and focused on the Moroccan problem. To please the army and silence Catalonia, he abolished the *Mancomunitat* and banned newspapers and periodicals in Catalan. He regrouped the army in Morocco into a few tenable positions. Freed of the Spanish threat, Abd el-Krim advanced on Fez in the French Protectorate. This, as Primo foresaw, caused the French to join the Spaniards against him. In 1925 Spanish and French naval units landed a reinvigorated Spanish army at Alhucemas Bay to advance into the Riff Mountains, while French forces with modern aircraft and equipment attacked from the south. Winning laurels with the Spanish Foreign Legion was Francisco Franco, who in 1926 became a brigadier general at age thirty-three. Abd el-Krim, beaten by overwhelming force, in 1926 surrendered to the French and was exiled to Réunion in the Indian Ocean. His heroics made world headlines, and in New York, a rousing "Riff Song" opened Sigmund Romberg's musical *Desert Song* (1926).

With Morocco pacified and an orderly Spain sharing the prosperity that at last came to postwar Europe, Primo appointed at the end of 1925 a largely civilian cabinet consisting of technocrats. José Calvo Sotelo, a financier, overhauled and refined the tax system, while Spain's railroads were brought together into a network directed by the state. Many of the lines were electrified, as new hydroelectric power plants and lines appeared. The construction of modern highways began, and motoring became popular, led by a king who loved fast cars. New bus lines joined railroads to facilitate public travel, and if electricity was slow to reach Spain's rural villages, buses were not. They brought rural and urban Spain into far closer contact than ever before. Aviation came to Spain, and in 1926, the year of Lindbergh's flight from New York to Paris, army aviator Ramón Franco, Francisco Franco's younger brother, hip-hopped from Spain to Buenos Aires, becoming the first to fly across the South Atlantic. Primo did not neglect agriculture, still the largest sector of Spain's economy, and his government carried out large-scale irrigation projects and tried to make credit more readily available to small farmers.

Although the standard of living for most Spaniards had increased perhaps 25 percent overall since 1900, Spain remained poor by the standards of northern Europe or North America. The poverty of more than 2 million landless agricultural workers remained desperate, and great landowners still wielded more political clout than industrialists and bankers. Primo was not unsympathetic to the poor and labor, and he set up a national arbitration system in which the more disciplined UGT participated; the CNT did not. The chief of the UGT, Largo Caballero, sat on Primo's Council of State.

The many who liked and supported Primo's regime formed a loose political front called the Unión Patriótica (UP—Patriotic Union), but they had no program apart from their enthusiasm for the dictator. Such enthusiasm in the army began to wane when Primo attempted to overhaul the strict seniority system in the Artillery Corps. One general remarked that "UP," the initials of the Patriotic Union, also stood for *urinal público*, public urinal.

Primo began to favor the idea of a new constitution that would embody the kind of corporate state Mussolini established in Italy. He even favored giving the vote to women, his reason being that they would prove more conservative than men. A National Assembly appointed from various corporate bodies took up the matter. Primo's health weakened—he was a diabetic who overate—and his supporters divided. Criticism of his regime began to mount.

The king felt left out and became impatient. The court aristocracy derided Primo's common ways, and his fellow generals had never been comfortable with him. Rich landholders and industrialists were not happy with state intervention and arbitration and called Primo's labor minister the "white Lenin." Catalans were angry because he had abolished the *Mancomunitat* and prohibited Catalan newspapers and periodicals. Most outspoken were intellectuals and university students who rankled at the limitations imposed on freedom of the press and speech.

In the first years of the twentieth century, the intellectual life of Spain had entered what many called a second golden age. It began with the so-called Generation of '98 that opened a public debate on the nature of Spain, its civilization, its people, and government in the wake of the defeat by the United States. The chief questions had been posed in a collection of thoughts (*Idearium español*, 1897) by a young diplomat, Angel Ganivet, who committed suicide in 1898 over a love affair. The Generation of '98, with which most Spanish writers and thinkers who first published between 1898 and 1920 get identified, enjoyed a significant pedigree that stretched back into the previous century, to the lively discourse of the Ateneo de Madrid and the teaching of Julián Sanz del Río, a professor at Madrid's university. Sanz, while a student in Germany, became enamored of the philosophy of Friedrich Krause, a disciple of Immanuel Kant. Called *Krausismo* in Spain, it promoted a sense of moral urgency, humanity, and regeneration. Because it did not include formal religion, Sanz and his chief pupil and successor, Francisco Giner de los Rios, quickly ran afoul of the Church and its conservative allies but became heroes to liberals and anticlericals. Forced from his chair at Madrid in 1875 when he refused to take a loyalty oath to dynasty, state, and Catholic Church, Giner and his associates withdrew to Cádiz, where they founded the *Institución Libre de Enseñaza* (Free Institution for Education). Giner believed that Spain's problems were above all rooted in a poor educational system, dominated by the Church and emphasizing rote learning and uncritical belief. In 1875, two-thirds of the population could neither read nor write. Giner's Institution, called free because it was private, trained teachers through practice and pioneered new educational methods, with a stress on elementary and secondary schooling. Students did pay tuition, and wealthy liberals and sympathetic foreign businessmen proved generous with endowments. It soon began to influence other educators in Spain, and when Giner was reinstated at Madrid by a Liberal government, its prestige and his influence expanded. Reform came to the universities in the aftermath of 1898, in response to more and more parents sending their sons abroad to study. For the task, the government established in 1907 the *Junta para Ampliación de Estudios* (Committee for the Improvement of Studies) and included Spain's first Nobel Prize winner in science, neurologist Santiago Ramón y Cajal. The medievalist Ramón Menéndez Pidal formed an institute for historical studies, and at Madrid a *Residencia para estudiantes* (Student Residence) was built for Spanish and foreign students and promoted close student-faculty relationships.

While the Generation of '98 was rich in thinkers, poets, writers, and journalists, the two who achieved the greatest worldwide influence were José Ortega y Gasset and Miguel de Unamuno. Each addressed the question of Spain and Spaniards, and each found a different answer. From a Madrid newspaper family, Ortega studied philosophy in Spain and Germany. He became a professor of philosophy at Madrid, but in his essays he treated the political life of Spain and Europe. Though he held the chair of metaphysics, his thought was existentialist, and he used Don Quixote as a focal point for his ideas. Spaniards, he came to believe, were above all Europeans, despite their idiosyncrasies, and as he watched disorders and political confusion spread after 1917, he deplored in *Invertebrate Spain* (1921) Spain's lack of a consistent and coherent elite to provide leadership. In his most famous work, *Revolt of the Masses* (1930), he expressed his prescient concerns about the growth of modern mass society dominated by amoral technocrats.

Although concerned with the perceived ills of Spanish society, Miguel de Unamuno focused more on the individual human being. Born a Basque, Unamuno identified with Spain and saw in Spaniards a common national character. He acquired the chair of Greek at the University of Salamanca, and like Ortega, he meditated on Don Quixote and is considered an existentialist. He wrote on the tension of faith and reason, mind and feeling, and each individual's longing for immortality. He believed that Spain was not like the rest of Europe but different and special. Modern Western civilization, he feared, had become soulless and materialistic, whereas Spaniards still confronted the tensions of human existence and retained the true "tragic sense of life," which became the title and theme of his most famous work, *The Tragic Sense of Life in Men and Peoples* (1913). For Spaniards it was all or nothing: There was no gray, only black and white, which Unamuno saw reflected in the stark light and shadow of the Spanish landscape. Because Unamuno spoke out against Primo's dictatorship, Primo fired him from Salamanca, locked him up, then forced him into exile in Paris.

Only one significant intellectual of the generation, Ramiro de Maeztu, supported Primo. The son of a Basque father and English mother, Maeztu became a London correspondent for the Spanish press. In his essays, he urged Spain to follow the English model of modern liberal government. But reporting the Great War broke his faith in liberalism, and in his notion of

Hispanidad (Spanishness) he came to promote a traditional, authoritarian, and Catholic regime for Spain and other Spanish-speaking nations.

Yet another Basque, Pío Baroja, came to be regarded as Spain's best novelist of the Generation of '98 despite his bleak treatment of Spanish life and manners. More flair, if less depth, can be found in the historical novels of Ramón del Valle-Inclán. An Argentine, Rubén Dario gave Spanish poetry a new vigor, but the Andalusian Antonio Machado caught best the vibrant rhythms and color of Spanish life. Juan Ramón Jiménez, a long-lived poet with a varied but rich style, began to publish in 1903 and in 1956 received the Nobel Prize for Literature.

In music Enrique Granados charmed Europe with his piano pieces titled *Goyescas* (1911–1913). Manuel de Falla remained Spain's great composer and on occasion collaborated with the rising poet Federico García Lorca, who was born in 1898 and would soon be acclaimed as Spain's greatest playwright since the Golden Age. From Granada, García Lorca found his favorite themes in the life of Andalusia, which Ignacio Zuloaga caught with vivid color and stark imagery in his paintings.

Many Spanish painters left Spain for the international art centers of Paris and New York. Pablo Picasso, the greatest of them, came from Málaga and began his career in Barcelona, where he hung out with other artists, both budding and prominent, at Els Quatre Gats (the Four Cats) Cafe, over which wealthy historical painter Ramón Casas presided. Others who achieved fame abroad were Salvador Dalí and Joan Miró, both strongly influenced in their early careers by the great Catalan architect Antoni Gaudí. Already admired and active in Catalonia, Gaudí in the years after 1900 embarked on his most famous works in Barcelona: the Casa Milà on the Passeig de Gràcia, the structures in the Güell Park, and the multispired Basilica of the Sagrada Familia, unfinished at his death in 1926 and still under construction.

Foreigners who came to know Spain in the 1920s, such as writers Gerald Brenan, Ernest Hemingway, and Somerset Maugham, tended to agree with those Spanish writers, artists, and thinkers who found Spain and Spaniards different and special and saw in Spain an intensity of life that the more industrial countries of Europe had lost. Spain came to mean guitars and castanets, the taca-taca-tac of the flamenco dance, and colorful fiestas. Ernest Hemingway extolled the virility of bullfighters; tourists flocked to Andalusia for Holy Week and the springtime ferias and to Pamplona for the running of the bulls.

But Spain was a part of the industrial world, and the financial crises of 1929 and the Great Depression that followed had strong effects. Despite the efforts of Finance Minister Calvo Sotelo to prop it up, the peseta fell 20 percent in value, from forty to the pound sterling to thirty-two. The 1929 fairs at

Seville and Barcelona to ballyhoo Spain's successes came at the wrong time and cost too much. Bad harvests complicated matters, and as support for the dictatorship waned, Primo could not silence his critics. Although in 1927 he had commenced a new Ciudad Universitaria (University City) on the outskirts of Madrid to replace the downtown Central University, its students jeered him. When he received an honorary degree, the students gave a degree to a burro. Primo responded that there were too many students, they were frivolous and their professors lazy. He fired scores of professors and derided what he called the arabesques of unemployed intellectuals. Many intellectuals who had previously deplored the "old politics" now allied with the old-line politicians, who were either out of work or in exile. The exiled Conservative leader Sánchez Guerra landed in Valencia in July 1929 but was promptly arrested by the regional captain general, who reneged on his promise to join him.

A pamphlet that tied the king to Primo as his "dancing partner" proved the straw that broke the back of waning royal support for the dictator. When King Alfonso discovered in January 1930 that Primo had sent a circular to the captains general to seek their support, and it proved to be lukewarm, he suggested that Primo resign. Primo did and departed for Paris, where he died six weeks later.

Alfonso XIII appointed General Berenguer to succeed Primo de Rivera at the head of government. Berenguer turned to the old politicians, but most had been so alienated by the king's association with the dictatorship that they refused to serve. The Liberal Romanones and the Conservative Alba demanded elections for a Cortes. Conservative leader Sánchez Guerra, released from jail, asserted that Spain might justly become a republic. While Cambó thought Catalan autonomy might yet be achieved through the monarchy, more and more Catalans were becoming Republicans. Several Republicans on vacation met in San Sebastián that August: the old Radical Lerroux; Niceto Alcalá Zamora, a Catholic Conservative turned Republican; leftist journalist and intellectual Manuel Azaña; and a few maverick army officers. Making a pact to conspire for a republic, they formed a Central Revolutionary Junta. Neither the UGT nor CNT cared to join what they saw as more bourgeois politics. The UGT resumed its revolutionary stance, and the CNT reemerged in Barcelona more intent on revolution than ever. Workers all over Spain became militant and sang revolutionary songs in their barrios.

Generals Emilio Mola and Gonzalo Queipo de Llano, who held important civil security positions, raised the question of loyalty to Spain over loyalty to a discredited king. In December the garrison of Jaca pronounced for a republic, and Ramón Franco, who had been expelled from the service for insubordination, flew over Madrid and dropped leaflets that vainly urged its garrison to join them. While the rising in Jaca was crushed and its leaders executed, republican sentiment became more blatant. In February, Ortega y Gasset met with Gregorio Marañón, the king's physician, and other intellectuals to prepare for a republic.

Berenguer at last recommended elections for the Cortes, but the politicians demurred, questioning his sincerity. They believed that the municipal governments appointed by Madrid would rig them. Berenguer resigned, Sánchez Guerra and Alba would serve only on their own terms, and so Alfonso appointed nonpolitical Admiral Juan Bautista Aznar to be prime minister. Aznar agreed that municipal elections precede elections to the Cortes, and some old politicians, such as Romanones, joined his government, which faced persistent popular unrest. In Madrid students confronted the Civil Guard, and shots were fired. Aznar granted the students amnesty and hoped that the elections would return a strong monarchist majority.

When the results of municipal elections in Madrid and the provincial capitals came on the evening of Sunday, April 12, Republicans and Socialists appeared triumphant. Monday seemed calm, while the election count made clear that forty-six of fifty provincial capitals voted against the monarchy, although the rural returns gave the monarchists a slight majority of seats in small towns and nationally. In rough figures, of some 80,000 councillors, 34,000 were republicans and 4,900 Socialists, the rest monarchists. However, it was the capitals that represented the more developed and better educated parts of Spain that mattered. At once both Barcelona and Seville proclaimed a republic. That evening celebrations erupted in the workers' barrios of Madrid. In the Puerta del Sol a crowd formed that called for the end to the monarchy and the establishment of a republic. The well-to-do feared that the crowds might turn violent, and generals doubted that their troops would open fire on popular demonstrations. In the wee hours of the morning, royalist politicians, professors, and journalists anxiously gathered at the bar of the Ritz Hotel, while concerned courtiers whispered in the corridors of the Royal Palace. A consensus developed that the king had to go. By morning Alfonso agreed to absent himself from the country until the Cortes made its decision on the monarchy. "We are out of fashion," he admitted. That evening he left Madrid in a motorcade, and the next day he boarded a cruiser at Cartagena and sailed for France and exile. Alcalá Zamora, provisional head of the Republic proclaimed as Alfonso departed, feared that had the king motored directly to France, the monarchist north might have rallied to him and stirred up violence.

The queen left Madrid on April 15 with the rest of the royal family, save for the Infante Don Juan, a naval cadet at Cádiz, who proceeded via

Gibraltar. Alfonso would die in Rome in 1941, soon after he had designated his surviving son Don Juan, count of Barcelona, as his heir.

10

Republic and Civil War

We now reach that part of Spain's history that lies within living memory. People still argue about the Second Republic and what followed. Objectivity is not easy. The tumultuous politics of those days unfolded against the backdrop of the Great Depression. Italy had already come under Mussolini, the Soviet Union, under Joseph Stalin. In 1933 Adolf Hitler took power in Germany, and the United States embarked on Franklin Roosevelt's New Deal. Britain and France, too, experienced economic and political convulsions. The conditions of modern life—such as rapid transportation, telecommunications, the variety of things to do—had fragmented the old sense of community and shared experience. Those with money conspicuously did more things and had less to do with those who had less, who became resentful. In *Don Quixote*, Sancho Panza saw the human race divided into two families, the haves and the have-nots. With so many more material possibilities available, Spain's far more numerous have-nots wanted what they thought to be their just share, and many heeded the rhetoric of anarchists and Socialists who promised it.

While most Spaniards in 1931 felt relieved that minimal violence attended the birth of the Republic, Alcalá Zamora filled his cabinet. Elections for a Cortes to draft a constitution was their chief business, but problems festered that needed quick attention. Regionalism was one. In Barcelona, separatist Colonel Francesc Macià proclaimed Catalan independence and invited the rest of Spain to join in an Iberian federation. Cooler heads reined him in. There was the need to achieve industrial peace and agricultural land reform. Everywhere, urban and rural workers agitated for better pay and conditions and, some of them, to make a revolution and establish socialism. In agriculture the liberal ideal of the small farmer clashed with anarchist and Socialist calls for collectivization. The army was still bloated, costly, and political. And there was what seemed to liberals and leftists the key to all of Spain's problems: the perceived power and wealth of the Catholic Church. Addressing these problems, the provisional government began to alienate the army, the Church, and the wealthy even before the elections.

The Vatican hesitated to recognize the Republic, and devout Catholics questioned what loyalty they owed it. In May, Minister of Education Marcelino Domingo announced that religious instruction would no longer be mandatory in public schools. The archbishop of Toledo protested and urged Catholics to resist attacks on religion. Scuffles between Catholics and republican militants led to mob violence against Church property in Madrid. Because lives did not seem endangered, the government hesitated to call in the Civil Guard. Desecration of Church property spread quickly to other cities, forcing Alcalá Zamora to impose martial law and use the Civil Guard and army to end the violence. The damage was done: The infant Republic and the old Church were at virtual war.

Wealthy businessmen and landowners saw the Republic take the side of labor and higher wages. Largo Caballero overcame scruples about serving a bourgeois government and became labor minister. Urban and rural strikes proliferated, not without violence, and the UGT began to rival the CNT in organizing farmworkers. As finance minister, Socialist publisher Indalecio Prieto inspired little confidence, and the value of the peseta dropped further when an international banking group, who propped it up for Calvo Sotelo, backed out. The wealthy began to move their money out of Spain.

A civilian, Manuel Azaña, became war minister. What Azaña knew of army life came from his historical studies. A civil servant, he had never before held public office and gained prominence as president of the literary Ateneo of Madrid. Admired by some, loathed by others, he headed the new Republican Action Party. Spain's army needed reorganization, and Azaña took up the task with zeal. It had some 25,000 commissioned officers, including eighty generals, for 120,000 men who on paper formed sixteen divisions. He reduced the number of divisions to eight and offered officers retirement at full pay in order to trim the officer corps. He abolished the captaincies general and replaced them with district commands that had little civil jurisdiction. He reviewed promotions made under the dictatorship, to the irritation of those promoted in the Moroccan campaign. Although many took early retirement, the officer corps griped incessantly about Azaña.

Elections for the Cortes were held in June. The provisional government wanted to ensure a Republican victory and achieve parliamentary stability. All Spaniards aged twenty-three and over, including women, could vote. Ballots carried party slates of candidates rather than candidates by district so the big capitals could carry the provinces and elect Republicans. To provide parliamentary stability, the winning slate would receive four-fifths of the province's seats, and the slate with the second highest number of votes would take the remainder of seats. As the other slates would elect no one, parties and factions formed coalitions and put their leaders on slates where they had the best chance to win. Nationwide, nearly fifty parties, mostly new, fielded candidates.

When votes were counted, Republican parties and Socialists had some 250 of the 457 seats. The Socialist PSOE elected 119, the largest number, while Azaña's Republican Action Party and its allies got some 80. Added to these were the Catalan Left (Esquerra), with 37 seats, some 20 Galicians, and a few leftist strays. Lerroux's Radicals anchored the center with 97 seats. With them sat intellectuals Ortega y Gasset, Unamuno, and Marañón. A scant 40 went to the disorganized Conservative parties.

The Cortes symbolically opened on July 14 (Bastille Day) and began to draft the Constitution of 1931, which declared Spain a "Republic of workers of all categories." Like the 1812 Cortes of Cádiz, it established a unicameral legislature. With one seat for every 50,000 people, the Cortes would be elected by province: The winning slate would win from two-thirds to four-fifths of the seats, based on the proportion of votes won, and the second place slate would get the remainder. The Cortes would serve for four years and meet annually. The Cortes and an equal number of elected commissioners would form an electoral college to choose a president for a six-year term. If the Cortes could not function, the president could dissolve it and call for elections, but if it happened a second time, the next Cortes would review his decision and, if not in agreement, might remove the president from office.

The Constitution provided for elected municipal councils and the prospect of autonomy for regions with shared historic and cultural traditions. To uphold the civil rights of Spaniards, it established a Court of Constitutional Guarantees. Foreign relations, the armed forces, the monetary system, interregional commerce and public works, and the regulation of religious cults remained the preserve of the central government.

While a telephone strike gripped the nation, the regulation of religion created the greatest excitement in Madrid. The Constitution and legislation that followed provided for the complete separation of church and state and removal of clergy from the state payroll within two years. Outraged, Alcalá Zamora resigned as prime minister, to be succeeded by Azaña, who proved relentless in his determination to reduce the Church to a nullity in Spanish life and expel the Jesuits. "Spain," he declared, "is no longer a Catholic country." Few apart from women, the middle classes, and children, paraded to Mass from school or regularly attended church. Azaña would get the clergy out of education as soon as Spain had enough lay teachers for the task. When crucifixes were removed from public schools, schoolchildren from devout families conspicuously wore crucifixes. School construction became a priority, and thousands were built. By 1936, nearly 30,000 new lay teachers were trained. In the summers university students went to remote villages and introduced peasants to Spain's cultural traditions.

When the Cortes ratified the Constitution of 1931 in December, Azaña, in a conciliatory gesture orchestrated the election of Alcalá Zamora as president of the Republic. The Cortes next addressed the Catalan question and in September 1932 established an autonomous Catalonia with a regional government, the Generalitat, that had a president, *Corts*, (Cortes in Catalan) and prime minister. Old Macià became president. Neither the Basque Country nor Galicia had made equal preparations for autonomy. Moreover, the devout Basques opposed the religious policies of Madrid and wanted regional control over religion.

The urgent land question did not wait on the Cortes, even as Largo Caballero favored field workers and the Cortes debated what all agreed was the most important issue in Spain. In December 1931 impatient agricultural laborers in Extremadura killed four Civil Guards and mutilated their corpses. The culprits were tried and six of them convicted to life imprisonment, though hard-line General José Sanjurjo was replaced as head of the Civil Guard. In the summer of 1932, he issued a pronunciamento against the government, which failed. He was court-martialed and incarcerated.

In September 1932 the Cortes, divided between traditional liberals concerned about private property and Socialists who favored collectivization, passed an agrarian reform the law full of half measures. The Institute for Agrarian Reform that the law established confiscated some latifundios, but for most affected properties, it had to compensate the owners, for which it lacked sufficient funding. Although thousands of peasants received land, critics complained that it would take a hundred years to complete its redistribution. Spain's rural proletariat numbered almost 2 million, not counting women who worked at harvest time. In rural southern Spain, anarchist unrest persisted. With high expectations, the landless often took matters into their own hands.

Madrid created a new republican police, the Assault Guards, to supplant the Civil Guard in cities. In January 1933, both Assault and Civil guardsmen battled a wave of anarchist uprisings in Andalusia, Aragón, and urban Barcelona, killing dozens and wounding hundreds. A national uproar ensued over guardsmen's conduct at Casas Viejas in Cádiz province. Having killed two Civil Guards, local anarchists fled to the cottage of an old relative, "Seisdedos" (Six-fingers). An Assault Guard was shot trying to arrest them. Reinforced guardsmen burned the cottage and killed eight men and women inside, including Seisdedos. An Assault Guard captain then rounded up twelve village men and executed them at the scene. It was claimed that Azaña ordered him to "shoot them in the belly."

Azaña, whose government enjoyed considerable popularity through most of 1932, found himself under mounting fire from all sides. Trying to ignore it, he continued his assault on religious education and in May 1933 rammed a law through the Cortes by a vote of 258 to 50, with over 150 abstentions, to close Catholic secondary schools in October and primary schools in 1934. The new archbishop of Toledo, who tolerated the Republic, urged the faithful to accept the constituted government, as early Christians had pagan Rome, but also to ensure that their children receive a Catholic education. He meant to keep Catholic schools open. Elections that summer to municipal councils revealed a shift to the right. Before the law closed Catholic schools, Alcalá Zamora dissolved the Cortes and called for elections in November.

Spanish conservatives, monarchists, and traditionalists had recovered from their shock over the triumph of the Republic. Catholic leader José María Gil Robles forged a coalition known by its initials CEDA (Confederación Española de Derechas Autónomas—Spanish Confederation of Autonomous Rights), which elected the largest group to the Cortes, aided by the women's vote, still largely Catholic and traditional. Lerroux's Radicals had the second largest bloc, while the PSOE, who broke with their leftist Republican allies, came in third. Azaña's leftist Republicans were routed. Alcalá Zamora, suspicious of CEDA monarchist tendencies, instructed Lerroux to form a government without CEDA ministers. Though Lerroux tried to placate the CEDA by leaving Catholic schools open, he could not provide effective government without them. In October 1934, Alcalá Zamora allowed three CEDA ministers in the cabinet. Immediately leftist Republicans walked out of the Cortes. Extremists of the Catalan Left and Socialists called for general strikes and even rebellion. A Catalan uprising failed when the middle classes provided no support, and new Generalitat president Lluys Companys refused to arm unruly workers. In Madrid and elsewhere the firm response of authorities limited unrest. But in Asturias striking coal miners seized control of Oviedo, its capital, and its chief port Gijón. Socialist, anarchist, and Communist unions forged a government for Oviedo but did little to prevent looting. Madrid summoned the army, which was reinforced by elite forces from Spanish Morocco, including Moroccans. War Minister Diego Hidalgo turned to General Franco to oversee the campaign. Before order was restored, 1,000 people had died. Atrocities were committed on both sides. The left and liberal press focused on the savagery of the Moroccans and the right on the murder of policemen and clergy by strikers.

Martial law prevailed in much of Spain; the press was censored. In Barcelona, Azaña was arrested, charged with fomenting all the strikes and risings in Spain, and became a hero to the left. When Azaña was cleared, Lerroux amnestied Sanjurjo to placate the outraged right. However, thousands of left Republicans, Socialists, anarchists, and Communists remained in detention. Even Companys and his Catalan government were jailed. Trials of the accused leaders of the Catalan and Asturian risings further exacerbated divisions between left and right, which Lerroux vainly tried to bridge. Thousands were convicted and imprisoned. When Lerroux commuted several death sentences, Gil Robles broke with him and brought down his government. He soon relented and agreed to serve a Lerroux government with five CEDA ministers. He became war minister, revived the captaincies general, and began to replace liberal generals appointed by Azaña with conservative officers. Franco became army chief of staff.

In the countryside, landlords and the Civil Guard settled scores, and supported by sympathetic arbitrators, agricultural employers reduced wages. Many big landowners left their land fallow, hoping to cow workers with the threat of unemployment. Middling landowners who employed labor complained about tight domestic and shrunken world markets. Even conservative politicians became alarmed about the rural situation, and Gil Robles denounced the tactics and policies of big landowners as un-Christian. Yet when he attempted to pass legislation that permitted sharecroppers to acquire title to their farms, his own allies watered down the legislation.

In cities and towns people took sides, and cafes where they met became hangouts for the right or left. Discussions in *tertulias*, Spain's informal afternoon discussion groups, grew heated. Party youth organizations formed and fought in the streets. Young people got killed. The Communist Party (PCE—Partido Comunista de España), which adhered to Stalin's Third International and denounced Largo Caballero's Socialist PSOE as spineless, enjoyed rapid growth. Largo Caballero ceased to cooperate with the left Republicans, and his rhetoric grew increasingly revolutionary. As the left parties turned militant, extremist parties developed on the right and proclaimed Fascist ideals. In 1933, José Antonio Primo de Rivera, son of the late dictator, founded the Spanish Falange and won followers through his fiery eloquence, which called for national rejuvenation and a just corporate society. He won a seat in the Cortes and forged a union of his Falange with the National Socialist Offensive Junta (JONS—Junta Ofensiva Nacional Socialista). Openly monarchist organizations appeared as exiled monarchists like Calvo Sotelo returned to Spain. In Navarre, Carlist *requetés* sporting red berets drilled in the mountains.

Despite political tensions, Spain's cultural life flourished. With student groups poet García Lorca staged classic Spanish plays and gained the theatrical experience evident in his great dramatic trilogy, *Bodas de Sangre* (*Blood Wedding*, 1933), *Yerma* (1934), and *Casa de Bernarda Alba* (*House of Bernarda Alba*, 1936). To wild acclaim he staged the first two in Madrid, where early in 1936 he read the third to friends. For a bullfighter friend who was gored and died, he wrote the haunting elegy *A las cinco de la tarde* (*At Five in the Afternoon*), with its opening line repeated again and again as the poem unfolds. In film, Luis Buñuel produced his documentary masterpiece *Las Hurdes: Tierra sin Pan* (*Las Hurdes: Land without Bread*), a scathing indictment of the rich and the Church, about life in impoverished Extremadura. Already he had won fame in Paris for his surrealist films done with Salvador Dalí. From his earnings, renowned Catalan cellist Pablo Casals subsidized symphonic music in Barcelona. Both Unamuno and Ortega y Gasset remained active.

Beneath the cultural brilliance, all the problems of Spain festered, while under the center-right government, the poor seemed to get poorer and the rich, richer. Alcalá Zamora despaired of a democracy that could be maintained only under emergency laws and aspired to find a stable center coalition in place of the divisive alternation of left and right. Financial scandals in the fall of 1935 involving several Radical ministers gave him a chance to dissolve the Cortes and call for elections. With Largo Caballero's PSOE and Azaña's Republican left at odds, and the right fragmented between CEDA and Calvo Sotelo's monarchists, Alcalá Zamora hoped for a victory of center parties, even though scandals tarred the largest of them, the Radicals.

The small but growing Spanish Communist Party, encouraged by Stalin, frightened of Nazi Germany, expressed interest in an alliance with the Socialists and Republican Left. The executive committee of the PSOE accepted both the Communists and Azaña's Republican Left as allies, over Largo Caballero's objections. In January 1936 Socialists, the Republican Left, and Communists forged a Popular Front, and Largo Caballero and Azaña, each with a different vision of Spain's future, became its most eloquent spokesmen. They agreed to maintain democracy, revive land reform, favor labor, remove the Church from education and public life, and grant amnesty to thousands still imprisoned for the events of October 1934.

The right formed a National Front and collected a lot of money. Gil Robles ran on a platform of social Catholicism and opposition to "Red" revolution but did not embrace the restoration of monarchy. Calvo Sotelo headed the monarchists. The government ended censorship of the press, and the parties held noisy and sometimes unruly rallies. The police were restrained and violence was less than in 1933, primarily because the left parties had united and did not fight each other. Seventy-three percent of eligible voters voted on Sunday, February 16, and the vote proved close, nearly 4.7 million for the Popular Front to almost 4.6 million for the right, center, and others. Even many anarchists voted, because the Popular Front promised amnesty to their imprisoned fellows. The center and right had expected to win but narrowly lost. After runoff elections were held and credentials determined, the method used to allocate seats gave the Popular Front 271 of 473, with 137 for the rightist coalition, 40 for the center, and the remainder for Basque Nationalists and other splinter and regional parties. The Popular Front had the majority in the Cortes it wanted, whereas the opposition cried the election had been stolen. Among themselves, the politicians of the center and right did much soul searching. Miguel de Maura called their reactionary politics after 1934 "political suicide."

The nervous caretaker government stepped down before the Cortes met. Reluctantly Azaña became prime minister and formed a cabinet from the Republican Left. He continued the state of emergency declared by his predecessor to quiet exuberant demonstrations by the left but granted amnesty to some 30,000 political prisoners and restored power to Companys and the Generalitat in Catalonia, as well as to Socialist municipal governments suspended in 1934. He also moved to renew land reform in Extremadura and Andalusia. From Madrid he removed several generals whose names cropped up too often in talk about overthrowing the Republic, including Chief of Staff Franco, whom he sent to the Canary Islands. When he finished shuffling generals around, he believed that he had loyal Republicans in all key commands.

Workers paraded through the streets of industrial centers and drew parallels with Russia, where the republican February revolution was followed by the October Bolshevik revolution. All over Spain, shootings and mayhem settled political scores between and within the political left, right, and center. In Madrid Falangist students tried to assassinate a Socialist member of the Cortes, and in retaliation a Socialist mob damaged Calvo Sotelo's newspaper presses and two churches. Azaña outlawed the Falangist party and had its leader Primo de Rivera arrested. The right protested that he was not equally harsh in dealing with violence from the left.

When the Cortes met, Azaña submitted his program of land reform and school construction, greater authority for municipalities, regional autonomy for the Basque Country, and the reemployment of all workers dismissed for political activity since 1933. To convince the right that they should continue to support the Republic, he insisted that he did not intend to socialize land, banks, and industry. He urged the PSOE and Communists to eschew revolution and go along with his moderate program. In the poorer provinces, however, landless peasants invaded big estates, while the censored press led people to believe all was peaceful and calm. Because turbulence and political murders persisted, Azaña postponed scheduled municipal elections.

As prescribed by the Constitution, the Cortes reviewed Alcalá Zamora's decision to hold elections a second time and deposed him from office. Most right and center members, who believed Alcalá Zamora favored the left, abstained. Dominated by the left, the electoral college chose Azaña to succeed him, to the horror of the right and devout Catholics. As president, Azaña knew he could achieve less than as leader of the Popular Front in the Cortes, but he seemed worn out by efforts to forge a cabinet from the Republican Left and Socialists ideologically reluctant to serve in a bourgeois regime.

Azaña considered moderate Socialist Indalecio Prieto for prime minister, but the PSOE majority would not have him. Largo Caballero accused Prieto of cowardice because in a May Day speech he had warned against leftist violence and predicted it would lead to a Fascist dictatorship under Franco. Azaña next turned to ailing Republican Santiago Casares Quiroga, who loyally took the post.

The pace of political violence continued unabated, and every week more strikes occurred. Madrid was paralyzed in June by strikes involving 70,000 workers. Businesses conceded huge increases in wages and benefits to workers, then shut down because they could not afford to pay them. Spanish exports and shipping ceased being competitive.

Because of sporadic violence against Church institutions, the government ordered Catholic schools closed for their own protection. Although the Popular Front government had so far avoided a direct confrontation with the Church, Catholics feared that it intended to shut down their schools permanently. In June Catholic leader Gil Robles reported to the Cortes that since the elections political violence had claimed 269 lives and left over 1,200 injured, that over 400 churches had been destroyed or damaged, and that there had been over 300 general strikes or near general strikes. If his figures were high, given the confused reports by authorities and the press, they were not high by much.

Army officers watched the mounting disorder with alarm. Some conspired with General Sanjurjo, an exile in Portugal. Portuguese dictator António Salazar, an economist backed by the military, watched events in Spain with anxiety and sympathized with Sanjurjo. In Spain General Emilio Mola headed the conspirators. He seemed a good Republican, and Azaña posted him to Navarre, ignoring warnings about Mola's contacts with Carlists. Soon active in the conspiracy was Queipo de Llano, another seeming Republican and military chief of Seville. An in-law of Alcalá Zamora, he loathed Azaña. Franco, though approached by the conspirators, remained noncommittal. Republican and leftist junior officers suspected a conspiracy and formed an anti-Fascist officers' association

Sanjurjo and his associates agreed to rise between July 10 and 20. On Sunday, July 12, a Falangist gang assassinated an Assault Guards officer active in revolutionary circles. His comrades sought revenge, and commandeering a police van, they falsely arrested Calvo Sotelo, took him for a midnight ride and shot him, then dumped his corpse in the morgue. Shocked, Azaña promised to find and punish the culprits. The army conspirators went into action and set Saturday afternoon, July 17, for the rising in Spanish Morocco, to be followed on Sunday by a rising in Spain. Franco agreed to join, and an airplane was hired in England to fly him to Morocco, where he was a hero to the Spanish Foreign Legion and Moroccan regulars. In Morocco, matters went smoothly for the insurgents. On Sunday from Tenerife, Franco broadcast to the nation the reasons why the army rebelled to save Spain from anarchy and destruction. On Monday he flew to join the Army of Africa in Morocco. Sanjurjo was not so lucky: Flying from Portugal to Spain, his plane crashed and he was killed.

In Spain, Mola and the Carlists quickly secured Navarre. In neighboring Aragón army insurgents seized Zaragoza from confused Republicans and workers. In Burgos and Valladolid junior officers executed Azaña's chosen commanders and gained control of Old Castile and León, a conservative region of middling farmers. In Galicia, a Republican stronghold, the insurgents posed as loyal Republicans determined to ensure order and seized the main centers, including the naval base of El Ferrol. Asturias, which the miners' unions dominated, proved not so easy. The army commander at Oviedo proclaimed for the Republic and armed detachments of miners, whom he sent by train to aid Madrid. When they left and Oviedo seemed lulled, he seized it for the insurgents with soldiers, police, and Civil Guards. In Seville, Queipo de Llano used armored cars and trucks to speed soldiers, guardsmen, and police to trouble spots and by radio told the stunned population that the army was in control. In Granada, as elsewhere, Falangists joined the insurgents, and as they seized the city, they took revenge on their enemies.

Alongside hundreds of leftists, union leaders, and militant workers, Falangists shot poet and playwright García Lorca for no good political reason but rather because he was "queer."

In Madrid, loyal officers distributed arms to workers despite the misgivings of authorities. The garrison was divided, and workers and loyal troops stormed the insurgents holed up in the Montaña Barracks. Some rebel officers committed suicide, and others were lynched before their former comrades could hustle them to prison. In Barcelona the rebellion neither enjoyed success, and General Manuel Goded, who had flown from Majorca to lead it, was arrested and forced to broadcast his submission and apologize to the nation. He was court-martialed and shot.

In Valencia the rebellion got nowhere, and an armed workers' junta emerged as the de facto government. In Bilbao the alert civil governor short-circuited the army plot and kept the Basque Country for the Republic. At the naval base of Cartagena, sailors overpowered their insurgent officers and gained control of the squadron there, including battleship *Jaime I*. They steamed into the Strait of Gibraltar to prevent Franco's Army of Africa from crossing to Spain.

The revolt took the government and most Spaniards by surprise. Many had started out on summer vacation. Azaña and Casares Quiroga now considered a government of national unity to include the Republican center and right, which Miguel de Maura had urged in June. Largo Caballero said no. When reached by telephone, Mola and other insurgent generals also said no. Casares Quiroga resigned, and Azaña appointed another crony, José Giral, as prime minister. But the government in Madrid had effectively lost control of things. In Catalonia, the Basque Country, Valencia, La Mancha, and Extremadura, local authorities and workers' juntas took charge. As in 1808, Spain became a federation of regions. Constituted authorities often found their powers usurped. In Madrid workers' councils, loyalist officers, and militias took matters into their own hands and ignored the municipal government. In Catalonia the CNT formed a junta with the UGT, the Communists, and the Catalan Left that eclipsed the Generalitat.

For the moment both sides assessed the situation, organized their resources, and considered their next moves. Crucial to the insurgents was getting the Army of Africa to Spain before loyal forces and armed workers crushed the insurrection. Both Hitler and Mussolini quickly saw advantages in aiding the insurgents, and a Nazi businessman in Morocco arranged for Junkers transport planes to airlift Franco's troops to Spain. Between July 28 and August 5, 15,000 troops and their equipment landed at Seville's airport. Mussolini sent Franco warplanes, and the Junkers also served as bombers. They attacked the Republican navy in the Strait of Gibraltar and disabled *Jaime I*. By August 6, troopships safely carried men and munitions across the Strait.

The Madrid government sought aid from France, where Léon Blum's Popular Front government held power. At first supportive, Blum found that the British had little sympathy with developments in Spain and preferred to keep out. Because France had to maintain its bonds with Britain in the face of Hitler's Germany, Blum acquiesced and, on August 8, closed the Franco-Spanish border. The British and French Allies promoted non-intervention and attempted to quarantine Spain from foreign aid. Nor did the United States wish to get involved. Republican Spain soon discovered that only Stalin's Soviet Union would provide material aid and in late August received Stalin's first ambassador. The Soviet Union, Nazi Germany, and Fascist Italy only paid lip service to the Allies' call to quarantine Spain.

Mola consolidated the insurgent position and at Burgos formed a junta to provide government. Most regional authorities and judges acquiesced and continued to provide law and order. Mola moved quickly against Madrid and reached the passes of the Sierra de Guadarrama, where loyalist troops and Madrid's militias stopped him. In Toledo Republican militias besieged over 1,000 insurgents in the Alcázar. By late August they had artillery in action, but the insurgents fought on, even after the commander's son was put on the telephone to tell his father he would be shot if the Alcázar did not surrender. The father told him to die for Spain. He did.

In Madrid, Azaña tried desperately to provide a government to which Republican Spain could rally and convinced Largo Caballero that in the present emergency he should accept the post of prime minister. At the beginning of September Largo Caballero, aged sixty-nine, formed a government that included five Socialists, three left Republicans, a Catalan Leftist, two Communists, and a crypto-Communist. For arms credit and safekeeping, Socialist Finance Minister Juan Negrín sent most of Spain's gold reserves to the Soviet Union, where Stalin kept them.

The attention of both sides focused on Toledo's Alcázar. Franco with his Army of Africa had battled through Extremadura toward Toledo. He met fierce resistance from Republican militias at Badajoz, where his Moroccans shocked the world when they herded perhaps 2,000 loyalist captives into the bullring and machine-gunned them to death. Franco reached Toledo on September 28 and relieved the Alcázar. On October 1, the Burgos junta acknowledged Franco as head of state and *generalísimo* of the insurgent forces, who began to style themselves Nationalists.

Spain had divided in civil war, and then and since people have asked why. The answers tend to be long and complex and can occupy a book such as *The Spanish Labyrinth* by Gerald Brenan, written at the time and still as

good as any. It is difficult now in the material comfort of a developed economy to catch the fervor of those days. Our narrative reveals a Spain economically not among the most advanced countries of Europe or America,
yet affected by the same intellectual and economic currents. What seemed
too much grinding poverty existed beside not enough obvious progress.
Flowery and inflammatory political rhetoric exacerbated differences. Too
many believed that they knew the cure for all of Spain's ills, be it anarchism,
fascism, free enterprise, Marxism, monarchy, or traditional Catholicism.
They knew Spain's enemies, whether anarchists, atheists, the army, the
Church, Communists, Fascists, Freemasons, Jews, Monarchists, or Reds.
What had traditionally been jocular if impudent relationships between rich
and poor had soured: Too many rich in thoughtless moments compared the
poor to animals, and the barely literate poor perceived the rich as heartless
oppressors, the Church and police as their henchmen. Too few sought the
center. Miguel de Unamuno, who favored the insurgents, warned them
against intransigence and anti-intellectualism and was publicly humiliated.
Only the intervention of Franco's wife, Doña Carmen Polo de Franco, saved
him from angry soldiers and Falangists. He died a broken man soon after.
But was civil war inevitable? Might it have been avoided? Even those involved do not agree on the answer, although a few admit that a compromise
here or there might have helped.

In October, from their positions in the sierras and Toledo, Nationalists
under General José Varela commenced the siege of Madrid. It would be
taken, Mola boasted, by four columns of Nationalist soldiers and—in a term
that has enriched our language—a "fifth column" of supporters inside the
capital. Italian and German bombers bombed Madrid, concentrating on
workers' barrios, and Russian fighters rose to defend it. President Azaña,
and soon after Largo Caballero and the government, headed for the security
of Valencia, while a member of the Spanish Communist politburo, Dolores
Ibárruri, used radio to rally Madrid's Republican defenders with fiery
speeches that earned her the name "La Pasionaria." Into Madrid behind
Russian tanks marched the International Brigades, recruited worldwide
through Communist parties, to join the local militias. Some were veterans of
the Great War, others idealistic students. In bloody fighting vividly reported
in the world press, Madrid held, under the leadership of General José Miaja
and Colonel Vicente Rojo of his staff. A desultory siege of over two years followed. Although Madrid was not cut off from Valencia till the last days of
the war, supply became difficult and life was hard.

Nationalist hope of swift victory evaporated at Madrid, though Italy and
Germany recognized Franco's government. The Nationalists held almost
half the country. Among the rich, the middle classes, small farmers, and de-

vout Catholics they enjoyed warm support, but much of the poorer population remained sullen and resistant. Police, aided by Falangists and in the north by Carlists, terrorized perceived enemies and executed thousands of the most dangerous, including teachers, journalists, and labor leaders. However, in the Nationalist zone, which included the granaries of Old Castile and enjoyed an open border with friendly Portugal through which commerce flowed, most people had at least the bare necessities of life.

On the Republican side, anarchists and Socialist extremists spontaneously commenced a social revolution in July 1936 and began to eliminate their enemies. They murdered nearly 7,000 Catholic clergy, including almost 300 nuns. They murdered hundreds of landlords and factory owners, foremen, technicians, and policemen and caused most of the rest to hide or flee. They collectivized industries and large estates and ran them with workers' councils that sometimes included former owners who had been kind to labor and technicians who settled for the same wages as the others. For anarchists and extreme Socialists it was a heady experience and, as goods and food were still more or less produced, apparent proof that a proletarian paradise was possible. Yet over time, production, hampered by shortages of raw material and rivalries of competing unions, became chaotic, and food and basic necessities became increasingly scarce.

Among the leftist idealists who flocked to Spain to fight for the Republic was George Orwell, a onetime British policeman in Burma turned Socialist. Orwell joined the militia formed by the Workers' Party of Marxist Unification (POUM—Partido Obrero de Unificación Marxista) and in his *Homage to Catalonia* (1938) extols the excitement of those days. War correspondents and photographers swarmed over the Spanish landscape and provided a horrified world with dramatic stories and unforgettable images. In countries with a free press, most conservatives, Catholics, and Fascist-sympathizers favored the Nationalists, whereas most liberals, Socialists, and Communists favored the Republic. There was little middle ground though most preferred to leave the fighting to the Spaniards. Burdened with world depression, people had not forgotten the Great War yet feared another. Totalitarian regimes booming bellicose rhetoric ruled Germany, Italy, and the Soviet Union. The League of Nations lacked teeth. In 1935 Mussolini's Italy conquered Ethiopia and broke with its former allies Britain and France. Partners in Spain, Mussolini and Hitler would form the Rome-Berlin Axis to which militarist Japan soon adhered.

In Spain during the winter of 1936–1937, both Nationalists and Republicans focused on training and prepared for a long war. The main front between the two sides (see Map 4) began at the Pyrenees in Aragón and ran south past Nationalist-held Zaragoza and Teruel, then looped west to Re-

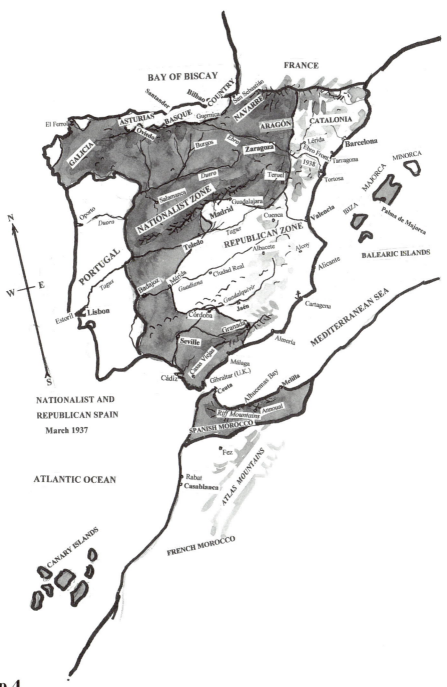

BAY OF BISCAY

FRANCE

Santander
Bilbao
BASQUE
COUNTRY
San Sebastián

NAVARRE

CATALONIA

El Ferrol
ASTURIAS
BASQUE
Guernica
ARAGÓN

Oviedo

Lérida

Barcelona

GALICIA
Burgos
Ebro
Zaragoza
Ebro Front
1938
Tarragona

MINORCA

Duero
Teruel
Tortosa

MAJORCA

Oporto
Salamanca
NATIONALIST ZONE
Guadalajara

Palma de Majorca

Duoro

Madrid

Cuenca

Valencia

IBIZA

N

REPUBLICAN ZONE

Tagus

BALEARIC ISLANDS

Toledo
Albacete
Alcoy

PORTUGAL
Ciudad Real

Alicante

W   E
Tagus
Badajoz
Mérida
Guadiana
Guadalquivir

Cartagena

Estoril
Lisbon
Córdoba
Jaén

MEDITERRANEAN SEA

S
Granada
Almería

Seville
Casas Viejas

Cádiz
Málaga

Gibraltar (U.K.)
Alhucemas Bay
Melilla

NATIONALIST AND
Ceuta
Annoual

REPUBLICAN SPAIN
Riff Mountains

March 1937
SPANISH MOROCCO

ATLANTIC OCEAN
Fez

ATLAS MOUNTAINS

Rabat
Casablanca

CANARY ISLANDS
FRENCH MOROCCO

Map 4

publican Madrid, then arced south again through La Mancha, where Republicans held Ciudad Real, and into Andalusia, where the Nationalists clung to Córdoba and Granada and Málaga (taken in February). The Republicans held Jaén and Murcia. The Basque Country stood for the Republic but was cut off, even from France, when Mola's people took Irún. San Sebastián was abandoned to avoid destruction. In Asturias, Nationalist Oviedo lay under siege. Franco's best formation, the Army of Africa, suffered heavy casualties against the defenses of Madrid, and his Falangist militiamen needed training. Italian "volunteer" regulars shored up the Nationalist front and spearheaded the capture of Málaga, where they were appalled by the number of people Falangists executed after its capture. On the Republican side reigned high enthusiasm and hatred of the Nationalists, but anarchists and extreme Socialists had problems accepting discipline and a command structure. In Alicante the local governor had Falangist chief José Antonio Primo de Rivera shot, after his trial and conviction, without waiting for Largo Caballero in Valencia to approve the sentence.

In the Republican government, middle-class Left Republicans did not like the wholesale appropriation of private property by anarchists and extreme-socialists, though small proprietors and professionals were seldom affected. Both Left Republicans and the Stalinist Communist Party, whose membership had jumped from 20,000 when the war began to more than 200,000, despaired of the lack of discipline. Both worried about the alienation of public opinion in the Western democracies and wanted an end to the British and French Allies' arms embargo, which they felt unjust when applied to a recognized regime. Spanish Communists also knew that Stalin desired an alliance with Britain and France against Hitler. Largo Caballero agreed that discipline and restraint were necessary if the Republic was to win, but neither he nor his PSOE wanted Stalinist communism in Spain. Given his prestige, the Communists and their Soviet advisers decided to get rid of him.

Anarchists and extreme Marxist parties such as the POUM opposed any call for discipline and restraint. Although anarchist leaders had put principle aside and joined government, they still believed it possible to win the war and carry out a social revolution simultaneously. Over their objections, Largo Caballero, who was also war minister, incorporated the party militias into the regular Republican army. By then, many officers who stood by the Republic in 1936 had defected to the Nationalist side. More and more who remained joined the Communist Party, which stressed needed discipline.

Largo Caballero and the Communists did agree on the return of power from the juntas that appeared in July 1936 to constituted governments. By May 1937, Catalonia's Generalitat, had recovered much of its power from the workers' junta, weakened by internal quarrels, and ordered police to take control of the Barcelona telephone exchange building, which had been in the hands of the CNT since July 1936. Fighting erupted, and in streets, plazas, and buildings the CNT, POUM and various youth groups battled policemen, Communists, and units of the Republican army. The CNT was humbled and the POUM destroyed. POUM leader Andrés Nín was later tortured and killed by secret police, and George Orwell barely escaped Spain with his life.

Largo Caballero despaired over the tragic events in Barcelona. The Communists called him an old man out of touch with reality. When he persisted in his own war strategy, to attack in Extremadura and cut Nationalist Spain in two, the Communists enlisted General Miaja, the hero of Madrid, against him. They demanded that Azaña relieve him of the war ministry, which precipitated his resignation as prime minister. With Communist input, Azaña made moderate Socialist Juan Negrín prime minister. Before entering politics, Negrín had been a professor of physiology. To the world the Republic presented the respectable bourgeois front Stalin thought necessary to win British and French support, while the Communists extended their control over the police and army. Britain and France maintained the embargo, which Hitler, Mussolini, and Stalin subscribed to but ignored. Mussolini had already put 100,000 men into Spain, and the Portuguese border was like a sieve. Hitler had no difficulty sending his Condor Legion of aircraft, artillery, and tanks to Spain, but Stalin found it increasingly difficult to get arms to the Republic. The munitions supply from Russia dropped off after mid-1937. British and French diplomacy seemed governed chiefly by anticommunism and the hope that Hitler would in time attack or neutralize Stalin. The United States hid behind its Neutrality Act and revoked the passports of Americans who enlisted in the Abraham Lincoln Brigade to fight for the Republic. However, oil was not embargoed, and Texaco continued its shipments to the Spanish state oil and gasoline monopoly, which the Nationalists had taken over in their conquest of Andalusia.

In mid-1937 the Nationalists attacked Vizcaya and Asturias, defended mainly by militias. Between Catholic Basques, who fought for home rule, and leftist Asturian miners, there was little in common. Nationalist forces concentrated first against Vizcaya. Nazi bombers shocked the world in April 1937 with their destruction of the historic town of Guernica, to which Pablo Picasso responded with his memorable painting. In June the Nationalists marched into Bilbao. Although some Basque politicians and priests were executed by Falangists, there were fewer atrocities by either side in the Basque Country than elsewhere. Even though the Basques lost their autonomy, Franco wanted to harness Basque industry and finance to the Nationalist cause. But the victors never understood why Catholic Basques fought for the Republic and in the following years did all they could to destroy the spirit of Basque nationalism. Franco next took Santander, then Asturias, inflicting bloody reprisals on the miners. By the end of 1937, despite guerrilla activity, Asturias, Galicia, and the Basque Country lay in Nationalist hands.

Franco planned to capture Madrid next. After a plane crash killed Mola, he was the undisputed leader of the Nationalist cause. The Republicans anticipated his plan and in December, after delays caused by a strike, launched an attack on Teruel, which they took in fierce fighting. Franco abandoned the planned assault on Madrid and shifted people to counter the tired Republicans at Teruel. With air superiority and heavy equipment, he recovered Teruel and struck toward Valencia. The Republicans fought bravely, only to have a sudden attack shatter their fragile discipline and lead to bloody rout. In April 1938 Franco's forces reached the mouth of the Ebro to cut Catalonia from the rest of the Republic. The Republicans prepared a counterattack. Léon Blum briefly reopened the French border, and material aid from northern Europe and munitions from Russia flowed to Spain. Juan Negrín tried to rally the population and restored limited worship to Catholics. To the world he reasserted the Republic's commitment to civil liberties and the League of Nations. But the bourgeois face the Republic showed the world disillusioned most leftists other than Communists, who consolidated their well-camouflaged grip on the Republic's government.

The Republican counterattack opened at night on July 24, 1938, in rugged country along the lower Ebro. It quickly bogged down when the Nationalists opened dams upriver that caused flooding. With planes, tanks, and artillery, the Nationalists ground down the Republicans in a series of head-on battles that cost both sides 40,000 men and provoked criticism of Franco, who chose not to attempt the Republican flank and strike for Barcelona. Mussolini became impatient. Negrín, hoping to win international support for a negotiated settlement, disbanded the International Brigades and in September 1938 flew to Switzerland and met secretly with Franco supporters. Franco was not prepared to compromise. A few days later in Munich, the British and French governments sacrificed Czechoslovakia to appease Hitler and avoid war. Stalin would have to make his own arrangements with Hitler; Spain mattered less.

On December 23, 350,000 Nationalists attacked some 90,000 bedraggled Republicans on the Ebro front. In mid-January they marched into Tarragona. Panic swept Catalonia; hundreds of thousands fled for France. On January 22, with scarcely a shot fired, the Nationalists entered Barcelona, which they looted for three days before order was imposed. At the beginning of February, Azaña, Negrín, Companys, and a half million others trudged into France on foot. Piled high were the surrendered rifles of Republican soldiers. The Nationalists soon sealed the border.

Negrín flew back to Valencia in late February, while Britain and France recognized Franco's regime. In France, Azaña resigned as president, and his designated successor refused to take office. Now utterly dependent on the loyalty of the Communists, Negrín promoted Communist officers to head the Republic's remaining armed forces. A confused mutiny broke out in the navy, and in hungry Madrid, veteran Colonel Segismundo Casado pronounced against the Communists and government. Madrid's Republican defenders fell to fighting among themselves, and Republican forces from Ciudad Real marched to support Casado. On March 5, Negrín fled for France. Casado capitulated to the Nationalists, and on March 30, they marched into Madrid. Everywhere Republican forces raised the white flag of surrender, and on April 1, 1939, Franco proclaimed total victory.

11

Dictatorship

Passions have not yet cooled about the dictatorship of Generalísimo Francisco Franco that would endure until 1975. At the beginning of the Civil War he was the most respected general in the Spanish army, whose support Sanjurjo and Mola wanted. He had taken no public political stance, although his private correspondence reveals concern for the direction taken by the Republic. He subscribed to a journal full of warnings about Communist designs and the role of Freemasons and Jews. During the Civil War, he developed a sense that Divine Providence had chosen him to save Spain from atheism and anarchy, which his wife further inspired. Sanjurjo and Mola died in accidents, leaving him head of the Nationalist cause. Franco refused to consider a compromise peace with Republican leaders he believed responsible for Spain's plight.

While Spain's upper and middle classes rallied to the Nationalists where they could, and the Church provided wholehearted support, Franco found the greatest commitment for his cause among Falangists and Carlists, who already had paramilitary organizations. Because Falange founder José Antonio Primo de Rivera had been jailed and executed, his disciples competed for leadership of the party. For their Syndicalist social policy and anticapitalist rhetoric, many Nationalists called them "our Reds," although Falangist doctrine was akin to Fascism and Naziism, without irreligion or Nazi racism. Franco turned for political advice to his wife's brother, Ramón Serrano Suñer, a successful lawyer once active in the CEDA, who had known José Antonio in their school days. In the days of his highest influence, Serrano Suñer became known as *cuñadísimo* (most high brother-in-law). Franco and Serrano deftly manipulated the factious Falangist leadership and pressured the reluctant and less numerous Carlists to merge into a single national party, the Falange Española Tradicionalista (FET—Spanish Traditionalist Falange). Making army officers members, Franco was acclaimed party chief or caudillo (leader, like "duce" for Mussolini and "führer" for Hitler) and fell into step with his Italian and German allies. As Mussolini's Fascists wore black shirts and Nazis wore brown shirts, the Falange had adopted the blue shirt. Although Franco's apparent posture as a Fascist hardly went well in Britain, France, and the United States, the two Allies were more concerned with Hitler and Stalin, and the United States with the depression.

Franco waged the Civil War with cold ruthlessness, but as his Nationalists advanced, he made sure food followed for the war's hungry victims, to feed and placate them. When he declared the war over on April 1, 1939, Spain lay in ruins. While "One Million Dead" from a population of some 25 million, became the popular figure for the loss of human life, historians have yet to settle on a final figure and probably will not until the passions on both side are spent. During the war, over 100,000 died in battle, from some 1.5 million mobilized by both sides. Political murders and mass slaughters may account for 20,000 people on the political right and well over 100,000 on the left. When the war ended, Franco remained unforgiving. For those who fought for or served the Republic, there was no amnesty. Perhaps 200,000 perished from exhaustion in forced labor or neglect in concentration camps in the first five years after the war or were executed. If these are added to the war dead, the total dead reaches a half million or more. The majority of prisoners were eventually released and returned home broken men.

Over a half million people fled Spain, and under 200,000 returned, some voluntarily, some forcibly repatriated after the fall of France in 1940 to Hitler. Azaña died in France. Largo Caballero was sent to a Nazi prison, whence he was liberated in 1945; soon after he died in Paris. Negrín escaped France for the United States. Other refugees escaped to Spanish America. Alcalá Zamora died in Buenos Aires. Most Spanish intellectuals and artists also chose exile. Diplomat Salvador de Madariaga settled in London and wrote *Spain: A Modern History*, a moving personal account. Medievalist Claudio Sánchez Albornoz taught in Buenos Aires. Poet Juan Ramón Jiménez settled in Puerto Rico. Salvador Dalí fled Paris in 1940 for Greenwich Village. Flamenco star Carmen Amaya danced for Allied troops during World War II, although she eventually returned to Spain. Cellist Pablo Casals established a music festival at Prades, a French sliver of Catalonia in the Pyrenees, and refused to set foot on Spanish soil while Franco lived. When he once had to change airliners in Barcelona, bemused Spanish attendants carried him to his next flight.

Franco's Spain was, its motto proclaimed, "Una, Gran, Libre" (unitary, great, free). Catalan autonomy was ended, the Catalan language forbidden in the press, public address, publishing, and schools. Even Catalonia's dance, the *sardana*, was forbidden. When the Vichy French government in 1940 extradited former Catalan president Lluys Companys to Spain, he was tried, convicted, and executed for treason. The Basques likewise lost their autonomy.

In Spain, the politics of Franco's regime became Byzantine, insider intrigue with little public dimension save for staged rallies and military parades. Generals, Falangists, old-line Conservatives, church leaders, and technocrats around Franco debated what course Spain should take. Historians sometimes refer to these interest groups as "families." Franco reshuffled cabinets from time to time, to keep Hitler and Mussolini happy, to maintain a discrete balance between the army and the Falangists, and to placate the Church. Franco listened to criticism but invariably had the last word. He adroitly promoted and demoted ministers and moved generals to one post or another to keep them under control without losing their loyalty. His authoritarian regime consciously depoliticized Spain's people. All the political liveliness of the years after 1808 disappeared. Noisy conversation in cafes and cafeterias settled on harmless issues like football, bullfights, and movie actresses. Spanish movies focused on the glories of Spain's past and were only relieved by Mexican comedies and westerns. Using ghostwriters, Franco himself wrote a novel, *La Raza* (*The Race*), whose hero was a thinly disguised version of himself. It was made into a film.

For local government, Franco used municipal regimes that were appointive rather than elective. Finding reliable civil servants was not always easy, and army officers frequently filled civil administration posts. A new national police force for guarding urban areas and government institutions, the Armed Police (*policia armada*), replaced the Assault Guards. To police rural Spain, the Civil Guard was enlarged. For ordinary crime and traffic control, each municipality had its municipal police force.

By 1939 Spanish production and income had dropped dramatically below the levels of 1936, inflation soared, and the peseta lost further value in international exchange, in part owing to Franco's determination to keep it artificially high. Fields lay fallow; half the livestock had perished. Roads, railroads, and bridges had been shelled, bombed, and neglected. A third or more of Spanish railroad equipment, trucks, and private automobiles had been lost. Bombardment destroyed entire blocks in many cities and damaged factories and dock facilities. Factory workers were sullen in defeat. Landless field hands, back to starvation wages and the tender mercies of landlords and the Civil Guard, were bitter. Protests about sorry conditions sometimes came from left-leaning members of the Falange and chastened Catholic clergy, who realized they needed to pay more heed to Christ's poor. Because Europe once more stressed arms production, Spain had to turn to Latin America for food supplies, with little credit to pay for them.

At Burgos in 1938 Franco had promulgated a Law of Labor, based on the Falangist ideal of corporate syndicalism that brought owners, management, and workers together by industry and stressed a fair share of profits for all. Twenty-nine national syndicates represented manufacturing, public utilities, transportation, and agriculture, while professionals were grouped into approved associations. A modest social security system for factory workers was established. The first ministers of labor were Falangists who took their ideals seriously. Complaints by management soon got them replaced by less zealous ministers. To feed his side during the Civil War Franco extended government authority over grain production. Though secure in their property, landowners were unhappy with regulation. While the regime talked of rural reconstruction, encouraged cooperatives, and established agricultural colonies on uncultivated land, life remained grim for the landless in zones of latifundios. Some small gains were made by building dams and providing improved irrigation in arid regions, but a shortage of capital prevented greater development.

On one subject the Nationalists agreed with the Republicans, that Spain needed a better educational system, but they differed over what that meant. For two generations Giner's Free Institution for Education had set the tone for instruction; now it was shut down. The Republicans wanted the Catholic religion out; the Nationalists made religious instruction central. Education Minister Juan Ibáñez Martín, a conservative Catholic, repaired and built schools as best he could with little money. By law, all children between ages six and twelve received a free education, segregated once more by sex where it was feasible. For years after the war, schoolteachers remained in short supply, and army officers taught reading and writing to illiterate recruits from remote villages. Religious orders and above all the Jesuits again dominated secondary education, although the government revived *colegios mayores* in the old university towns as elite state-run residential colleges. At the university level, where students specialized, the regime concentrated on the University of Madrid and rebuilt the Ciudad Universitaria that had been a battlefield during the war. Of Spain's university professors, more than half fled or were killed in the Civil War. Only a few of the more distinguished, such as septuagenarian Ramón Menéndez Pidal, remained. It took years to rebuild the stature of Spain's faculties, although bright Spaniards persisted in scholarly and scientific activities. In the humanities, scholars concentrated on research fields that were safe and avoided modern intellectual and political controversies. The star was Catalan historian Jaime Vicens Vives, who brought the new methodologies of French social and economic historians to his work and to students at the University of Barcelona. Spanish scholars did receive support from the Superior Council of Scientific Research (CSIC—Consejo Superior de Investigaciones Científicas), which replaced former Republican institutions for the promotion of research.

In the constructive work of the Franco regime, a clandestine, Catholic, and to some, sinister organization had a hand: Opus Dei (Work of God). Founded by a conservative priest, José María Escrivá de Balaguer, it received in 1941 recognition from the bishop of Madrid, and in 1950 from the Vatican. Escrivá urged on its members an austere life dedicated to moral improvement, personal achievement, and doing good. While its leaders were priests, most members were well-educated and often wealthy laymen, who became increasingly important in the later years of the Franco regime. They also took the lead in education.

To deal with Spain's disrupted manufacturing, a successful businessman and boyhood friend of Franco, Juan Antonio Suanzes, took charge and held office until 1963. It proved no easy task, especially after Franco's nationalization of Spain's railroad network frightened many Spanish and foreign investors. No economist, Franco thought in terms of autarchy, a self-sufficient Spain not dependent on imports or foreign credit. Once Europe went to war in September 1939, conditions in Spain went from bad to desperate. He maintained an obedient army of 500,000 men to keep public order and workers working, at near starvation levels for most.

Five months after the end of Spain's Civil War, World War II erupted. Mussolini and Hitler counted on Franco while the Allies courted him. Franco favored the Axis powers but knew that Spain was in no position to go to war. He declared Spain's official neutrality and waited on events. Hitler conquered Poland and then overwhelmed France in the spring of 1940. Mussolini joined him. Great Britain was isolated, and Hitler urged Franco to come in. Spanish ports would allow German submarines to extend their operations against Britain, and Spain would give Hitler's army access to Gibraltar. Franco was eager enough and changed Spain's international posture from neutrality to nonbelligerence, in favor of the Axis. Spain, he insisted, would need considerable help before going to war. He prepared a laundry list of railroad stock, transport and heavy equipment, arms and munitions for his army, and food for his hungry people. Moreover, he wanted Spain to supplant France in French Morocco and western Algeria. Hitler met with Franco at Hendaye on the French frontier in October 1940, but nothing was settled. At the end of the nine-hour meeting, Hitler admitted he would rather have three or four teeth pulled than talk with Franco again. Not only did Hitler have little materiel to spare for Spain, but the Vichy government in unoccupied France proved useful to Nazi aims. Hitler did not want to make an issue of French North Africa. Serrano Suñer met Hitler in Germany in November and reiterated what Franco had asked, while Franco remarked to German envoys in Madrid that he dared not provoke the British navy since Spain had to import vital foodstuffs from Latin America and the United States. Hitler began to doubt Franco's reliability and canceled the planned German march through Spain to Gibraltar. Although some in Berlin talked of invading Spain, they remembered the disaster Spain had proved for Napoleon.

Hitler hoped that Mussolini could yet persuade Franco to enter the war. Franco repeated his case to Mussolini in February 1941 at Bordighera on the Italian Riviera. By then the British had won the Battle of Britain and stopped the Italians in North Africa. Mussolini acknowledged Franco's need for massive assistance and advised Hitler that for the time being it seemed best simply to keep Franco in the Axis camp. On his return journey, Franco met with Vichy leaders at Montpellier. Although Vichy returned to Spain documents and art looted by Napoleon, it refused concessions in North Africa.

Later German victories in the Balkans reassured Franco, who cheered the German invasion of Stalin's Soviet Union in June 1941. Falangists clamored for a Spanish declaration of war. Franco allowed the formation of a volunteer Spanish "Blue Division," which the Germans equipped, to fight alongside the Nazis in Russia. General Augustín Muñoz Grandes, a 1937 convert to Falangism, commanded.

In December 1941, the United States entered the war, and by the summer of 1942 an Axis victory seemed less certain. In July Franco issued a Law of the Cortes, which reestablished a representative assembly, although its membership was determined by the Falange, the army, the Church, and loyal corporate bodies. He also permitted limited elections for municipal governments. In November, U.S. and British forces invaded French North Africa, the Germans occupied Vichy France, and French forces overseas joined the Allies. Franco returned Spain to strict neutrality. By May 1945, the Allies had won in Europe. They no longer had to deal circumspectly with Franco and linked him with Hitler and Mussolini. While Stalin was most vociferous, Britain's new Labor prime minister Clement Atlee and U.S. President Harry Truman agreed that Franco's regime should be replaced before

Spain could join the newly formed United Nations. In response, in July Franco published his Law of the Rights of Spaniards, a list of civil rights with emphasis on obligations and obedience to authority. Spain was Catholic, though tolerant of the private practice of other faiths, the family was central to Spanish society, and labor was to be respected. The term *National Movement*, though in use since 1936, now began to supplant Falange Española Tradicionalista for the official political party.

The diplomatic offensive against Franco grew. France closed its border with Spain, although Spanish Communist guerrillas sneaked across it to fight Franco's soldiers. A Spanish government in exile formed, with José Giral as president. Despite a show of unity, fissures soon appeared between his Republicans, Prieto's Socialists, disgruntled monarchists, Gil Robles's Catholics, and assorted Communists, many settled in Moscow. The pretender to the throne, Don Juan, count of Barcelona, issued a declaration at Lausanne, Switzerland, that called for Franco to step down and restore constitutional monarchy. Several generals held secret talks with him. The United Nations accepted a Mexican resolution, pushed by Spanish exiles, that all members withdraw their ambassadors from Madrid until Spain had a more democratic government.

In Spain the regime orchestrated large rallies to demonstrate support for Franco and denounce foreign meddling in Spain's internal affairs. To appeal to the Catholic world, Franco stressed Spain's Catholicism and downplayed the role of the Falange. He made Alberto Martín Artajo, a devout Catholic, foreign minister and evoked the idea of Hispanidad (Spanishness, in the sense of a shared culture) to woo Spanish America. He called UN attacks on Spain's human rights record hypocritical and pointed at Stalin's tyranny in the Soviet Union and the Communist takeover of eastern Europe. As the Cold War developed, Franco touted his own credentials as an anti-Communist and in a new coinage that bore his likeness proclaimed himself "Caudillo by the Grace of God."

The conditions of life in Spain, as elsewhere in Europe, remained harsh, and in the spring of 1947 a series of strikes and demonstrations rippled through the Basque Country, Catalonia, Madrid, El Ferrol, and the depressed rural south. The United States, in response to the widespread misery of postwar Europe and the threat of Soviet communism, unveiled the Marshall Plan for economic recovery but did not include Spain. President Harry Truman harbored a vehement dislike of the Spanish dictator. Diplomatically isolated and short on credit, the Franco government found a friend in Argentine dictator Juan Perón, who provided Spain with vital foodstuffs. That summer Argentine first lady, Evita Perón, payed a state visit to Madrid and added glamour to the lavish ceremonies Franco arranged.

In July 1947 Franco proclaimed Spain a Catholic and representative constitutional monarchy in another effort to win international respectability. He formed a Council of Regency, which would choose a king from the Bourbon dynasty to replace him when he died. For representation he had already provided a pliant Cortes. Franco's constitutional monarchy was overwhelmingly approved by Spain's voters in a plebiscite that outside observers called a farce. It did not get the approval of the pretender Don Juan, who rebuffed Franco's envoys sent to Estoril, Portugal, where he had moved to be closer to Spain.

Franco did not give up, and in the summer of 1948, Don Juan agreed to meet him in secret. Franco sailed aboard his yacht to fish in the Bay of Biscay, where Don Juan sailed in his yacht to meet him. Franco shed effusive tears as he greeted Alfonso XIII's heir, but he drove a hard bargain. He made no promises about a restoration but persuaded Don Juan to permit his ten-year-old heir Juan Carlos to be educated in Spain. That November Juan Carlos arrived in Spain to begin his tutelage under Franco's supervision. While there has been much speculation about its nature, its story remains to be told. Although Don Juan had surrendered his son to Franco, he played a significant role in his son's upbringing. But with Juan Carlos in Spain, Franco no longer feared a monarchist plot.

Franco did not give up on his efforts to win the support of the United States. He sent suave diplomat José Félix de Lequeria to Washington as an "Inspector of Embassies" after the Truman administration dubbed him a Fascist and refused to accredit him as ambassador. New York's Francis Cardinal Spellman, conservative U.S. senators and representatives, and many business executives were duly impressed and came to favor full diplomatic relations with Franco's Spain. Late in 1948, Franco proposed that Spanish bases might prove useful to U.S. naval and air forces in the Cold War. Given Spain's poverty, he fixed a high price. In early 1949 the United States and its World War II western Allies formed the North Atlantic Treaty Organization (NATO) for mutual defense against the Soviet Union. Portugal joined, but the European democratic left would not consider Franco. A late 1949 visit by Franco to Portugal reaffirmed the bonds between him and Salazar. The wedding in 1950 of Franco's daughter to the marquis of Villaverde, a physician, took place on a royal scale.

Though Franco had achieved some success in winning friends in the United States, Spain remained isolated and impoverished. Even as much of western Europe could ease up on the rationing of food and vital supplies, Spain could not. The population had grown slightly since the end of the Civil War, but reconstruction lagged. Around major cities shanty towns spread. Prices were seven times what they had been in 1936 and still rising.

Government efforts to regulate the economy led to corruption, as entrepreneurs bribed officials for favors. The *enchufe* (connection) became important. With production and wages low and goods scarce, a black market flourished that charged outlandish prices for those who could afford to pay them and, worse, flaunt their wealth. Widespread misery could not be silenced in a people used to speaking their minds. Old-line Falangists, with their notions of corporate fairness, protested, and underground Communists printed leaflets that circulated widely. Businessmen angry with bureaucratic red tape and corruption bellowed their outrage and browbeat their cronies in government. The appearance of a socially conscious clergy led to calls for justice from the pulpit.

In the second half of 1950, following the outbreak of the Korean War, people talked seriously of a Soviet invasion of western Europe and wondered if NATO could repel it. The Pyrenees might become a battle front, and NATO, despite the misgivings of many, had to consider anti-Communist Spain as an ally. In November, the United Nations, prompted by the United States and Spain's Latin American friends, repealed their prohibition of ambassadorial relations with Spain. The United States allowed Franco a large loan.

It would take time for the loan to affect Spain's economy. In response to workers' protests about stagnant wages and rising prices, Franco admitted that Spain was a poor country and there was little to go around. In the spring, protests led to demonstrations and strikes. Although the government blamed underground leftists hankering for a Soviet victory, local issues most often provoked the outbreaks. Three hundred thousand people, reflecting most shades of opinion, paraded in Barcelona following an increase in tram fares, to protest corruption and conditions in general. In Madrid strikers boycotted government services and business and refused to ride public transit to their rallies. There were strikes in Bilbao. The army and police responded swiftly, but none could deny that political divisions in Spain remained deep. A fear that Spain might fall to the Communists or into civil war, which may seem far-fetched now but in 1951 seemed real enough, led to more loans and deals with Franco's government by U.S. business interests and serious talks about bases by U.S. admirals and generals. Franco reshuffled his cabinet to replace hard-liners with more accommodating men. Old Falangist Raimundo Martínez Cuesta, who favored labor, took charge of official political life as head of the National Movement. To improve relations with the outside world, a Ministry of Information and Tourism appeared. The notion of autarchy was scrapped, labor gained a greater voice in the syndicates, and conditions improved sufficiently by 1952 that Spain could end rationing.

Franco negotiated a new concordat with the Vatican in the summer of 1953, which reaffirmed that Spain was Roman Catholic, privileged the Church in education, and gave Franco the right to nominate bishops in Spain. In September 1953, the U.S. government of President Dwight Eisenhower signed a pact with Franco to establish U.S. air and naval bases on Spanish soil, over which both flags would fly. Backed by the United States, Spain began to participate in United Nations activities and in 1955 gained full membership. The next year, Spain ended its protectorate over Spanish Morocco, although by an agreement with the Moroccan government, it kept the enclaves of Ceuta and Melilla with their largely Spanish Christian populations. Over the next twenty years, Spain would surrender its few other African colonies.

With the U.S. military presence in Spain came more economic aid. Spain had foreign credit to improve its industry, although the archbishop of Toledo murmured that Franco was selling Spain's Catholic soul for U.S. Protestant dollars. Yet when Gerald Brenan returned to Spain in the mid-1950s, it still seemed impoverished. (From the author's own first experience of Spain in 1956 springs recollections of taxicabs that burned charcoal for fuel.) The indicators suggested, however, that matters were slowly improving. Spain's big banks became more efficient and more willing to make loans to stimulate economic activity. Foreign investment was again encouraged. Between 1950 and 1960 the number of active corporations increased by 50 percent and their worth tripled. Steel production was ten times what it had been in 1914. A Spanish train, the *Talgo* from Madrid to the French frontier, pioneered fast light-rail transport in Europe. Paved roads and electricity were reaching the most remote villages. Improved highways, with big Spanish-made Pegaso trucks barreling along them, joined telecommunications to quicken the process of forging a national economy. And at last there was money to build the schools long talked about.

Endless jostling to get a share of the growing wealth, coupled with a steep rate of inflation, sustained continued labor unrest. Spanish students, with the enthusiasm of the young, sided with labor. Some of them, through various grants, such as the Fulbright exchange of scholars with the United States, had studied abroad under freer conditions. Although the government offered scholarships to poor youths who showed promise, most students came from middle- and upper-class families that supported or at least accepted Franco, which meant that the government had to deal with them gingerly. In 1956 antigovernment demonstrations by students led to the arrest and trial of four prominent student leaders. Like an apparition from the past, José María Gil Robles, recently returned from exile, emerged to defend them. The token sentences they received were taken as a victory.

That year Franco again juggled his cabinet and appointed three members of Opus Dei, known for their expertise in economics: Alberto Ullastres to Commerce, Mariano Navarro Rubio to Finance, and Laureano López Rodo as assistant to Admiral Luis Carrero Blanco, Franco's right-hand man. With their vision of a free economy with a social conscience, the new ministry reduced government regulation and pushed the integration of Spain's economy into the larger economy of Europe. In a step hurtful to Franco's pride, they worked with the International Monetary Fund to reorganize the Spanish currency and devalued the peseta from PTA 42 to PTA 60 to U.S. $1. To help weather the painful period of readjustment, Spain received a $420 million U.S. loan. The government also liberalized its law for syndicates, and labor gained a stronger bargaining position in handling local disputes. Although strikes officially remained outlawed, they continued to occur.

In agriculture the new ministry continued irrigation programs and encouraged owners of scattered tiny plots of land to consolidate their holdings into fewer but larger and more viable plots. The larger agrarian problems of latifundios in the south or excessively small plots in the north that had long haunted Spain were gradually solved by migration rather than by any government act. The rural poor migrated to booming cities for better-paying jobs or became guest workers in France, Germany, and Switzerland, where labor was in demand. With a dwindling supply of labor for field-work, those who remained to do it demanded higher wages. Owners began to spend money on capital improvements that allowed fewer hands to become more productive. Between 1940 and 1960, the percentage of Spaniards employed in agriculture dropped from over 50 to barely 40 percent in a growing population. By 1975, agriculture employed only 25 percent.

When Franco proclaimed on April 1, 1964, "Twenty Five Years of Peace," Spain's rising prosperity was becoming evident almost everywhere. In Madrid, Barcelona, and other big cities, it became a game to watch license plate numbers rise through the 100,000s, indicating the increasing number of private cars on the streets. The devalued peseta not only encouraged exports by Spanish industry and agriculture but also invited tourism. Spain was a bargain for foreigners and retirees. On what the tourist ministry dubbed the Costa del Sol (Coast of the Sun), resorts sprung up near Málaga, such as Torremolinos, which gained a racy reputation with the young, and Marbella, which catered to the rich. Many retirees and year-round vacationers favored the Balearic Islands, or Alicante and Benidorm, south of Valencia. Summer holidays found the Costa Brava between Barcelona and the French border packed with Dutch, English, French, German, and Scandinavian vacationers, brought at first by tour bus and later by private car. New resort hotels and restaurants lined Spain's coasts, which wags dubbed the *costa concreta* (concrete coast). Not only were there jobs for construction workers; there was a demand for waiters, guides, clerks, and chambermaids. Young Spanish men and women came from distant villages to find summer work and mingle with foreigners and Spaniards from other parts of Spain.

To encourage travel in the interior, the tourist ministry established *paradores* (travelers' hotels) that provide comfortable lodgings, often in refurbished castles or monasteries, and set high standards meant to promote improvements in commercial hotels. Karl Baedeker's admonition in 1900 that decent hotels and restaurants could not be found outside Spain's chief cities ceased to be true. Bargain prices also brought foreign visitors to those cities, where they discovered the glories of the Prado Museum in Madrid, wondered at Gaudí's architecture in Barcelona, saw El Greco's paintings in Toledo, walked the gardens of the Alhambra in Granada, gasped at the splendor of the *mezquita* (mosque) in Córdoba, and climbed the Giralda Tower in Seville. Restaurants offered—and too often bastardized—paella, a Valencian peasant dish that became the national dish of Spain. Other regions had their specialties: Castile prized its roast suckling pig and lamb; Andalusia, its cold soup, gazpacho, Navarre, its trout with mountain ham. Coastal Spain lavished its attention on seafood.

To entertain tourists in a Spain advertised abroad as "different," uniquely Spanish spectacles flourished. Flamenco dancing enjoyed a golden moment as a high art form. Just before she died in 1962, Carmen Amaya partnered with Antonio Gades in the brilliant film *Los Tarantos*. The team of Antonio and Rosario dazzled audiences in capitals and leading resorts, and troupes of less famous dancers, singers, and guitarists brought money into the Spanish gypsy community. Folkloric dances shared the stage, as costumed young men bounded for swirling ladies in lively jotas or stately *castellanas*. In university towns young men formed groups called *tunas* and, clad in sixteenth-century costume, sang traditional songs for tourists and locals in restaurants and on terraces (sidewalk cafes). Guitarist Andrés Segovia had made a classic instrument of the Spanish guitar, for which Joaquín Rodrigo wrote his brilliant and popular *Concierto de Aranjuez*. To the despair of humane societies, bullfighting also boomed. Although the great Manolete fell to a bull in provincial Linares in 1947, Dominguín carried the pure style of the bullfight into the 1960s, while a new generation headed by photogenic El Cordobés took a more flamboyant approach that appealed to the younger set and tourists.

Tourism and Spaniards working abroad had as profound an effect on Spain as did the increased availability of primary education, which dropped the illiteracy level from about 25 percent in the 1930s to less than 12 percent by 1960 and less than 5 percent by 1970. Spain became integrated into the life of Europe as never before, and Spaniards found the dictatorship with its censorship and restriction of political and labor union activity an embarrassment. Yet Franco retained powerful support from the army and rightist political groups, and most agreed that he provided stability. However, under foreign prodding as well as his awareness that things in Spain were changing, Franco and his government eased up on restrictions, although occasional crackdowns reminded people of Franco's determination to destroy all that he believed caused the Civil War. In 1962 technocrat and Opus Dei member Manuel Fraga Iribarne, aged forty, became minister of information and tourism and worked to ease restrictions on publishing. In 1966 a new press law limited prior censorship, though newspapers remained cautious in what they printed. Once more the plays of García Lorca graced the Spanish stage. The public image of Franco began to change from that of the stern soldier to that of the grandfather. He wore civilian clothes and was often pictured with his wife, daughter, and grandchildren.

For Franco, the growing question became the preservation of his system of government, which he believed suited Spain. Turning age seventy in 1962, he appointed General Agustín Muñoz Grandes as vice president of government, who, if Franco died, would head the Regency Council to determine Spain's future. But Muñoz Grandes's health began to decline, and moreover, he had no enthusiasm for the restoration of the monarchy. In 1967 Franco replaced him with Admiral Luis Carrero Blanco, the man long closest to him. Carrero Blanco agreed with Franco that the system would survive better under a monarchy and was confident that Prince Juan Carlos was their man. In 1962 the prince married Princess Sofía of Greece, sister of King Constantine II, in Athens. He underwent military training, led an exemplary life, and seemed both open-minded and yet committed to Franco. In July 1969, Franco announced that Prince Juan Carlos would succeed him as head of state and reign as king of Spain.

A year before, there had been big student demonstrations in Madrid that demanded liberalization of the regime. A growing faction of "ultras" around Franco blamed Fraga and the elimination of many restrictions on the press and free speech. More than a million workers had participated in strikes that year, but efforts to liberalize the official syndicates foundered. Carrero Blanco feared their infiltration by Reds. Worse yet was the appearance in the Basque Country of the ETA (Euskadi ta Askatasuna—Basque Land and Liberty), a separatist movement that espoused violence and terror to achieve its goal, an independent Marxist Basque state.

Franco and his military regime, with their vision of a centralized Spain unified in the Castilian spirit, had done all they could to eradicate any sense of autonomy and cultural identity in the Basque Country. The Basques had fought for the Republic and paid the price. Soldiers and policemen from other parts of Spain garrisoned the region like an occupied territory. Yet the Basque provinces were among Spain's richest, and Basques owned and managed much of Spain's heavy industry and two of its biggest banks. From poorer parts of Spain non–Basques came to Bilbao and other Basque industrial centers in search of work and introduced what seemed an alien and disruptive element into Basque life. Basque organizations opposed to Franco's policy grew rapidly inside and outside Spain. The separatist ETA was the most extreme and in 1968 gunned down a police official. In 1969–1970 they killed several more policemen. The police cracked down, often indiscriminately, winning sympathy for their victims and increased support for the ETA. In 1970 at Burgos, a court martial tried seven accused terrorist leaders and condemned them to death, outraging liberal world opinion. Franco, on the advice of his cabinet, commuted the sentences to life imprisonment, because, as he put it, his regime was secure enough to be merciful.

Although a growing middle class reluctant to risk its gains was likely the regime's chief prop, the armed forces remained its most conspicuous. The army had become more effective and professional, while its numbers were reduced to 250,000 men, of whom half were draftees who served for eighteen months. The salaries of some 19,000 officers still consumed too much of its budget. Its equipment had been modernized with U.S. hand-me-downs. The air force had some new warplanes, though the navy remained small.

The Catholic Church had started, following the conclusion in 1965 of Ecumenical Council Vatican II, to criticize the regime openly and move toward the opposition. Christian-Marxist dialogues took place, and in 1971 Cardinal Vicente Enrique y Tarancón, head of Spain's council of Bishops, asked forgiveness for the failure of the Church to reconcile Spaniards rather than perpetuate their divisions. The Vatican, unhappy with Franco's more conservative episcopal nominees, left over a dozen sees without bishops.

Franco grew visibly feeble as he reached age eighty. Among the ultras, a bunker mentality developed and won them the appellation "the Bunker." Many, who fought for Franco in the Civil War and became provisional lieutenants, held government jobs or contracts and depended on him. There were die-hard Falangists, committed to the cause, and veterans of the Blue Division who fought alongside the Nazis in Russia. In their cafeterias they complained of the way things were going and argued about what needed to be done. They regretted the submergence of the Falange into the Movement and saw the Movement adrift, without leadership. They believed that rock music and loose morals were seeping in from western Europe and the United States and corrupting Spanish youth. They denounced the Church and clergy for going "red" since Vatican II. Even Spain's anti-Communist allies were tainted by Freemasonry. Neither were the diehards sure of Prince Juan Carlos, son of the liberal Don Juan, as Franco's designated successor. Against the ETA and leftist terrorist groups such as FRAP (Frente Revolucionario Antifascista y Patriota), they undertook vigilante action in which off-duty policemen often joined.

The wedding in 1972 of Franco's granddaughter, María del Carmen Martínez Bordiu y Franco, to Alfonso de Borbón, duke of Cádiz, caused many ultra Francoists to recommend that he, rather than Prince Juan Carlos, be designated Franco's heir. Because his father was the deaf-mute older brother of Don Juan, he had a strong claim on the crown. Although Franco's wife Doña Carmen toyed with this possibility, Franco and Carrero Blanco remained committed to Juan Carlos.

In the Basque Country ETA violence escalated and repression became more brutal. The ETA hoped that repression would trigger a mass revolution that they would lead. To dramatize their cause, they took their tactics to Madrid, where they dug under a boulevard and, in December 1973, blew up Carrero Blanco in his car as he left Mass for his office. Franco was shattered by the death of the man intended to guide Juan Carlos. Civil Guard chief General Carlos Iniesta Cano ordered his men from rural posts into urban areas to make wholesale arrests, and freed them to shoot antiregime demonstrators and any who resisted. Realizing that Iniesta had exceeded his authority and risked bloodshed, Acting Prime Minister Torcuato Fernández Miranda, president of the Cortes, and the chiefs of the armed forces stopped him. A few days later Franco appointed a loyal functionary, Carlos Arias Navarro, to be prime minister.

On February 12, 1974, Arias announced that the government would be open to change, which encouraged the opposition. Faced with massive labor unrest, student demonstrations, and continued ETA violence, his government scrambled to maintain order and forgot openness to change. Martial law was extended, and over widespread foreign and Spanish protest, an accused Catalan terrorist was executed by garrote. Monster rallies by Franco's die-hard followers roared their support for the ailing Caudillo. At the same time, disgruntled government functionaries and junior army officers met in secret to plan the anticipated transition to democracy. The officers formed a clandestine Democratic Military Union (UMD—Unión Militar Democrática). Arias and his cabinet tried to work out a new law of political associations that would give the opposition some vent. Already broached under Carrero, the idea was to recognize and allow limited expression to three groupings within the Movement: the Falangist left, the Opus Dei technocrats, and conservative Christian Democrats.

In the meantime the Mideast oil embargo and ensuing world energy crisis hit Spain. Also affecting Spain was a military coup in Portugal in April 1974 by leftist officers who overthrew the dictatorship and established a Socialist democracy. Then in July, Franco had to be hospitalized and Prince Juan Carlos became acting head of state. Franco's die-hard followers feared a monarchist coup, and Franco worried that the prince might give way to his father, Don Juan. Even as Arias attended the human rights conference in Helsinki that month, army intelligence arrested nine officers associated with the UMD. On September 3, a weak but alert caudillo took back the reins of government, to the relief of the diehards.

Terrorist activity reached a new level ten days later with the bombing of a cafeteria frequented by policemen on Madrid's Puerta del Sol. Twelve people died and eighty were wounded. The only police employee killed was a woman clerk. All of Spain was shocked, the ETA admitted responsibility, and the diehards called for blood. Yet Arias persisted in his efforts to get a law of political association for groups committed to the Movement. Public opinion polls made clear that Spaniards wanted parliamentary democracy. Although distracted by financial scandals involving Franco's brother, Arias got his law through the Cortes and the Council of State in December, but restrictions made it almost meaningless. Outside Spain, political parties, old and new, rallied and won converts inside Spain, who only waited on the right opportunity to surface. All felt that Franco's days were numbered. The revived PSOE found a new and energetic young leader, Felipe González, in its assembly at Suresnes, near Paris. A range of Christian Democratic parties formed as top people in government, finance, and industry held clandestine meetings in Madrid and abroad to prepare for the inevitable changes they believed would follow Franco's death.

In March 1975, Arias formed a new cabinet dominated by moderates and Opus Dei technocrats rather than Francoist diehards and right-wing generals, yet it made scant progress in finding ways to open up political life. Franco would not risk it. He doubted that Spain, given the option, would restore the monarchy that he believed vital to its future, and he thus believed it necessary to keep his regime intact until the minute he died. One reform-minded minister did form an association, the Unión del Pueblo Español (Union of the Spanish People), under the law but soon after died in a car crash. His chief associate, Adolfo Suárez, who had been a popular head of Spanish television and vice secretary of the Movement, resigned his government posts in order to captain the new association. People began to talk openly of rats leaving the sinking ship.

Continued ETA and leftist acts of terror met with retaliation from right-wing death squads and enraged police forces. In September the government declared a national state of emergency to deal with terrorism and tightened censorship of the press. Journalists, academics, and labor leaders were arrested alongside terrorist suspects. In the Basque Country, repression by police and right-wing death squads became particularly brutal and kindled more resentment in the Basque population. Rich and poor, priests and left-wing atheists, joined in protests. Death sentences were handed down against eleven convicted ETA and leftist terrorists. Franco and his cabinet reprieved six, including two pregnant women and a handicapped person. Five were shot, in the face of international protests from liberals and the left and the condemnation of Pope Paul VI. Thirteen countries recalled their ambassadors, and leftist mobs in foreign capitals set fire to four Spanish embassies. On October 1 in Madrid the Movement produced a rally of tens of thousands of people before the Royal Palace to cheer Franco when he appeared on the balcony. He ascribed everything going on to the leftist-Masonic conspiracy in cahoots with the Communists. His voice sounded weak, he was tearful and for a moment had to be held up by Juan Carlos. On the same day, a new terrorist group, GRAPO (Grupos de Resistencia Antifascista Primero de Octubre), emerged to kill four policemen.

Franco made his last public appearance on October 12. Within a week, a combination of ailments had him on life support. His son-in-law, the physician Villaverde, took over his treatment while the government clamped down on dissent. Several operations did little more than prolong his suffering, which he bore like the old soldier he was. His daughter, backed by Cardinal Tarancón, finally insisted that he be allowed to die. On November 20, Franco quietly passed away. Spain stood at the edge of a new era.

12

Democracy

We now reach that point, many of the people who appear on these pages are not only alive but also active. Many official papers remain classified, and few memoirs have been written. We have reports from the press, televised broadcasts, and popular accounts and biographies. We have interviews with participants in print, on radio, and on television. To try to arrive at a history of what really happened, we must analyze everything critically, with common sense, goodwill, and care.

At ten o'clock on the morning of November 20, 1975, Arias Navarro read Franco's last testament. The dictator claimed that he would face the judgment of God with a clear conscience. He forgave his enemies and asked their forgiveness. He had done all for Spain and Christian civilization and urged Spaniards to maintain the unity of their country and strive for social justice and the good of Spain. Hundreds of thousands passed his bier as he lay in state. The irreverent claimed that the crowds only wanted to make sure he was dead. In the Basque Country and Catalonia, people broke out champagne and danced in the streets. On November 23, Franco's body was taken to the Valle de los Caídos (Valley of the Fallen), the vast basilica dug into the Sierra de Guadarrama close to the Escorial. Built by Republican Civil War prisoners in the name of reconciliation, it served as a mausoleum for José Antonio Primo de Rivera and mainly Nationalist war dead. Franco was placed in a tomb near the founder of the Falange. The only important foreign head of state among the mourners was Chilean dictator General Augusto Pinochet, who believed that Franco's model for Spain suited Chile and other Spanish-American nations.

King Juan Carlos I had assumed his royal office before the Cortes on November 22. He reappointed Arias as prime minister and Torcuato Fernández Miranda as president of the Cortes. An expert on constitutional law, Fernández Miranda once served as his tutor. As president of the Cortes, he also chaired the seventeen-member Council of the Realm, a bastion of backers of Franco's system. The king used his military connections to maintain close links with the army and its generals. They had sworn oaths of loyalty to him: He was both Franco's designated heir and their legitimate king. To demonstrate his identification with the army, he flew to Spanish Sahara to hearten its garrison, as it withdrew in line with an agreement to restore the region to Morocco.

Most Spaniards hoped that there would be progress toward democracy, though they were not agreed on the pace. The left wanted a swift break (*ruptura*) with Francoism. The diehards of the Bunker wanted no break. Few on either side wanted to jeopardize Spain's prosperity and stability. When the Cortes reassembled in January 1976, Arias proposed a new statute of associations, but said nothing of increased autonomy for the Basque Country and Catalonia, changes in the law of syndicates that would permit labor unions, or an end to the state of emergency against terrorists. In March the generals made their commitment to the continuation of Francoism clear when a court-martial convicted the UMD leaders arrested the previous July, booted them from the army, and sentenced them to prison. When the new Law of Political Associations passed the Cortes in June, it excluded separatist parties and the Communists. It transferred recognition of what amounted to political parties from the Movement to the minister of the interior, but the Cortes did not repeal the laws that outlawed political activity.

All spring, strikes and random acts of terror sporadically disrupted the routine of Spanish life. Hundreds of thousands participated in demonstrations to call for change and amnesty for political prisoners. People joked that history would dub Juan Carlos "the Brief," for the shortness of his reign. Strikes by public employees and railroad workers made the depth of discontent clear, and top men in government sought contact with opposition leaders to find a solution. Of this Juan Carlos was in favor. Through friends and former teachers, he was in contact with pragmatic reformists who had served under Franco and were called "Tácitos," from the Roman historian Tacitus, whose *Agricola* relates how loyal men did good service under bad emperors. They had formed a loose association during Franco's last years and contributed articles to the conservative newspaper *Ya* under the pen-name "Tácito." Franco and Carrero Blanco tolerated them, as they seemed more thoughtful than threatening. The king, unhappy with Arias's progress regarding political associations, obtained his resignation in July and appointed Adolfo Suárez to be prime minister, with the connivance of Fernández Miranda, who chaired the Council of the Realm. While most regarded Suárez as one more Franco functionary, Suárez at some point had come around to believe that Spain must become democratic. The king knew Suárez's thinking and believed that Suárez and Fernández Miranda would provide the team he needed for a genuine transition to democracy. From the evidence it appears that the three agreed that the peaceful achievement of their goals required them to work within the laws and institutions bequeathed by Franco. Suárez used his television image and charm with opposition leaders, including Socialist Felipe González and Communist Santiago Carrillo, to convince them to work within the legal guidelines. He met with generals and won their grudging support. He persuaded the Cortes to repeal the laws against political activity. Still, intermittent violence continued, and the army and political right grew restive as clamor for change mounted. As commander in chief, the king reshuffled the high command and appointed the relatively liberal General Manuel Gutiérrez Mellado to be chief of staff. The most intransigent general, Jaime Milans del Bosch, he took from command of the Brunete Armored Division quartered outside Madrid and posted him to Valencia.

By decree in December 1976, the king transferred trial of political crimes from military to civil courts. By decree he permitted the public use of Catalan and Basque. A new Law of Political Associations passed that set elections for a bicameral Cortes, which would draft a constitution. In accordance with Franco's Fundamental Laws it was submitted to a plebiscite that December and received overwhelming approval. The king, Suárez, and Fernández Miranda now worked to prepare for the first free elections in Spain since 1936. The political parties were already in the field. Manuel Fraga Iribarne formed the right-wing Alianza Popular (AP—Popular Alliance). Gil Robles and Joaquín Ruiz Giménez formed a conservative Christian Democrat coalition. Felipe González had his Socialist PSOE running hard. In April the Movement was abolished, and Suárez lifted the ban on the Communist Party. Carrillo swung into action. La Pasionaria returned from exile to exhort the party faithful and remind people that Spanish Communists had provided the most consistent opposition to Franco during the dictatorship. Communist-led clandestine Workers' Commissions had given labor an alternative voice to that of Franco's syndicates. The recognition of the Communists outraged the generals and Francoist diehards, who accused Suárez of reneging on his word. Suárez rummaged through the political center to form an uneasy coalition called the Union of the Democratic Center (UCD—Unión de Centro Democrático), which he held together by dint of personality and access to state funds and television. The chiefs of the UCD's parties were called "barons." As prime minister, Suárez persuaded a compliant Cortes to legalize trade unions and to dismantle the syndicalist bureaucracy that once directed labor.

In the Basque Country, conservative and moderate Basque nationalist parties vied with the more militant ETA-oriented groups for votes. Over a period of time the ETA had divided into the political-military ETA-PM (*político-militar*), willing to talk with other Basque factions, and the uncompromising military ETA-M (*militar*). In Catalonia conservative and leftist regional parties likewise competed for votes. For press coverage of the electoral campaign, a remarkable national newspaper, *El Pais*, appeared in Madrid. Editorially liberal, its reportage proved thorough and balanced, and all over Spain, citizens began to read it alongside their local newspapers. The better newspapers from the Franco years, such as *ABC* and *Ya*, struggled to overcome their image of dullness and caution. More strident journals flourished on the right and left.

Despite outrages all spring by the ETA and left- and right-wing extremists, over 80 percent of voters cast ballots in the elections of June 15, 1977. The results returned Suárez and his UCD coalition to power. To his left stood González's PSOE and the Communists, who won far fewer votes than they had expected. Fraga's Popular Alliance did worse than the Communists had. All the main parties had proved remarkably responsible during the campaign. The Church, more liberal than in 1936, was no longer a big issue. And Spain was more prosperous than in 1936, which gave most Spaniards a sense of optimism when the new Cortes assembled to draft a constitution.

In Catalonia, the regional parties had won, and by decree in October, the king restored the Generalitat under its aged president Josep Tarradellas, who had returned from exile. In the Basque Country unrest continued unabated. The ETA and its allies organized marches to demand amnesty for Basque political prisoners, mostly convicted terrorists, or to hold their trials in Basque courts and keep them in Basque jails. Though not unsympathetic, most conservative and moderate Basques eschewed the marches, which right-wingers and off-duty policemen harassed. Right-wing provocation and rivalries within the ETA factions escalated the violence. Interior Minister Rodolfo Martín Villa backed the Civil Guard, despite its contribution to violence in the Basque Country, in hopes of getting it under control. Over 300 Civil Guards were transferred from the Basque Country and several were court-martialed after a mutiny. Senior generals demanded that Suárez send the army in support of the Civil Guard, which he refused to do. They then began to conspire against him.

In addition to these problems Spain was still affected by the world energy crisis and rampant inflation. To address the grim socioeconomic situation, Suárez held a series of meetings at the Moncloa Palace, residence of the prime minister, on the weekend of October 8–9, 1977, with leaders of the parties in the Cortes, including the Socialists and the Communists. Their frank discussions and agreements led to the so-called Moncloa Pacts, which the parties in the Cortes ratified later that month. In a significant spirit of compromise, Suárez and the center and right party leaders agreed to take up needed social legislation once the new Constitution was in place. The Socialists and Communists for their part agreed to restrain labor from making exorbitant or disruptive demands and to maintain industrial peace. The government reformed the tax structure to make it less regressive, increased restrictions on the army and police, restored properties confiscated from labor unions after the Civil War, and provided subsidies to help the spread of a free press. The left toned down its rhetoric against U.S. military bases and NATO.

The following October, after months of committee work and debate, the Cortes approved the Constitution of 1978. It defined the place of the king, established a Cortes that consisted of a Senate and a Congress of Deputies and a Constitutional Court of twelve judges to rule only on constitutional issues. The Senate represented regional interests, although more populous regions received greater representation. The Congress enjoyed the chief legislative authority, and its dominant party or coalition selected the prime minister (president of government), who selected the cabinet. It provided for the establishment of autonomous regions—in effect, a federal Spain. It was decisively ratified by referendum in December.

At the same time, discontent reached a head in the army over the actions of the ETA and leftist terror groups and a perceived moral deterioration in Spain. During 1978 the ETA shot down over eighty people, mostly policemen but including a general and his aide, in the streets of Madrid. The crime rate rose, drug use increased, and varied kinds of sexual behavior became more blatant. New laws permitted divorce. Senior generals talked of a government of "national salvation" and tried to determine the attitude of the king. When Gutiérrez Mellado, now defense minister, confronted them, one of them called him a "Freemason, a pig and a coward." A harebrained plot to kidnap the government hatched in the Cafetería Galaxia, a rightist hangout, was uncovered at the last minute in November 1978, and its ringleaders, including Civil Guard Lieutenant Colonel Antonio Tejero, were arrested. Some suspicion fell on army and other intelligence services for failing to warn Suárez sooner. The plotters were tried and convicted in May 1980 but received only light sentences from a government fearful of further alarming the right. Tejero was soon back on duty.

On March 1, 1979, the first elections for the Cortes under the 1978 Constitution took place. Suárez's UCD won again, taking 168 seats of the 350 in Congress. González's PSOE got 121 seats after a campaign that won him wide respect for his professed moderation. Smaller parties won the rest. But as ETA violence raged unabated, May local elections indicated a rightward trend.

For Suárez and his government the Basque problem became the chief dilemma: how, on the one hand, to placate the army and Civil Guard and, on the other, to find an acceptable solution that would keep the rich Basque Country Spanish. Over half the voters in the Basque Country abstained from the constitutional referendum, and of those who voted, almost a quarter voted no. Though growing numbers objected to ETA violence, they remained distrustful of Madrid, the army, and the national police. In the elections for the Cortes, a leftist Basque party backed by the ETA, Herri Batasuna, took second place to the moderate Basque Nationalist Party (PNV—Partido Nacionalista Vasco). With moderate Basque leaders headed by Carlos Garaicoetxea, Suárez hammered out an autonomy statute. The ETA, which in July extended its attacks to tourist beaches, rejected the statute as a sellout, and all autumn its members clashed with those who favored it. Despite threats by the ETA, over 60 percent of Basque Country voters went to the polls, and over 80 percent approved the statute.

ETA murders of police and army personnel, the kidnaping of businessmen for ransom, and extortion of money from others kept the generals in an uproar. The right-wing press blasted the government as weak and vacillating. The left also blasted the government, for catering to the army and its failure to amnesty the convicted UMD army officers. Inflation continued to run rampant, and the weak world economy left well over a million Spaniards without work. Felipe González claimed that Suárez's time was past. Suárez's own political allies began to abandon him as they saw his popularity wane. Ailing and evidently disillusioned, Suárez resigned office in January 1981. He was succeeded by moderate conservative Leopoldo Calvo Sotelo, nephew of the man whose murder in 1936 had triggered the Civil War.

As Calvo Sotelo formed a new cabinet and sought the approval of the Cortes, King Juan Carlos and Queen Sofía paid a state visit to the Basque Country. In ceremonies at Guernica, intended to evoke the traditional lordship of Castilian monarchs and their respect for the *fueros* of the Basque Country, members of Herri Batasuna made unpleasant scenes. The king proved gracious but firm, and as the royal couple continued their visit, their welcome became warmer. The ETA persisted in its campaign of violence and kidnap. From a nuclear power station they took an engineer hostage and demanded that the station be destroyed. When it was not, they executed their hostage. Mass indignation followed, and over 300,000 people marched in Bilbao, San Sebastián, and Vitoria to protest the murder.

Army conspirators decided the time had come to act, though they differed over details and ends. General Alfonso Armada Comyn, once with the Royal Household, apparently believed that he could win the cooperation of the king and acquiescence of the political leadership in the establishment of a government of national salvation, perhaps with himself at the head. Milans del Bosch, in command of the III Military Region in Valencia, and inveterate plotter Lieutenant Colonel Antonio Tejero listened to Armada and agreed that they needed the king with them, although they preferred a military dictatorship like those current in Chile, Argentina, and Turkey.

On February 23, 1981, they struck. The Cortes had assembled to confirm Calvo Sotelo in office but failed to give him enough votes. At 6:30 P.M. Tejero, in his Civil Guard uniform with its patent leather hat, and a band of armed guardsmen burst into the chamber, brandishing their weapons. The photographic coverage is remarkable. Defense Minister Gutiérrez Mellado ordered Tejero and his men out, but instead he and the chief party leaders were sequestered in separate rooms. While other units seized Madrid's television studio, Tejero telephoned Milans del Bosch in Valencia, and Milans took to radio and television to declare a state of national emergency in the king's name. His troops deployed in the streets to maintain order. By telephone he reached the regional captains general and divisional commanders. They did not join him, though he expected they would come around when the coup succeeded. In Madrid word reached the Zarzuela Palace on the outskirts, where the king resided. He and his chief people debated how to respond. From the first moment, King Juan Carlos appeared determined to stand firm for Spain's new democracy.

The captain general of Madrid, Guillermo Quintana Lacaci, stood by the king and kept the Brunete Armored Division on tight leash. It was now known that Armada was not with the king nor expected at the palace. Loyal officers persuaded troops who occupied Madrid's television studio to yield. However, Tejero would talk with none but Armada, who reached the Palace of the Cortes at 12:30 A.M. Their talk about a government of national salvation foundered on Tejero's insistence that neither Socialists nor Communists be included. In the meantime, Juan Carlos donned full uniform as commander in chief of the armed forces and appeared on national television at 1:10 A.M. on February 24. He announced that he would not tolerate the disruption of Spain's democratic processes by anyone and reminded Spain's armed forces of their oath of loyalty to him and the nation. By telephone he told Milans that he would not go along with the plot, and the plotters would have to shoot him first. At 4:00 A.M. Milans recalled his troops and the plot collapsed. Armada negotiated Tejero's surrender at noon, and the Cortes was freed. Suspicion fell on several hundred officers for what came to be called F-23. Thirty-two would face trial.

Spanish democracy had weathered its most dramatic threat, and Juan Carlos became a hero to the democratic world. In the days following, massive demonstrations of support took place in Spain's cities. A special bond had been established between Juan Carlos and Spaniards of almost every political persuasion. Even the die-hard right admitted his courage. And for a few months, the ETA did little.

The Cortes confirmed Calvo Sotelo in office, and he undertook to make good his program. In the wake of the F-23 coup attempt, he got a law to defend the Constitution that allowed the government to proceed against inflammatory material in the press, both left and right. Eager for Spain to join NATO, he hoped that contact with professional NATO officers would take Spain's military officers from their insularity. The left, with its knee-jerk anti-Americanism, antimilitarism, and historic sympathy for the Soviet Union, opposed Spain's joining NATO. Calvo Sotelo and the left also differed over Spain's economy. Calvo Sotelo favored free enterprise and wanted labor to exercise restraint in their demands. The left felt labor had given enough and wanted more social programs. Calvo Sotelo's concern with the ETA led him not only to consolidate operations against them but also to propose a law that would place restrictions on regional autonomy. Although this pleased the army and Civil Guard, it alarmed Catalonia, the Basque Country, and Galicia (which gained autonomous status in April). The Socialist Party (PSOE), which was nationwide in organization, went along with Calvo Sotelo and, with him and the army, incurred the wrath of the regionalists.

Renewed murders by GRAPO that summer kept matters on edge. The generals and right-wing press demanded stronger government action. The king restructured the high command in favor of generals firm for democracy, on the argument that the army needed stricter discipline if it were to become a part of NATO. In February 1982, the trials of the F-23 plotters began. On the witness stand, they did their cause little credit with their arrogant posturing and self-righteousness. Milans and Tejero were each sentenced to thirty years in prison, Armada to six. The remaining twenty-two convicted received light sentences, and most would return to duty. For

Spain's officer corps it proved a cleansing experience. In March 1982, Spain became a member of NATO.

The ETA resumed its campaign of murder and kidnap with the beginning of 1982. The centrist UCD that rallied to Calvo Sotelo after Suárez's resignation began to weaken once more, and its party barons had to be bought off by cabinet shuffles and concessions to army hard-liners. As elections for a new Cortes, scheduled for late October, drew near and polls suggested that Felipe González's Socialists might win, unregenerate right-wing officers entered into one more conspiracy. Three colonels, in touch with imprisoned Milans del Bosch, contrived a coup that would seize the government the day before the elections and depose the king as a traitor to the Francoist Movement. Uncovered on October 3 by intelligence services that had been overhauled since F-23, the plot was swiftly defused. The elections of October 28 returned the eloquent González and his PSOE with 202 seats, an overwhelming majority, with Socialist deputies elected from every corner of Spain. The center had crumbled, and the Popular Alliance of Fraga Iribarne, who moderated his attitudes and moved closer the center, came in second with 106 seats. The UCD had 12 seats, but Calvo Sotelo was out. Carrillo's Communists won only 4 seats. Splinter and regional parties shared the remainder. The Catalan Convergence and Union (CiU—Convergència i Unió) got the most, with 12; the Basque Nationalist Party (PNV) won 8.

The PSOE that won big in 1982 had moderated its Marxist doctrines to become in effect a social democratic party, as Socialist parties in France, Italy, Germany, and Scandinavia had done for similar reasons. It had come a long way from the heady days of October 1974, when the exiled party was reborn at its congress in Suresnes, France, and Felipe González and his followers had wrested control from tired old-timers and proclaimed the party's commitment to revolutionary Marxism. In December 1976, the PSOE had reiterated its Marxist faith during its first congress in post-Franco Spain, to distance it from the moderate Popular Socialist Party (PSP—Partido Socialista Popular). Attendance at that congress of Europe's Socialist elite —François Mitterrand of France, Willy Brandt of West Germany, Pietro Nenni of Italy, Michael Foote of the United Kingdom, and Olof Palme of Sweden— legitimated the PSOE in its own eyes and the eyes of the Spanish left as the champion of muscular socialism. Fear that legalization of the Communist Party threatened the PSOE's dominance of the left evaporated after the PSOE's strong showing in the 1977 elections and the Communists' dismal performance. Following the elections, González played a key part in the Moncloa Pacts and the drafting of the Constitution and won a reputation for pragmatism and moderation. He and his chief associate, Alfonso Guerra, saw in moderation the ticket to electoral victory. The moderate PSP soon merged with the PSOE. In the PSOE congress of May 1979, González used his popularity to outmaneuver more orthodox Marxists. A special congress followed in September, dominated by González's people, which relegated Marxism to a tool of theoretical analysis rather than an instrument of social revolution. González consolidated his grip on the PSOE in the 1981 party congress. Clad in a sweater, open-collar shirt, and corduroys, and adapting a relaxed style, González seemed "a regular guy," whom rank-and-file Socialist workers saw as one of their own.

With a commanding majority in the Cortes, forty-year-old González began to govern. He made Alfonso Guerra, considered his alter ego, deputy prime minister (vice president of government).During the electoral campaign of 1982, González had promised to create 800,000 jobs, something always easier said than done. Like other Socialists in power, Mitterrand in France and Bettino Craxi, who in 1983 became Italy's first Socialist prime minister, González had to recognize the realities of a market-driven global economy of which most nations were part. Spain was particularly dependent on imported oil, which fueled a high 65 percent of its energy needs. González was also aware of a broad conservative backlash against the statist policies favored by Socialists, which brought Margaret Thatcher to power in Great Britain (1979), Ronald Reagan in the United States (1980), and Helmut Kohl in West Germany (1982). A major task for González would be to keep the support of organized labor and in particular the Socialist UGT. Though shared by all, Spain's new prosperity benefited the rich and the growing middle class to a conspicuously greater degree. Spain's more numerous workers had been repeatedly asked to show restraint, such as settling for wage increases that in percentage terms fell well below the rate of inflation. With the PSOE in power, they believed it would be their turn to get a bigger share of Spain's new wealth. In real terms, wealth must be created by increased productivity. To free money for productive purposes, González had to trim Spain's historically bloated bureaucracy and end subsidies to inefficient industries. Some jobs would be lost so that more might be created. To ease the process, he had to increase unemployment and retirement benefits.

Of the other domestic issues González tackled, abortion proved the most rancorous, with the Catholic Church thundering its opposition. A law allowing abortion in cases of rape or incest, of a malformed fetus, or of saving the life of the mother passed in October 1983. After the Supreme Constitutional Court overruled it, on grounds of ambiguity, a similar law passed in 1985. Education proved to be another bone of contention. The Catholic Church, which operates most of Spain's private schools, objected to PSOE legislation to bring its schools under closer regulation, although its schools receive government subsidies, which the Church favors. The controversial legislation passed in 1984 and extended the upper age for guaranteed free schooling from fourteen to sixteen.

The PSOE legislated reforms for Spain's universities and curtailed the power long held by senior professors (*catedráticos*—chair holders). Although junior faculty and students gained a greater say in university governance, they objected to tuition charges and fees that limited access to higher education for poorer students. Student grievances led to a series of strikes in January 1987 that caused the government to make concessions on tuition and fees and offer more grants to poor students. Many of the students' grievances regarding university governance were less simple to address. Much remains antiquated about Spain's universities, as is also the case with other European universities. Professors remain too few for the number of students. Complutense University of Madrid has over 100,000 students, the Central University of Barcelona, over 80,000. Laboratory facilities remain inadequate, and new developments in computer technologies have been almost impossible to accommodate. As with most European universities, students mainly educate themselves in the intense give and take of student intellectual life. But with more distractions and opportunities for entertainment, traditional student life is losing that intensity, as it is elsewhere, and Spanish students have become more career oriented.

González continued to reduce the size of the armed forces that had begun under Suárez and shortened the length of obligatory military service by three months, to between twelve and fifteen months' active duty. In 1986 he reinstated the UMD members court-martialed ten years earlier, although they preferred to remain in the civilian sector and were satisfied with reserve status. In line with other countries, Spain opened its armed forces and military academies to women. González reversed himself about Spain's membership in NATO. In the debates of 1981–1982 he and the PSOE had objected to Spain's entry into NATO. During the 1982 elections, he promised to hold a referendum on the issue. The referendum was not held until March 1986, following Spain's entry into the European Community (EC). Most other members of the European Community are also members of NATO, and González now urged voters to keep Spain in NATO. In framing the referendum, he stated that Spain would remain free of nuclear arms and called for the elimination of the U.S. military presence in Spain. Manuel Fraga, leader of the right and once a proponent of Spain's joining NATO, urged voters to abstain in order to deny González a victory. His move backfired when most voters voted—over half of them yes. In 1995, a Spaniard, González's former foreign minister Javier Solana, became secretary general of NATO.

Spanish membership in the European Community was perhaps González's greatest achievement. Although he and most Spaniards knew that a period of painful adjustment might follow, most wanted membership in the EC and felt certain in the long run that it would prove to be to Spain's economic advantage. Whereas Franco's dictatorship had touted Spain's "difference" from the rest of Europe, Spain's new democracy hankered for acceptance by Europe and the larger democratic world. Negotiations were hard and drawn out. Spain would soon be in full competition with the more advanced industrial facilities and financial organization of EC power-houses such as West Germany, France, and Italy. Faced by French and Italian agricultural interests, Spain had to forego gaining early advantages in agricultural exports, a strong sector of its economy, though it did get concessions for its extensive fisheries. Onerous to many Spaniards would be the EC's basic value-added tax (VAT), which taxes each phase of production and adds to the cost of consumer goods. Britain had gone through the pain of it earlier, with a good deal of griping. Although the VAT increased the cost of basic necessities by 3 to 5 percent and provoked bitter complaints, its promoters argued that it hit harder the rich who consume more, especially high-priced luxury goods. Negotiations with the EC were conducted by González himself, his foreign minister Francisco Fernández Ordóñez, and his minister for economics and finance, Carlos Solchaga. The agreement was signed in June 1985, and Spain's membership in the EC became official on January 1, 1986. Spain has since played an important role in the EC and participated in the framing of the 1991 Maastricht Treaty to form a European Union. In the first five years following its entry into the EC, Spain enjoyed one of the world's highest rates of growth in GDP among developed countries. Since Spain joined the EC, average household income has increased considerably.

In addition to joining the EC and remaining in NATO, Spain, under González, took a larger role in world affairs. It strengthened its bonds with Spanish America, where democracies also began to replace dictatorships. King Juan Carlos and Queen Sofia make frequent journeys to further friendly relations with nations that once formed part of his forebears' empire. In 1991 Spain participated in the first Ibero-American summit, held at Guadalajara, Mexico. Nations represented included Spain, and the Spanish-American republics including Cuba, as well as Portugal and Brazil. In 1992 Juan Carlos and González hosted the second summit in Madrid and urged that it become an annual event, which it has. Spanish business has become a significant investor in Spanish America, and Spain a promoter of stronger economic ties between Latin America and the EC. Spain's historic Mediterranean position also gave Spain a voice in the politics of North Africa and the Middle East. Spain only belatedly recognized Israel in 1986 and enjoyed a certain favor in the Arab world. It has provided the site for several important meetings in the Arab-Israeli peace process. Spain's relations with Morocco have been lately strained over illegal immigration of Moroccan workers seeking jobs in Spain and over drug trafficking.

The ETA proved González's most intractable problem and complicated his relations with the Basque Country. When first elected, González enjoyed good relations with moderate Basque leaders, while the Basque branch of the PSOE was an important element in Basque politics. Never associated with Franco's oppressive policies, González could be firm with the ETA and yet keep the confidence of the Basque majority. The mainstream Basque parties repudiated ETA violence but disagreed over how or whether to engage the ETA in dialogue. Over it, Carlos Garaikoetxea broke in 1986 with the PNV and formed his own Basque Solidarity Party (EA—Eusko Alkartasuna). Efforts by González's government to talk with the ETA in Algeria came to naught, and González continued the use of national police and the Civil Guard against them. Like his predecessors, he would not turn to the army, despite grumbling from die-hard senior generals that he do so. Using his close relationship with Socialist François Mitterrand, elected president of France in 1981, he obtained French help in pursuing the ETA, which has hideouts in the French Basque Country, where French police have made key arrests. When Jacques Chirac became French premier in 1986, he sustained Mitterrand's policy of cooperation with Spain against the ETA.

Also in the field against the ETA and its sympathizers were right-wing death squads who formed an Anti-terrorist Liberation Group (GAL—Grupo Anti-terrorista de Liberación), which looms as a serious problem in its own right. Basques and most others harbor little doubt that police are involved with GAL death squads. It remains ETA strategy to provoke the police and diehards into repressive measures, which they believe will drive the Basque Country to recognize the ETA as liberators, break from Spain, and support an ETA Marxist state. In light of all the evidence, the strategy seems insane. Between Franco's death and 1986 they killed over 500 people, among them dozens of innocent bystanders, including women and children, although most were police, civil guardsmen, and soldiers. In July 1986, an ETA bomb in Madrid killed ten Civil Guard trainees.

In the general elections held in June 1986, González and the PSOE kept their absolute majority in the Congress of Deputies, with 184 seats, though the figure represented a loss of 18 seats and an erosion in the percentage of the popular vote from almost 49 percent to barely 44 percent. Fraga's Popular Alliance won 105 seats. The center parties, under the leadership of a reinvigorated Adolfo Suárez, rebounded from 2 seats in 1982 to 19 seats, through a coalition called the Social Democratic Center (CDS—Centro Democrático Social). The Catalan Convergence and Union increased its representation from 12 to 18, whereas the Basque Nationalist Party dropped from 8 deputies to 5. Herri Batasuna, the ETA's political arm, won 5 seats, and the Basque Left, 2. A small increase of from 4 seats to 7 was made by the United Left (IU—Izquierda Unida), an affiliation that included Carrillo's Communists, old-line Communists with whom Carrillo split, and a new Marxist-Leninist Communist Party that backed Soviet intervention in Afghanistan. Carrillo himself failed to get elected. An improbable partner in the IU were the Carlists, who had become a populist party.

Again victorious, González appointed two women to cabinet positions in 1988, the first to occupy such posts since the last years of the Second Republic. For the first time ever he put civilians in charge of state security police and the Civil Guard. Both Civil Guards and the national police became more accountable, and the black patent leather hats long associated with the Civil Guards virtually vanished in ordinary wear. González negotiated the elimination of U.S. bases in Spain and the withdrawal of U.S. forces. However, during the Persian Gulf crisis and war of 1990–1991, Spain stood with the United Nations, and U.S. aircraft used Spanish arifields for strikes against Iraq. By 1992 the last U.S. planes had left, and the bases became entirely Spanish. By then both the Cold War and the Gulf War were over.

In July 1988 González had new labor laws enacted that he insisted both fulfilled PSOE promises and met European Community requirements. Labor was not happy, and the Socialist UGT pondered its relationship with González's Socialist Party. Spanish workers continued to believe they had not received their fair share of Spain's increased wealth and talked of González selling out to newly rich entrepreneurs and middle-class yuppies. The economy, while growing, began to overheat, and already high unemployment increased. Other unions and parties on the left agreed with the UGT and, on December 14, 1988, joined in a nationwide general strike, the first since 1934. It virtually paralyzed the country. González got the message, and with support from most of the opposition, early in 1989 he legislated large increases in workers' benefits, at the expense of defense and public works' projects.

The ETA problem persisted. In 1987 a French policeman was murdered, and an ETA bomb explosion in a Barcelona supermarket in June left a score of people dead. Mass protests against ETA ruthlessness became common in the Basque Country and elsewhere. The leadership of the ETA began to divide between embarrassed old-timers willing to talk about a settlement and implacable militants. In 1989 talks were held between González's Secretary for State Security Rafael Varón and ETA representative Eugenio "Antxón"

Etxebetse, which soon broke down. The Cortes expelled four ETA-backed deputies who refused to pledge loyalty to Spain.

In the fall of 1989, González decided to chance a new election. He tried to frighten labor with the specter of a conservative reaction, such as that in France which in 1986 made Jacques Chirac premier. Spanish conservatives seemed in disarray after Fraga resigned in 1986 as head of the Popular Alliance. During the elections, however, Fraga returned to keep what had been renamed the Popular Party in place with 106 seats, while the PSOE lost ground and returned only 175 deputies, exactly half of the Congress. The percentage of voters who voted for the PSOE fell below 40 percent. The more disaffected workers gave their votes to the United Left, which gained 11 seats to hold 18. The Social Democratic Center coalition dropped from 19 seats to 14, with new regional parties the gainers. The Catalan CiU kept their 18 seats, while the mainstream Basque PNV dropped from 5 to 4.

González formed a new government but no longer enjoyed the popular mandate that brought him to power in 1982 and had kept him there in 1986. The economy continued to slow and unemployment to grow. Unemployment figures exceeded 20 percent and reached 40 percent among the young. The reality was less grim. An underground economy in small shops, on the streets, in agriculture, and in domestic work, with wages paid but not reported, makes unemployment in Spain often seem greater than it is. Many of the unemployed are women or young people living in households headed by an employed wage earner. Some argued that unemployment contributed to the rise in crime, since many crimes, from embezzlement and fraud to extortion and robbery, are economically motived and lead to income redistribution. Still, Spain's crime rate remained among the lowest in the EC. Spaniards blame much of the crime problem on Spanish-American and North African immigrants.

During the Gulf crisis and war of 1990–1991, oil supplies became short and prices skyrocketed. González looked ahead to 1992, to the Olympic Games and Expo-92, and hoped the influx of visitors and money from around the world might resolve Spain's difficulties. Getting the Olympics for Barcelona was regarded as a major achievement and seemed to confirm Spain's place in the world community. Through Expo-92, an international exposition hosted by Seville and resplendent with spectacular festivities, Spain would celebrate in a big way the five-hundredth anniversary of Columbus's epic voyage that extended Spanish civilization over half the Americas. The construction of an Olympic Village and new athletic facilities in Barcelona, airport improvements, and the erection of international pavilions, highway bridges, and a new station in Seville (which would be connected to Madrid by a new high-speed rail line), would provide needed jobs. But financing the events strained Spain's resources, and when the games and Expo were done, the EC forced on Spain the first of a series of devaluations of the peseta. González also had to increase the rate of the VAT from 12 percent to 14 percent.

Tourism did increase in 1992, if not as much as hoped, and Madrid basked in the prestige of being named Europe's cultural capital for the year. The Olympic Games proved a success, and a spruced-up Barcelona reveled for a few weeks in being the center of the world's attention. During the Olympics, the ETA agreed to a cease-fire that did not last long afterward. Expo-92 in Seville also came off well. Some criticized the government for building the high-speed rail line to Seville rather than to busier Barcelona. But the government belived that cutting what had been a day's journey to two and a half hours would help to provide needed stimulation for Andalusia's economy.

During the preparations for the Olympics and Expo-92, a round of scandals involving finances and favoritism overtook the government, smug after eight years in power. Juan Guerra, brother of Deputy Prime Minister Alfonso Guerra, was convicted, fined, and imprisoned for financial shenanigans in Andalusia. Early in 1991, Alonso Guerra resigned. Private and government bankers were caught with their hands in the till. Ministers were accused of getting kickbacks or favoring relatives in granting government contracts. Accusations that the government waged an illegal "dirty war" against the ETA, in Spain and abroad, surfaced in the press and tarred the interior and security ministries. None of the scandals directly touched González, but some came close. Conservatives and disaffected leftists branded his pragmatic style of government "Felipismo" (Philipism). In parts of rural Castile, La Mancha, and Andalusia the promised prosperity had never arrived, and some hankered for the days of Franco. In many small towns streets and plazas continued to bear the names "Generalísimo" and "José Antonio," which in most big cities had been long effaced. The Church blamed González and his government for Spain's perceived moral decay, although the problem is worldwide and would better be attributed simply to modern secular society. González tried to please the right and nationalists when he visited British Prime Minister John Major in 1991 and insisted on negotiations for the return of Gibraltar to Spain. Talk but little more has followed. He also visited President Mikhail Gorbachev in the Soviet Union, to reaffirm his credentials with the left.

The Popular Party took full advantage of González's problems to increase its membership and appeal. In 1989 Fraga arranged for his succession by José María Aznar López, aged thirty-six and president of Castile and León. Fraga himself ran for the presidency of his native Galicia, which he won. Aznar won a seat to the Congress of Deputies from Madrid, the city where he was born in 1953, and in 1991 was confirmed as chairman of the Popular Party. He extended his coalition further into the political center and reached out to two groups who had remained suspicious of Fraga's authoritarian past. The first included the Christian Democrats and the Church. In 1990, as an observer he attended the world Christian Democrat convention in Dublin. He informed Church leaders that while his party would not be a parish of the Church, he favored the continuation of government funding for private schools and would allow them more freedom than the Socialists did. The second group, which backed old-fashioned liberal parties, was the Spanish Confederation of Entrepreneurial Organizations (CEOE—Confederación Española de Organizaciones Empresariales), which included Spain's leading industrialists and employers. To them he asserted his commitment to the free market and private enterprise. In 1991 he posed as a classic liberal, when he opposed a law introduced by González to permit the police more latitude in searches and seizure related to drug crimes.

In 1993, elections had to be held. Besmirched with scandal and blamed for all Spain's ills, González and the PSOE seemed, according to opinion polls, headed for certain defeat. Aznar and his Popular Party, now joined by Suárez's center coalition, would be the big winner. But when the votes were counted, González and PSOE won the most seats, 159 of 350. According to conventional wisdom, many voters feared a loss of benefits and entitlements, should the Popular Party win, and voted Socialist. Aznar and his party did make huge gains and took 141 seats. The others, the United Left, and regional parties held their own. The king asked González to form a government.

Crucial to González's continuation in power was the Catalan CiU, whose leader Jordí Pujol gave González the necessary support, although the cabinet remained in the hands of the PSOE. In 1995 the Cortes passed a new Penal Code, the long-promised revision of criminal law, and a reform of Spain's judiciary. Repercussions from the financial scandals and indictments of former ministers and officials for involvement with the secret GAL weakened Gonzalez's position, and Pujol withdrew CiU support. Gonzalez called for elections, which were held in March 1996.

Aznar's Popular Party and its immediate allies got 39 percent of the vote and a plurality of 156 seats in the Congress. They also won 111 of the 208 Senate seats determined by direct election. González's PSOE polled 37.5 percent of the vote and took 141 seats. King Juan Carlos asked Aznar to form a government. Aznar got the backing of Jordi Pujol, whose CiU had 16 seats, and the Canary Island Coalition of 4, to get his majority. He was approved by the Cortes in May.

Aznar had run on a platform crafted to win the support of business and Catholic interests and to allay any fear that his attitude toward civil rights might be authoritarian. He promised to trim the size and cost of government and entitlement programs and to root out corruption. To improve business conditions and stimulate economic growth, he would privatize more state-owned and -operated businesses, reduce government regulation, and curtail the power of labor unions. Although he did not identify his party with the Church, Aznar would continue state support of private, mainly Catholic, education, while easing government regulation. González passed into the opposition and soon turned the leadership of the PSOE over to Joaquín Almunia. Lately he has assumed the mantle of elder statesman and shares his reflections with journalists. He acts occasionally as a roving ambassador.

In office Aznar began to implement his program. He privatized the Spanish national telephone company and sold off other government enterprises. Many urge him to privatize Spain's national airline, Iberia, the railroads, and the state-run television network. They complain that the marginal tax rate of 56 percent on higher incomes and profits is too high. Aznar has continued to reduce or eliminate subsidies to antiquated industries, in the face of stubborn opposition, primarily from affected labor unions. Protests from Asturian miners forced him to delay his plans to shut down more inefficient mines. He has tried to rein in the costly but popular entitlements that plague most European economies. In the summer of 1997 he froze the pay of public employees, which a one-day general strike in December protested but did not reverse.

To carry out an economic program that brings pain and distress to many in order to improve matters over all requires that the economy grow and absorb those displaced. Government figures suggest that the rate of increase of GDP in Spain has improved to over 3 percent, and the proposed budget deficit has been trimmed to less than 3 percent of GDP, as demanded by the EC. Aznar claims to have reduced unemployment to 12 percent, but most analysts believe that the figure is closer to 20 percent, only slightly lower than it had been. The question remains of how many of those reported as unemployed are at work in the underground economy.

Toward the ETA Aznar has continued the tough policy adopted by González. He narrowly escaped an ETA bomb during the 1996 election campaign. Some have accused his government of attempting to cover up the "dirty war" González's ministers and the GAL are charged with waging against the ETA. While some Catholic churchmen and Basque leaders have urged Aznar to negotiate with the ETA without preconditions, he continues to demand that the ETA lay down its arms and observe a cease-fire before talks can start. Continuing are murders of government officials, policemen, and Basque businessmen who fail to pay the "revolutionary tax" demanded by the ETA. The total killed by the ETA at the end of 1997 has passed 800. In January 1996 the ETA took a simple prison employee hostage to force its demand that convicted ETA terrorists dispersed in prison cells throughout Spain be transferred to Basque Country prisons. The demand was refused. In the summer of 1997 police freed the hostage. In response the ETA seized and murdered a PP Basque municipal official. In mid-October 1997, ETA militants attempted to plant a bomb at the new Guggenheim Museum in Bilbao to disrupt its opening, which the king attended. A Basque policeman foiled them, although he was shot dead doing so. Recent studies of ETA members suggest that they are few in number, not well educated, and mostly over age forty. Though rejected by the overwhelming majority of Basques, they have not given up. On a more promising note, the place of Basques in Spain received further national confirmation by the wedding earlier in October of King Juan Carlos's daughter, Infanta Elena, to Basque athlete and commoner Iñaki Urdangarín in Barcelona.

Apart from the ETA and a diminishing number of right-wing diehards, the chief problems that face Spain are those of the modern industrial world. Large numbers of Spaniards own their own apartments and automobiles and enjoy the prosperity of a modern industrialized nation. Traffic jams are monumental. Spaniards are literate and fully committed to the democratic process. They still pack the streets in late afternoon and early evening to promenade and meet friends at sidewalk cafes and in cafeterias. All around them are reminders of their history, from Roman aqueducts and bridges to medieval castles, cathedrals, mosques, and synagogues. Philip II's Escorial stands but a few miles from Francisco Franco's Valley of the Fallen. Baroque churches crowd modern banks; beaux arts buildings share blocks in Barcelona with Gaudí's fanciful structures. In every Spanish town in spring, white-clad children still march to First Communion. In 1996 in Madrid over 300 veterans of the International Brigades met to mark the sixtieth anniversary of the beginning of its siege in 1936. F-23 was brought to mind in 1997 when a court released Tejero on parole.

Spain has ridden the waves of world economic growth so that by 1998 Spaniards approach the standard of living of their senior EC partners. However, the high wages, costly social security packages, subventions to government-owned or -favored industries, and an aging industrial plant have made Spain, like most other European countries, in many instances less competitive on world markets. No one can yet predict the progress of the European Monetary Union, of which Spain is a part. Aznar's peaceful accession to power, to attempt to deal with the problem, and the passage of González into the opposition give testimony to the maturity of Spanish democracy. It has the requisite broad middle class and high levels of literacy, and its leaders seem to have learned the art of sensible compromise and mutual respect for the public good. Increasingly, massive demonstrations in every part of Spain against ETA outrages have created a new sense of solidarity. As the twenty-first century nears, it would seem that Spaniards have retained their remarkable warmth and individuality and recovered their historic sense of community. Spaniards are no longer, as Aznar recently remarked, quoting poet Antonio Machado, frozen at birth into one of two Spains, each opposed to the other.

Notable People in the History of Spain

In most cases, the individuals listed are treated at some length in the text. No one still alive and active is included.

Abd-al-Rahman I (731–788), born in Syria into the Umayyad dynasty, which was overthrown in 750. He escaped to Spain and became emir of Córdoba.

Abd-al-Rahman III (891–961), emir of Córdoba, proclaimed himself caliph in 929. Under him, Islamic Spain reached its peak.

Alfonso X (1221–1284), born in Toledo, in 1252 succeeded his father Fernando III as king of Castile and León. He presided over the flowering of medieval Spanish culture and supervised the codification of Castilian law.

Alfonso XIII (1886–1941) became king at birth, as his father Alfonso XII had died. Charming but capricious in his reign, he vacated the throne in 1931 when elections made Spain a republic.

Aranda, Pedro Pablo Abarca de Bolea, count of (1719–1798), born in Aragón, entered the government of Carlos III. Believing in Enlightenment ideals, he tried to implement them in Spain.

Azaña y Díaz, Manuel (1880–1940), born in Alcalá de Henares, became a civil servant and political essayist. He formed the Republican Action Party in 1931, became prime minister, and from 1936 to 1939 served as president of the Second Republic.

Cánovas del Castillo, Antonio (1828–1897), born in Málaga, became a lawyer and historian. He admired England's political stability, which he tried to achieve in Spain after the restoration of the monarchy in 1874. He was assassinated by an anarchist.

Carlos III (1716–1788), son of the second marriage of Philip V, had been king of the Two Sicilies before becoming king of Spain in 1759. He gave Spain enlightened government.

Casas, Bartolomé de Las (1474–1566), arrived in the West Indies in 1502 as an adventurer. Becoming a Dominican friar, he denounced his fellow Spaniards for their mistreatment of New World Indians. Made bishop of Chiapas in Mexico, he influenced humane legislation.

Cervantes y Saavedra, Miguel de (1547–1616), author of *Don Quixote* (1605–1615), Spain's great novel, served as a soldier and, after being wounded and held captive, as a tax collector. Unsuccessful in the theater, he wrote the novel that made him famous.

Charles V (1500–1558), born in Ghent (Belgium), as grandson of Ferdinand and Isabella became **Carlos I of Spain** in 1516 and ruled in place of his unstable mother Queen Juana. His inheritance included Spain, Naples and Sicily, the Low Countries, Austria, and Spain's American empire. Elected Holy Roman Emperor as Charles V in 1519, he made Spain Europe's leading power. He abdicated in 1556.

Cid, El (Rodrigo Díaz de Vivar) (c. 1043–1099), hero of the reconquest of Spain from the Moors, was an aggressive border lord and became the subject of epic poetry.

Cisneros, Francisco Ximénez de (1436–1516), joined the Franciscan Order and served as Queen Isabella's confessor. He became cardinal-archbishop of Toledo and promoted church reform. After Isabella's death, Cisneros acted as Ferdinand's lieutenant in Castile.

Cortés, Hernán (1485–1547), after a stint at university, sought his fortune in the New World. In 1519–1521 he achieved the spectacular conquest of the Aztec empire in Mexico. Made marquis of Valle de Oaxaca, he died a rich man near Seville.

Espartero, Baldomero (1793–1879), born the son of a carter, rose in the army through talent to become a general. Becoming involved in politics, he championed the Progressive Party. He served briefly as regent for Queen Isabel II.

Ferdinand V and II (1452–1516) became King Ferdinand V of Castile in 1474 as consort of Queen Isabella and, in 1479, Ferdinand II of Aragon, on the death of his father. Dubbed Ferdinand the Catholic by the pope, he and Isabella restored order to Spain, improved government, and conquered Granada. He also inherited Sicily and acquired Naples in the Italian Wars against France.

Fernando III the Saint (c. 1201–1252) became king of Castile in 1217 and of León in 1230, uniting the two kingdoms. He conquered most of Andalusia from the Moors and was canonized by the Roman Catholic Church in 1671.

Franco y Bahamonde, Francisco (1892–1975), born in El Ferrol, entered the army and rose through combat in Morocco to become a respected general. In 1936 he joined an officers' revolt against the Republic and became its generalísimo. Victorious, he ruled Spain as dictator. Under him Spain modernized, and the monarchy was restored.

Giner de los Ríos, Francisco (1840–1915), was educated in Germany and became a professor at Madrid. Dismissed for his liberal politics, he took up educational reform through his influential Free Institution for Education (Institución Libre de Enseñaza) and started developments that over the next century eliminated illiteracy in Spain.

Godoy y Alvarez de Faria, Manuel de (1767–1851), born in Extremadura, joined the royal guards. He became Queen Maria Luisa's confidant and, most likely, lover. Loyal to her and the king, he entered government in 1792 and was their chief minister until 1808.

Goya y Lucientes, Francisco de (1746–1828), was born in Aragón and became one of the world's great artists, painting for court and society and satirizing popular life. Following Napoleon's invasion, he painted heroic canvases about the Spanish rising of 1808 and made etchings called *The Disasters of War*.

Isabella I the Catholic (1451–1504), arguably Spain's greatest ruler, was born in Madrigal de las Altas Torres. In 1469 she married Ferdinand of Aragon and in 1474 became queen of Castile. She encouraged Church reform although her establishment of the Inquisition and expulsion of Spain's Jews remain controversial. She shared Ferdinand's achievements and backed Columbus's epochal voyage that brought Europe to a New World.

Jaime I the Conqueror (1208–1276) became king of Aragon in 1213. In 1229 he conquered the island of Majorca and before his death added Valencia to his kingdoms.

Jovellanos y Ramírez, Gaspar Melchor de (1744–1811), born in Asturias, proved the most enlightened of Spain's reformist ministers. In 1808 he opposed Joseph Bonaparte, whom Napoleon tried to make king of Spain, and worked on Spain's Constitution of 1812.

Largo Caballero, Francisco (1869–1946), born poor in Madrid, became a plasterer and joined the Socialist Party. He rose to leadership and in 1936 became prime minister of the Second Republic. He fled to France, was imprisoned by the Nazis, and died in Paris.

María Cristina de Bourbon of Naples (1806–1878) married King Fernando VII in 1829 and bore his daughters, Isabel and Luisa. In 1833 Isabel became queen. María Cristina served as her regent until 1840 and brought Spain's liberals back to power in government.

Maura y Montaner, Antonio (1853–1925), born on Majorca, entered politics and led Spain's centrist conservatives after 1900. Though rigid in personal matters, he was open to change. His government of national unity failed in 1918, and Spain headed for dictatorship.

Narváez, Ramón (1800–1868), a successful general in the Carlist Wars, headed the Moderate Party and dominated Spanish politics during the last ten years of his life.

Olivares, Gaspar de Guzmán, count-duke of (1587–1645), born the son of Philip II's ambassador to Rome, he served Philip IV (1621–1665) as chief minister and favorite. Philip added the title "duke of Sanlúcar la Mayor" to his favorite's title of "count." Olivares involved Spain in foreign conflicts in order to make Philip "Number One." Brought down by revolt and intrigue, he died half mad.

Philip II (1527–1598), son of Charles V, succeeded to the Spanish crowns in 1556. During his reign Spain reached its apogee of world power with the acquisition in 1580 of Portugal and its empire. But the Dutch Revolt and war with England and France overtaxed Spain's resources and led to its decline.

Philip V (1683–1746), born at Versailles, grandson of Louis XIV of France and his Spanish-born queen Marie Thérèse, succeeded his great-uncle Carlos II to Spain in 1700. In the War of the Spanish Succession he kept Spain and its overseas empire but lost his crown's other possessions in Europe. He ended the autonomy of the crown of Aragon and centralized Spain's government along Castilian lines.

Pizarro, Francisco (1476–1541), illegitimate son of a poor nobleman of Extremadura and barely literate, conquered the Inca Empire through daring and treachery with a few hundred Spaniards. In 1533 founded Lima. He was murdered by supporters of an executed rival.

Primo de Rivera y Orbaneja, Miguel de (1870–1930), son of a prominent Andalusian family, became a successful army general. Widespread unrest led him in 1923 to assume dictatorial power with the approval of Alfonso XIII. At first effective, he was overwhelmed by the Great Depression and dismissed. His son **José Antonio** (1903–1936) founded the Falange, Spain's chief Fascist party.

Sagasta, Práxedes Mateo (1827–1903), born in Logroño, entered liberal politics and flirted with republicanism. After the restoration of the monarchy in 1874, he became the pragmatic chief of the Liberal Party. With Cánovas del Castillo, he arranged a rotation of power between Liberals and Conservatives to achieve political stability.

Theresa of Avila, St. (1515–1582), born Teresa de Cespedes y Ahumada to a minor noble family, became a Carmelite nun and reformed the order. A dynamic personality and mystic, she wrote a splendid spiritual *Autobiography*.

Velázquez, Diego Rodríguez de Silva (1599–1660), became prominent as a painter in Seville. Invited to the court of Madrid by the count-duke of Olivares, he served Philip IV and the royal family. His paintings stand among the greatest in the history of art.

Bibliographic Essay

I limit myself to works available in English. Most contain bibliographies for further reading. For university students, Stanley Payne, *History of Spain and Portugal*, 2 vols. (Madison, WI, 1973), is most useful. Basic historiographical questions to 1936 are well posed by Jaime Vicens Vives, *Approaches to the History of Spain* (Berkeley and Los Angeles, 2nd ed., 1970), with informative notes by Joan Connelly Ullman. His *Economic History of Spain* (Princeton, NJ, 1969) covers history until 1900. Charles E. Chapman, *History of Spain* (1918; paperback, New York, 1965), based on the work of Rafael Altamira, remains interesting. Color maps and illustrations complement text in Mary Vincent and R. A. Stradling, *Cultural Atlas of Spain and Portugal* (Oxfordshire and New York, 1994). Gerald Brenan, *Literature of the Spanish People* (Cambridge, 1951), introduces the subject in lively fashion. For Spain's provinces, see Robert W. Kern, *The Regions of Spain* (Westport, CT, 1995). A labor of love is Robert Hughes, *Barcelona* (New York, 1992).

A magisterial work that introduces Spanish history but stresses the last two centuries is Richard Herr, *An Historical Essay on Modern Spain* (Berkeley and Los Angeles, 1971). Efforts by Spanish scholars to explain Spain's historical experience include Américo Castro, *The Spaniards: An Introduction to Their History* (Berkeley and Los Angeles, 1971); Claudio Sánchez Albornoz, *Spain, a Historical Enigma*, David Reher, trans. (Madrid, 1975); and Ramón

Menéndez Pidal, *Spaniards in their History*, Walter Starkie, trans. (New York, 1950).

For Spain's beginnings, see R. J. Harrison, *Spain at the Dawn of History* (London, 1988), and S. J. Keay, *Roman Spain* (London, 1988). See Roger Collins, *Early Medieval Spain, 400–1000* (London, 1983), for Visigoths and early reconquest, and his *Arab Conquest of Spain* (London, 1989) for Muslim Spain. Gabriel Jackson, *Making of Medieval Spain* (London, 1972), is lively if idiosyncratic. Richard Fletcher offers an intriguing *Quest for El Cid* (London, 1989), which he complements with *Moorish Spain* (London, 1992). Comprehensive are Joseph F. O'Callaghan, *History of Medieval Spain* (Ithaca, 1975), and Jocelyn Hillgarth, *The Spanish Kingdoms, 1250–1516*, 2 vols. (Oxford, 1976, 1978). For women in medieval Castile, see Heath Dillard, *Daughters of the Reconquest* (Cambridge, 1984); for warfare, James F. Powers, *A Society Organized for War* (Berkeley and Los Angeles, 1988); for the Aragonese reconquest, R. I. Burns, S.J., *Muslims, Christians and Jews in the Crusader Kingdom of Valencia* (Cambridge, 1984). Queen Isabella has a fine biography in Peggy Liss, *Isabel the Queen* (New York, 1992). Townsend Miller, *The Castles and the Crown* (New York, 1963), reads like a novel. For Granada see, L. P. Harvey, *Islamic Spain, 1250–1500* (Chicago, 1990). Roger B. Merriman, *The Rise of the Spanish Empire in the Old World and in the New*, 4 vols. (New York, 1918–1934; reprint 1962), a standard, begins with medieval Spain and proceeds through the reign of Philip II. John H. Elliott, *Imperial Spain* (London, 1963), remains a perceptive minor classic. See also Henry Kamen, *Spain, 1469–1714* (London, 2nd ed., 1991). For the Inquisition, see Henry Kamen, *Spanish Inquisition* (London and New Haven, 1997), Norman Roth, *Conversos, Inquisition and the Expulsion of the Jews from Spain* (Madison, 1995); and the debatable Benzion Netanyahu, *Origins of the Inquisition in Fifteenth Century Spain* (New York, 1995). J. H. Parry, *The Spanish Seaborne Empire* (London, 1966), covers the discovery, conquest, and administration of Spain's overseas dominions.

For the Habsburg period, John Lynch, *Spain under the Habsburgs* (Oxford, 3rd ed., 1991, 1992), emphasizes the role of the Americas. Manuel Fernández Álvarez, *Charles V: Elected Emperor and Hereditary Ruler* (London, 1975) gives a Spanish perspective. Stephen Haliczer, *The Comuneros of Castile* (Madison, WI, 1981), details that episode. Philip II, long subject to controversy, has three recent good biographies: Peter Pierson, *Philip II of Spain* (London, 1975), a concise political introduction to the reign; Geoffrey Parker, *Philip II* (Boston, 1978), an intimate if not always sympathetic portrait; and Henry Kamen, *Philip of Spain* (New Haven, 1996), which adds more detail and provides a sympathetic look at Philip. Philip's era enjoys one of the great historical works of our times, Fernand Braudel, *The Mediterranean and the Mediterranean World in the Age of Philip II* (English trans., London, 1972). The

1588 Spanish armada also enjoys a classic account, Garrett Mattingly, *The Armada* (Boston, 1959), which garnered a Pulitzer Prize in 1960. More recent accounts include Colin Martin and Geoffrey Parker, *The Spanish Armada* (London, 1988), and Peter Pierson, *Commander of the Armada* (New Haven, CT, 1989). I.A.A. Thompson, *War and Government in Habsburg Spain, 1560–1620* (London, 1976), details Spain's fundamental military problems. Also see R. A. Stradling, *Europe and the Decline of Spain, 1580–1720* (London, 1981), and his *Philip IV*, 2 vols. (Cambridge, Eng., 1988). Seminal are John H. Elliott, *Revolt of the Catalans* (Cambridge, Eng., 1963,) and *Count-Duke of Olivares* (New Haven, CT, 1986). Elliott and art historian Jonathan Brown collaborate on *A Palace for a King* (New Haven, CT, 1980). Also by Jonathan Brown, *The Golden Age of Painting in Spain* (New Haven, CT, 1991) and *Velázquez* (New Haven, CT, 1986), both with lavish illustrations.

The eighteenth century has John Lynch, *Bourbon Spain 1700–1808* (Oxford, 1989). Richard Herr, *The Eighteenth Century Revolution in Spain* (Princeton, NJ, 1958), is a classic. Also see William Callahan, *Church, Politics and Society in Spain, 1750–1874* (Cambridge, MA, 1984). See Gabriel H. Lovett, *Napoleon and the Birth of Modern Spain,* 2 vols. (New York, 1965), for a narrative account. For the nineteenth century and most of the twentieth stands the magnificent Raymond Carr, *Spain, 1808–1975* (Oxford, 2nd ed., 1982). David Ringrose, *Spain, Europe and the Spanish Miracle, 1700–1900* (Cambridge, Eng., 1996), takes a long and convincing view of Spain's economy. Carolyn Boyd, *Historia Patria* (Princeton, NJ, 1997), looks at Spanish education through how history was taught. For the Spanish labor movement, see Benjamin Martin, *The Agony of Modernization: Labor and Industrialization in Spain* (Ithaca, NY, 1990). Special is Joan Connelly Ullman, *Spain's Tragic Week* (Cambridge, 1968), about 1909 in Barcelona. For the 1920s, Ben Ami Shlomo, *Fascism from Above: The Dictatorship of Primo de Rivera* (Oxford, 1983).

Like Imperial Spain, the Second Republic and Civil War have attracted legions of English-speaking writers and scholars. Gerald Brenan, who resided in Spain, begins with 1874 for his perceptive *Spanish Labyrinth* (Cambridge, Eng., 2nd ed., 1950). Gabriel Jackson, *The Spanish Republic and Civil War* (Princeton, NJ, 1965), became the first standard account. A more critical look is Stanley Payne, *Spain's First Democracy* (Madison, WI, 1993). Also by Payne are *Falange* (Stanford, 1961), about Spanish fascism, *Politics and the Military in Modern Spain* (Stanford, 1967), and *The Spanish Revolution* (New York, 1970), about the Spanish left. More sympathetic is Gerald H. Meaker, *The Revolutionary Left in Spain* (Stanford, 1974). For the agrarian issue, see Edward Malefakis, *Agrarian Reform and Peasant Revolution in Spain* (New Haven, CT, 1970). For rural anarchism, see anthropologist Jerome Mintz, *The Anarchists of Casas Viejas* (Chicago, 1982). Burnett Bolloten exposes communism in the Republic in *The Spanish Revolution* (Chapel Hill, NC, 1979). The standard military history is Hugh Thomas, *The Spanish Civil War* (London, rev. ed., 1977). Based on firsthand accounts is Ronald Fraser, *Blood of Spain: The Experience of the Civil War, 1936–1939* (London, 1979). Valentine Cunningham, ed., *Spanish Front: Writers on the Civil War* (Oxford, 1986), presents English-speaking authors' views. George Orwell, *Homage to Catalonia* (London, 1938), is a classic. For the Basques, see Marianne Heiberg, *The Making of the Basque Nation* (Cambridge, Eng., 1989).

For Franco and his regime, Paul Preston's *The Politics of Revenge* (London, 1990) and *Franco* (London, 1993) offer a harsh view. More favorable is Stanley Payne, *The Franco Regime* (Madison, WI, 1987). Spain since Franco is just entering the province of history. Raymond Carr and Juan Pablo Fusi Aizpura, *Spain: Dictatorship to Democracy* (London, 1979), detail the first steps. Paul Preston has an enthusiastic *Triumph of Democracy in Spain* (London, 1986). A longer view appears in E. Ramón Arango, *Spain: Democracy Regained* (Boulder, CO, 2nd ed., 1995). For the ETA, see Robert P. Clark, *The Basque Insurgents* (Madison, WI, 1984) and John Sullivan, *ETA and Basque Nationalism* (London and New York, 1988).

Index

Medinaceli, 31
Melilla, 3, 7, 10, 53, 126, 164
Mendizábal, Juan Álvarez de, 97–98
Mendoza, Pedro de, cardinal-
   archbishop, 50
Menéndez Pidal, Ramón, 130, 159
Menéndez y Pelayo, Marcelino, 114
Mérida, 6, 20, 21
Mérimée, Prosper, 114
Meseta, 3, 23
Mesta, 44–45
Mexico, 54, 55, 56, 63, 161; treasure,
   78; Spanish and French in, 101;
   Guadalajara summit, 184. *See also*
   America, Spanish
Miaja, Gen. José, 147, 151
Middle East, 18, 19, 24; modern, 170,
   184–85
Milan, 75
Milans del Bosch, Gen. Jaime, 175,
   179–80, 181
Military Orders (Alcántara, Calatrava,
   Santiago), 37, 44, 49
Militias: urban, 94, 98, 101, 108; mili-
   tias in Civil War, 145–51 passim
Ministries, 8–9; establishment, 75; and
   Constitution of 1812, 92
Minorca, 74, 75, 82, 85
Miró, Joan, 131
Missionaries, 54, 82
Mississippi Valley, 82, 84
Mitterrand, François, 181, 182, 185
Mobile (Alabama), 84
Moderates (*Partido Moderado*), 97–102,
   107
Mola, Gen. Emilio, 132, 144–46, 147,
   150, 152, 155
Monarchists, 103, 133. *See also* CEDA
Monarchy: medieval 32, 33–34; en-
   lightenment, 77–78; absolute, 91;
   constitutional, 105, 107, 110; Franco
   and, 162. *See also* Constitutions
Moncloa Pacts, 177
Montemolín, Carlos Luis de Borbón
   (Carlos VI), count of, 96, 100
Montero Ríos, Eugenio, 118
Montesquieu, Charles de Secondat,
   baron de, 91
Montijo, Eugènie de, empress of the
   French, 102

Montjuich (citadel), 88, 122
Montpensier, Antoine of Orleans,
   duke of, 100, 104, 105, 110
Montserrat, 31
Moors, 8, 24, 29, 37, 38, 50, 52; in
   France, 30; expulsion, 52. *See also*
   Berbers; Muslims
Moret, Segismundo, 118, 123
Morillo, Gen. Pablo, 95
Moriscos, 51, 52; revolt of, 64; expul-
   sion, 67–68
Morocco, 7, 18, 24, 35, 45, 174, 185; Ro-
   man Mauretania, 21; 1859–1860
   War, 101; Spanish army in, 122, 125,
   144; Spanish and French Protector-
   ates, 124, 127–28; Franco's ambi-
   tions, 160; end of Protectorate, 164
Mota, Pedro Ruiz de la, bishop, 59
Movement, National (*Movimiento Na-
   cional*), 161, 163, 168, 169, 170, 171,
   181
Mozarabs, 25, 30, 35, 36
Mudejars (*Mudéjares*), 37
Muhammad, Prophet, 24
Muhammad I, emir, 30
Mühlberg, battle of, 61
Muñoz, Augustín, duke of Riánsares,
   99, 100
Muñoz Grandes, Gen. Agustín, 160,
   167
Murat, Joachim, marshal of France, 88,
   89
Murcia, 5, 49, 150; *taifa* 33, 38
Muret, Battle of, 40
Musa ibn Nusair, 22, 23
Music, 15, 77, 79, 114–15, 141, 166;
   rock, 15, 168. *See also* Flamenco;
   Zarzuela
Muslims, 23, 25, 26, 29, 30, 35, 38; con-
   quest of Spain, 23–24; Balearics, 40;
   Valencia, 40; expulsion, 52. *See also*
   Islam; Moors
Mussolini, Benito, 127, 128, 135; and
   Civil War, 145, 148, 151, 152, 156;
   World War II, 157, 159–60
Muwalladun (*muladíes*), 25

Naples, kingdom of, 48, 52, 74, 76

About the Author

PETER PIERSON is Lee and Seymour Graff Professor of History at Santa Clara University. The history of Spain is one of his main interests, and he regularly undertakes research trips to Spain. A former Fulbright fellow in Spain, he is a member of the Society for Spanish and Portuguese Historical Studies and author of *Philip II of Spain* (1975), *Commander of the Armada* (1989), and numerous articles and book chapters on early modern Spanish history.